Investment Strategies

How to Create Your Own and Make It Work for You

STEVEN KELMAN & SEYMOUR FRIEDLAND

Penguin Books

PENGUIN BOOKS
Published by the Penguin Group
Penguin Books Canada Ltd., 10 Alcorn Avenue, Suite 300, Toronto, Canada M4V 3B2
Penguin Books Ltd., 27 Wrights Lane, London W8 5TZ, England
Viking Penguin Inc., 40 West 23rd Street, New York, New York 10010, USA
Penguin Books Australia Ltd., Ringwood, Victoria, Australia
Penguin Books (NZ) Ltd, 182-190 Wairau Road, Auckland 10, New Zealand
Penguin Books Ltd., Registered Offices: Harmondsworth, Middlesex, England

Published in Penguin Books, 1994

10 9 8 7 6 5 4 3 2 1

Copyright © Financial Times of Canada, 1994
All queries should be addressed to the Financial Times of Canada, 440 Front Street West,
Toronto, Ontario M5V 3E6 (416) 585-5555

Canadian Cataloguing in Publication Data
The National Library of Canada has catalogued this publication as follows:

Kelman, Steven G. (Steven Gershon), 1945 –
    Investment strategies

(Financial times personal finance library)
Annual.
At head of title: Financial times.
Following title: How to create your own and make it work for you.
ISSN 1193-9028
ISBN 0-14-024383-6 (12th ed.)
1. Investments – Canada – Periodicals. 2. Finance, Personal – Canada – Periodicals. I.
Friedland, Seymour, 1928 – 1992. II. Title. III. Title: Financial times. IV. Series.

HG179.M25   332.6'78'097105   C93-030702-X

Cover design: Creative Network
Cover illustration: Peter Yundt
Charts: Ivy Wong

The information contained in this book is intended only as a general guide and may not be
suitable for certain individuals. If expert advice is warranted, readers are urged to consult a
competent professional. While the investment, legal, tax and accounting information
contained in this book has been obtained from sources believed to be accurate, constant
changes in the legal and financial environment make it imperative that readers confirm this
information before making financial decisions.

CONTENTS

Tables and Illustrations

Introduction

ONLY A FEW CANADIANS, perhaps 25 percent, invest in anything other than the guaranteed investments offered by banks, trust companies and other institutions. By excluding alternatives such as bonds, stocks and mutual funds, most investors deprive themselves of significant opportunities for increasing their financial returns. Indeed, many people fail to realize that even small differences in rates of return mean huge differences in results over time. For example, $1,000 a year invested for twenty-five years at 5 percent brings in just over $50,000. At 8 percent you end up with almost $79,000; with 10 percent, you end up with $108,000; with 12 percent, $149,000; and with 14 percent, $207,000.

The purpose of this book is to make you aware of your investment alternatives and how they work. It won't show you how to get rich overnight, but it will show you how to accumulate wealth by using the investment alternatives available to Canadians. It will also demonstrate how other investors have increased their wealth by putting money into varied investment vehicles and, just as important, will help you avoid the pitfalls that have prevented many people from meeting their financial goals. Even if you've given some thought to financial planning, this book can be a valuable aid. Recent changes in investment and taxation have made it necessary to review your goals and financial planning strategies.

Federal and provincial tax reform continues to evolve. In 1988, there were three federal marginal tax rates, 17 percent, 26 percent and 29 percent. Since then, Ottawa has added a 3 percent surtax on top of the basic tax and another 5 percent surtax on tax greater than $12,500. Provincial tax rates as a percentage of federal tax have been rising too – and they've been boosted even further by surtaxes.

At the same time our disposable income has been eroded by higher taxes and, for some government employees, by unpaid holidays, the investment income from deposits has been eroded by the decline of interest rates. While this is good news for borrowers, particularly for home buyers, more and more people are looking beyond deposits to other kinds of investments. They realize that they cannot meet their financial goals at current interest rate levels.

About the authors

Born in the United States, Seymour Friedland took his doctorate at Harvard University and came to Canada as professor of finance and economics at York University's faculty of administrative studies. His forty-year teaching career included terms at New York University, Claremont Graduate School, Rutgers State University, the Massachusetts Institute of Technology and Harvard.

He published nine books and numerous articles in academic journals and served as a consultant to many U.S. and Canadian companies, as well as governments. He was chief economist for Dominion Securities Ltd. from 1969 to 1974 and for many years an associate editor of the *Financial Times*. He often appeared as a business and economics commentator on television and radio and was business editor of CBC Television's *The Journal*. He won a National Business Writing Award in 1980. He died on October 15, 1992.

Steven G. Kelman is an investment counsellor and a vice-president of Dynamic Mutual Funds, part of the Dundee Bancorp Inc. group of companies. He is a chartered financial analyst and a member of the Toronto Society of Financial Analysts. He has also lectured at York University's faculty of administrative studies.

After obtaining his MBA from York University in 1969, Mr. Kelman worked as an analyst and portfolio manager for a major insurance company before becoming a senior analyst with a stock brokerage house. He began his association with the *Financial Times* as a staff writer in 1975, becoming investment editor in 1977. A recognized expert on Canadian mutual funds, he acts as a consultant to Southam Information and Technology Group on its *Mutual Fund Sourcedisk* and fund tables, and is consulting editor of the *Mutual Fund Sourcebook*. As well, Mr. Kelman is author of *RRSPs 1995 and Understanding Mutual Funds*, both published by the *Financial Times of Canada,* and co-author of *Investing in Gold*.

He joined the Dundee Group of Companies in 1985.

CHAPTER 1

How to Make a Million: Save

IT IS ABSURDLY EASY TO become a millionaire. It doesn't take clever gimmicks or blind luck or risks that will keep you awake at night. Becoming a millionaire only takes a bit of knowledge, sound investment strategies and time.

Time is the critical ingredient, for it is time and the power of compound interest that will have the most significant impact on your ability to build your wealth. Compound interest is interest earned and then added to the original investment so that it too begins to earn interest. It's interest on interest.

Suppose $1,000 has been invested at 10 percent compounded annually. In the first year, interest earnings are 10 percent of $1,000 or $100. If the first year's interest remains invested, the principal in the second year becomes $1,100, and the second year's interest earnings are $110. In the third year, the principal becomes $1,210, and interest earnings are $121. As long as the interest is not withdrawn, compound interest generates a rapidly ascending curve of wealth.

At the end of five years, the investment will have grown to $1,610.51. With simple interest – where interest is not earned on past interest – the value of the $1,000 at 10 percent in five years would be only $1,500.

If the interest is compounded semi-annually, rather than just annually, interest in the second six months of the first year would include interest on the first half-year's earnings. With semi-annual compounding, the value of the $1,000 at 10 percent would be worth $1,628.89 after five years, an increase of $18.38 over annual compounding and $128.89 better than simple interest. Interest that compounds every three months is better still, and monthly compounding better yet.

An easy way to see the impact of time and compounding on your investments is to use the Rule of 72. To determine the time it takes

How an Investment of $1,000 a Year Can Grow over Time at Different Rates of Return

COMPOUNDED ANNUALLY

Years	4%	6%	8%	10%	12%	14%
1	1,040	1,060	1,080	1,100	1,120	1,140
2	2,122	2,184	2,246	2,310	2,374	2,440
3	3,246	3,375	3,506	3,641	3,779	3,921
4	4,416	4,637	4,867	5,105	5,353	5,610
5	5,633	5,975	6,336	6,716	7,115	7,536
6	6,898	7,394	7,923	8,487	9,089	9,730
7	8,214	8,897	9,637	10,436	11,300	12,233
8	9,583	10,491	11,488	12,579	13,776	15,085
9	11,006	12,181	13,487	14,937	16,549	18,337
10	12,486	13,972	15,645	17,531	19,655	22,045
11	14,026	15,870	17,977	20,384	23,133	26,271
12	15,627	17,882	20,495	23,523	27,029	31,089
13	17,292	20,015	23,215	26,975	31,393	36,581
14	19,024	22,276	26,152	30,772	36,280	42,842
15	20,825	24,673	29,324	34,950	41,753	49,980
16	22,698	27,213	32,750	39,545	47,884	58,118
17	24,645	29,906	36,450	44,599	54,750	67,394
18	26,671	32,760	40,446	50,159	62,440	77,969
19	28,778	35,786	44,762	56,275	71,052	90,025
20	30,969	38,993	49,423	63,002	80,699	103,768

TABLE I

an investment to double simply divide seventy-two by the annual interest rate. $1,000 invested at 10 percent will double in value in 7.2 years. At 5 percent, it would take 14.4 years for $1,000 to grow to $2,000. At 15 percent, doubling takes place in just 4.8 years.

To find the interest rate that would double your investment in a given number of years, divide seventy-two by the number of years. For example, to double an investment in six years, one must earn 12 percent. Another example: the population around the Great Lakes is expected to double in the next forty years. Using the Rule of 72 – dividing seventy-two by forty – we discover that the annual population growth is expected to be 1.8 percent.

Of course, the rule is only an approximation. In reality, it would take 7.273 years, not 7.2, to double $1,000 at 10 percent compounded annually. If the compounding period is shorter, the Rule of 72 overstates the length of time needed to double your invest-

How a Single Deposit of $1,000 Can Grow over Time at Different Rates of Return
COMPOUNDED ANNUALLY

Years	4%	6%	8%	10%	12%	14%
1	1,040	1,060	1,080	1,100	1,120	1,140
2	1,082	1,124	1,166	1,210	1,254	1,300
3	1,125	1,191	1,260	1,331	1,405	1,482
4	1,170	1,262	1,360	1,464	1,574	1,689
5	1,217	1,338	1,469	1,611	1,762	1,925
6	1,265	1,419	1,587	1,772	1,974	2,195
7	1,316	1,504	1,714	1,949	2,211	2,502
8	1,369	1,594	1,851	2,144	2,476	2,853
9	1,423	1,689	1,999	2,358	2,773	3,252
10	1,480	1,791	2,159	2,594	3,106	3,707
11	1,539	1,898	2,332	2,853	3,479	4,226
12	1,601	2,012	2,518	3,138	3,896	4,818
13	1,665	2,133	2,720	3,452	4,363	5,492
14	1,732	2,261	2,937	3,797	4,887	6,261
15	1,801	2,397	3,172	4,177	5,474	7,138
16	1,873	2,540	3,426	4,595	6,130	8,137
17	1,948	2,693	3,700	5,054	6,866	9,276
18	2,026	2,854	3,996	5,560	7,690	10,575
19	2,107	3,026	4,316	6,116	8,613	12,056
20	2,191	3,207	4,661	6,727	9,646	13,743

TABLE II

ment. Compounded monthly, it takes only 6.96 years for $1,000 to double at 10 percent.

The real key to making a million
The magic of compounding is much stronger when applied to regular savings, rather than to a single deposit. At a savings rate of 8 percent compounded monthly, a thirty-two-year-old can be a millionaire at age sixty-five simply by saving $500 a month. If savings rates were in the 13 percent to 14 percent range, hitting the millionaire class would have taken ten years less. But when rates are about 6 percent, it would take seven years longer.

Tables I and II show the importance of time and rates of return in reaching your goal. The first demonstrates how annual investments of $1,000 grow over different time periods and at different rates of return. A more comprehensive table appears in appendix one.

Table II shows how a single investment will grow over time at differing rates of return. Again, a more comprehensive table appears at the end of this book in appendix two.

Regardless of the interest rate, the real issue is whether you can raise the dollars you need to save each month. A steady savings program is also the key to successfully using the strategies in this book.

The money for that first step into investing can come from only two sources. A fortunate few may inherit the money, but the rest of us have to get it the old-fashioned way – we must earn it and save it. For most of us, then, becoming rich is merely a dream if we cannot save. And the key to saving is controlling expenditures.

Many savers have found that a budget is essential to control spending. That's why a look at how the typical Canadian household spends money is a useful starting point in developing that all-important budget.

The three big expenses for most Canadians are food, shelter and transportation. Depending on where you live – for instance, it costs a lot less for housing in St. John's than in Vancouver – these three necessities of life can consume as much as two-thirds of the take-home pay of typical Canadians.

As earnings increase, these basic expenses take a smaller percentage of income. The family with an income of $50,000 or more is likely to spend a smaller percentage on food, shelter and transportation than the family with $20,000 of income. And the family with $100,000 will spend an even smaller percentage.

Credit hurts saving

Clearly, savings prospects are improved if you avoid extravagances. And if you avoid extravagant spending, you may also avoid another costly drain on the budget – interest payments on consumer debt.

Canadians owe about $105 billion of consumer debt, excluding their $312 billion in mortgage debt. Some of that borrowed money was used to buy cars but each year more of our debt is tied to credit cards. Still, there are times when it is necessary to borrow. If the borrowing is for a business or investment, such as investing in securities, some or all of the interest may be deductible for income tax purposes. If interest is deductible, a 9 percent interest rate shrinks to as little as 5.3 percent for a person whose marginal tax rate is 41 percent. But without the tax deduction, interest on consumer debt can be a heavy burden, particularly as the interest on an unpaid balance is compounded. That's when compounding turns vicious.

While deposit rates have plunged, your credit card may charge something like 0.05094 percent daily on unpaid balances. If that's the case, you could be paying an annual interest rate of 20.43 percent. At that rate your interest costs will exceed the original balance in three years and nine months.

It is much cheaper to go to a bank, trust company or credit union and borrow to pay off your credit card balance – as long as the personal loan rate is less than your card rate. It is cheaper still to operate on a tight budget and owe nothing for spending that is purely for personal consumption. Even at today's relatively low interest rates, it is far better to be a lender than a borrower.

The first thing you should do is create a budget using Your Family Budget (page 7), if only to get a clearer picture of how you spend your money. If you aren't saving anything now, set a target of 10 percent, then look for areas where you can cut spending to allow for those savings. Your pay slip will show you what you pay in taxes each pay period and your cheque records will provide information about where your money goes. You should also keep track of where your pocket money is spent. Don't forget to include everyone in the family on both the income and expenditure sides. Setting money aside each month is the first step toward becoming a millionaire. You must put in place spending limits that will shave a percentage point or two from those categories that can bear the cut.

Don't give up easily. Food costs can be cut by anywhere from 10 percent to 40 percent by seeking out sales, buying no-name products and shopping at food stores that sell out of shipping cartons and have you pack your own groceries. It may cause some inconvenience, but becoming a millionaire requires savings – and that is not painless. Those nickels and dimes you can save will add up. Remember, $10 a week is more than $500 a year. And $500 a year invested at 10 percent for twenty-five years is more than $54,000. That's a far cry from a million, but it's a start.

You're wealthier than you think

Admittedly, preparing a budget is almost as painful as holding to budgeted spending limits. But measuring wealth, particularly if it is your own, is a most gratifying experience. It is also a very useful exercise.

Most of us are wealthier than we think. Yet we rarely look at the things we own and the money we have in Canada Savings Bonds, a few stocks or mutual funds as an investment portfolio, and so we don't try to maximize gains in overall portfolio value. Furthermore, we too often hold a bag of undiversified assets – a risky practice. While diversification is more difficult for individuals than for professional investment managers, the results can be very rewarding.

To assess your wealth, you need to determine your net worth. You can do this by adding up the value of everything you own and subtracting from that everything you owe. But it isn't really that simple; you have to make some adjustments. You may think your furniture is worth a great deal, and in fact your house insurance should be based on its replacement value. But for net worth purposes, it should be given a value of $1. Your RRSP may be worth $50,000, but you have to pay tax on it when you withdraw. So its true value may be as little as $24,000. Whether you use a pre-tax or after-tax value depends on your circumstances. But most people should use the pre-tax value because that is the amount which will continue to grow untaxed until retirement when it will be used to generate a stream of income. You can use Your Financial Balance Worksheet as a guide to constructing your personal balance sheet. Don't be shy about changing it to suit your circumstances.

If you are a homeowner, your house is probably your biggest asset, although if you recently purchased a house, your assets may only slightly exceed your liabilities or even be less if you bought in those markets where house prices have since fallen from peak levels. Two of the trickier items to estimate on your balance sheet are life insurance and pensions. Term insurance can be ignored because it has no savings component, but the cash surrender value of whole life insurance should be included.

Estimating the value of pensions is also a problem, although this is made easier if your employer sends you pension investment information. Such information usually includes the present value of your pension, which is the amount to include on your personal balance sheet. It is quite difficult to estimate the value of some government retirement program payments because benefits are partly indexed to the cost of living and are subject to unforeseen legislative changes. Ottawa does, however, provide a statement on Canada Pension Plan benefits.

Your Family Budget

	Earner #1	Earner #2	Earner #3
INCOME			
Employment income			
Interest income			
Dividends			
Pension income			
Rental income			
Business income			
Other income			
TOTAL INCOME			
EXPENSES			
Taxes on income			
Mortgage or rent			
Utilities/property taxes			
Home maintenance			
Furniture			
Transportation/car			
Food			
Clothing			
Dental/medical			
Household contributions			
Loan payments			
Education			
Life and disability insurance			
Entertainment			
Charitable donations			
TOTAL EXPENSES			
SAVINGS			
RRSP/PENSION CONTRIBUTIONS			
OTHER INVESTMENTS			

The value of savings in RRSPs is easier to determine. For your balance sheet, include the current value, which is indicated on the statements sent to you by the financial institution holding your funds.

Once you've compiled a list of your assets, consider whether they are diversified enough. The older the head of the household, the more diversified the portfolio should be. Insufficient diversification means putting too many of your eggs in one basket – a pitfall for older people, who have less time to recover from financial disasters that might result when an investment goes sour. To introduce diversity into a portfolio, it may be necessary to borrow against other assets.

Typically, an undiversified personal balance sheet will consist mainly of pension claims and a house with a small mortgage, or with no mortgage at all. Borrowing against equity in the home, and using the proceeds to buy financial assets such as stocks and bonds, does more than just increase diversification. It allows the interest expense on the loan to be used as a deduction for income tax purposes. Furthermore, using investment vehicles which produce capital gains and dividends can offer significant tax benefits.

Home mortgages are the largest single liability for most Canadians. In fact, we have more than $290 billion in outstanding residential mortgages. Moreover, it is a huge pile of debt that is extremely expensive because mortgage interest is not deductible when calculating tax liabilities. If you have a 41 percent marginal tax rate and are paying $5,000 annually in mortgage interest, you must earn $8,475 to cover your after-tax mortgage interest. Those with a 52 percent marginal tax rate must earn $10,417.

You can save a bundle if you can reduce your mortgage by agree-ing to pay it off in less than the usual twenty-five years through a rapid amortization or by taking advantage of the annual pay-down most institutions offer. Look at the situation of a homeowner who has $10,000 in savings beyond rainy-day needs. If he's in a 41 per-cent tax bracket, earning even 10 percent before taxes on the savings is not as attractive as using the money to reduce the mortgage. That's because the 10 percent saving rate is reduced to 5.9 percent after taxes – a lot less than the 12 percent after taxes being paid on the mortgage.

For higher-bracket earners, the results are even more striking. That 10 percent before-tax savings rate is only 4.8 percent after

Your Financial Balance Worksheet

ASSETS	Earner #1	Earner #2
Bank accounts		
Canada Savings Bonds		
Other cash investments		
GICs		
Bonds		
Mortgage investments		
Annuities		
RRIFs		
Pensions		
RRSPs		
Stocks		
Mutual funds		
Other investments		
Cash value of life insurance		
Collectibles		
Furniture		
Cars		
House		
Cottage		
TOTAL ASSETS		
LIABILITIES		
Mortgages		
Bank loans		
Credit cards		
Investment loans		
Other debt		
TOTAL LIABILITIES		
NET WORTH		

taxes for someone paying a marginal tax rate of 52 percent. He would be far better off using the savings to pay off the mortgage. For these high-bracket earners, a risk-free rate of more than 20 percent would be necessary to break even after taxes with a 10 percent mortgage rate. In mid-1994 variable-rate mortgages were available at rates as low as 7 percent. Unless someone had investments which locked in higher returns on an after-tax basis it still made sense to pay off a mortgage as quickly as possible.

Most Canadians are well aware of the horrendous mortgage costs they face and attempt to reduce or eliminate the mortgage as soon as possible. For financial well-being, there's no finer aroma than the smell of a paid-up mortgage being burned to a crisp.

So fill out your balance sheet and tally your worth. After you have completed your balance sheet, review it with the aim of increasing returns and achieving diversification. Then prepare a target balance sheet, setting targets for both the next few years and the distant future. To make sure you're on track, review these targets each year.

Once you know where you are and where you would like to go, you can use the information and strategies in the rest of this book to build an investment program that will help ensure your financial life unfolds as you want. The remaining chapters of the book cover taxation of income, methods of putting your financial house in order, the setting of your investment objectives and your range of investment options.

These are the tools you can use to build your wealth. But there are other tools you must use, the most important of which is information. As an investor who wants to make the highest returns possible without ignoring the risks, you must have a fundamental knowledge of events that have an impact on investment.

CHAPTER 2

A Financial Tool Kit

MOST PROFESSIONAL INVESTORS in Canada make a point of reading the business press to keep themselves informed of developments in the economy, specific industries and individual companies. Basic reading material includes *The Globe and Mail Report on Business* or *The Financial Post* daily, possibly *The Wall Street Journal,* and a Canadian business weekly such as the *Financial Times of Canada* or *The Financial Post* weekly. In addition, there are numerous specialty publications covering the spectrum of investments.

But you have to learn to walk before you run so start with a paper that contains financial tables covering the investment areas that interest you, as well as information on economic or industrial developments and business trends. Start slowly and expand your reading as your understanding increases. Don't run out and buy subscriptions to every business publication available – most will end up unread.

The papers you choose should keep you informed about interest rate trends and the current rates available. Table III, the money market table, is taken from *The Globe And Mail Report on Business,* and includes several key short-term interest rates. The ninety-one-day treasury bill rate indicates what the federal government is paying for short-term money. The yields on T-bills are adjusted by the Bank of Canada to reflect its policies toward economic growth and the level at which it wishes to maintain the international value of the dollar.

All short-term rates, including the rate that banks pay on savings accounts, are based on T-bill yields. The Bank of Canada rate is the rate at which certain deposit-taking institutions can borrow funds from the Bank of Canada. But the key yield, as far as individual investors are concerned, is the T-bill rate.

MONEY RATES

ADMINISTERED RATES		UNITED STATES	Certificates of Deposit by dealer: 30 days, 4.74; 60 days, 4.80; 90 days, 4.85; 120 days, 4.90; 150 days, 5.11; 180 days, 5.16
Bank of Canada	5.72%	NEW YORK (AP) — Money rates for Thursday as reported by Telerate Systems Inc:	
Canadian prime	7.25%		
MONEY MARKET RATES		Telerate interest rate index: 4.910	Eurodollar rates: Overnight, 4.625-4.75; 1 month, 4.75-4.8125; 3 months, 4.875-4.93755; 6 months, 5.1875-5.25; 1 year, 5.6875-5.75
(for transactions of $1-million or more)			
3-mo. T-bill(when-issued)	5.45%	Prime Rate: 7.75	
1-month treasury bills	5.09%	Discount Rate: 4.00	
2-month treasury bills	5.25%	Broker call loan rate: 6.50	London Interbank Offered Rate: 3 months, 4.6875; 6 months, 5.00; 1 year, 5.50
3-month treasury bills	5.45%	Federal funds market rate:	
6-month treasury bills	5.87%	High 4.75 low 4.75 last 4.75	
1-year treasury bills	6.76%	Dealers commercial paper: 30-180 days: 4.77-5.16	Treasury Bill auction results: average discount rate: 3-month as of Aug. 22: 4.62; 6-month as of Aug. 22: 4.98
10-year Canada bonds	8.76%		
30-year Canada bonds	8.89%	Commercial paper by finance company: 30-270 days: 4.67-4.85	
1-month banker's accept.	5.33%		
2-month banker's accept.	5.43%		Treasury Bill, annualized rate on weekly average basis, yield adjusted for constant maturity, 1-year, as of Aug. 22: 5.63
3-month banker's accept.	5.53%	Bankers acceptances dealer indications: 30 days, 4.72; 60 days, 4.77; 90 days, 4.82; 120 days, 4.88; 150 days, 5.05; 180 days, 5.12	
Commercial Paper (R-1 Low)			
1-month	5.42%		Treasury Bill market rate, 1-year: 5.30-5.28
2-month	5.52%		
3-month	5.62%	Certificates of Deposit Primary: 30 days, 3.54; 90 days, 3.92; 180 days, 4.25	Treasury Bond market rate, 30-year: 7.54
Call money	5.37%		

SOURCE: THE GLOBE AND MAIL

TABLE III

Table IV shows the rates banks and trust companies are willing to pay for minimum deposits, usually of at least $5,000, and for terms ranging from thirty days to five years. Interest rates quoted by an institution can change at any time, depending on deposit levels at the institution. In fact, rates quoted by an institution on large amounts can change hourly to reflect marketplace trends.

It's also a good idea to keep an eye on bond yields so you can see what governments are paying for medium- and long-term funds. Trends in bond yields have a significant impact on mortgage rates and on insurance company annuity rates.

If you invest, or plan to invest, in the stock market you will require a publication containing stock tables. Those who trade their stocks daily would certainly want to follow their stocks in a daily newspaper. Otherwise, a weekly paper will suffice.

Stock tables provide trading information for the most recent period – including the share prices, price changes over the day or week, the number of shares traded and the price range over which the stock has traded during the past twelve months. They also include dividend information. The indicated dividend is the total

INTEREST RATES

This survey of rates offered by a sample group of companies was prepared by Cannex Financial Exchanges, Aug. 26, 1994, at 5:00 p.m. Savings rates are non-redeemable except where indicated by an 'r'. Rates are for information purposes only and should be confirmed by the company quoted.

SAVINGS RATES / MORTGAGE RATES

Company	Savings account ($1,000 bal.)	Chequing account	Min. deposit	30 days	60 days	90 days	120 days	180 days	270 days	Min. deposit	One year	Two years	Three years	Four years	Five years	Variable rate	6 month open	6 month closed	1 year open	1 year closed	2 year closed	3 year closed	4 year closed	5 year closed
BANKS																								
Banca Comm. Ital. Canada, Toronto	1.75	1.50	5,000	r4.50	r4.63	r4.88	r4.88	r5.38	r5.63	1,000	r6.63	r7.65	r7.88	r8.00	r8.25	-	8.38	-	9.25	8.45	9.50	9.88	10.13	9.95
Bank of Montreal, Toronto	2.00	0.25	5,000	r4.25	r4.38	r4.63	r4.63	r5.13	r5.38	1,000	6.25	7.25	7.63	7.88	8.00	7.50	8.38	7.25	9.25	8.45	9.50	9.88	10.13	10.25
Bank of Nova Scotia, Toronto	0.25	0.25	5,000	r4.25	r4.38	r4.63	r4.63	r5.13	r5.38	1,000	6.25	7.25	7.63	7.88	8.00	7.25	8.38	7.25	9.25	8.45	9.50	9.88	10.13	10.25
CIBC, Toronto	0.25	0.10	5,000	r4.25	r4.38	r4.63	r4.63	r5.13	r5.38	1,000	6.25	7.25	7.63	7.88	8.00	7.25	8.38	7.25	9.25	8.45	9.50	9.88	10.13	10.25
Citibank, Toronto	3.00	0.25	5,000	r4.50	r4.63	r4.88	r4.88	r5.38	r5.63	5,000	r6.38	7.25	7.63	7.88	8.00	-	8.38	7.25	9.25	8.45	9.50	9.88	10.13	10.25
HongKong Bank, Vancouver	0.50	0.50	5,000	4.25	4.38	4.63	4.63	5.13	5.38	1,000	6.25	7.25	7.63	7.88	8.00	7.25	8.38	7.25	9.25	8.45	9.50	9.88	10.13	10.25
Laurentian Bank, Montreal	0.25	-	10,000	4.50	4.63	4.63	4.88	5.38	5.63	1,000	6.38	7.25	7.63	7.88	8.00	-	8.38	7.25	9.25	8.45	9.50	9.88	10.13	10.25
Manulife Bank, Orillia	-	-	25,000	4.75	4.88	4.63	5.13	5.63	5.88	1,000	6.63	7.25	7.88	8.00	8.13	-	8.75	8.00	9.75	8.45	9.50	9.88	10.38	10.50
National Bank of Greece, Montreal	1.50	1.50	5,000	4.50	4.75	5.00	5.25	5.75	6.00	1,000	6.75	7.50	7.75	8.00	8.25	-	8.75	8.00	9.75	8.45	9.50	9.88	10.38	10.50
National Bank, Montreal	0.25	0.10	1,000	4.25	4.38	4.63	4.63	5.13	5.38	1,000	6.25	7.25	7.63	7.88	8.25	7.25	8.38	7.25	9.25	8.45	9.50	9.88	10.13	10.25
Republic National Bk NY, Montreal	0.50	-	50,000	5.00	5.00	5.05	5.05	5.05	5.05	50,000	5.60	6.94	7.31	7.66	7.77	7.25	8.38	7.25	9.25	8.45	9.50	9.88	10.13	10.25
Royal Bank of Canada, Montreal	0.50	0.25	5,000	r4.25	r4.38	r4.63	r4.63	r5.13	r5.38	1,000	6.25	7.25	7.63	7.88	8.00	7.50	8.38	7.25	9.25	8.45	9.50	9.88	10.13	10.25
Toronto-Dominion Bank, Toronto	0.25	0.25	5,000	4.25	4.38	4.63	4.63	5.13	5.38	1,000	6.25	7.25	7.63	7.88	8.00	7.50	8.38	7.25	9.25	8.45	9.50	9.88	10.13	10.25
TRUST COMPANIES																								
AGF Trust Co, Toronto	-	-	10,000	r3.00	r3.00	r3.00	r3.00	r3.00	r3.00	5,000	6.80	7.30	7.60	7.75	7.95									
Bayshore Trust, Toronto	-	1.25	5,000	5.00	5.00	5.25	5.25	5.75	6.00	1,000	6.75	7.75	8.00	8.13	8.25			7.75				9.75		
Bonaventure Trust, Montreal	-	-	5,000	4.38	4.38	4.63	4.75	5.00	5.13	1,000	6.38	7.38	7.88	8.00	8.13									
Canada Trust, Toronto	0.25	0.25	5,000	r4.25	r4.38	r4.63	r4.63	r5.13	r5.38	1,000	6.25	7.25	7.63	7.88	8.00	-	8.38	7.25				7.25		
Citizens Trust Co, Vancouver	2.00	1.25	5,000	r4.75	r4.75	r4.88	r5.13	r5.38	r5.63	1,000	6.38	7.25	7.50	7.88	8.00	-	8.38	7.25	9.25	8.45	9.50	9.89	10.13	10.25
Co-Operative Trust, Saskatoon	-	-	500	4.25	4.50	4.75	4.75	5.25	5.50	500	6.38	7.25	7.63	7.88	8.00	-	8.38	7.25	9.25	8.45	9.50	9.88	10.13	10.25
Community Trust, Toronto	-	-	5,000	4.38	4.50	4.25	5.00	5.25	5.50	5,000	6.25	7.25	7.63	7.75	8.00	-	9.00	8.00	9.75	8.75	8.75	10.25	10.50	10.50
Effort Trust, Hamilton	-	1.00	5,000	4.00	4.00	4.25	4.25	4.75	4.25	5,000	7.00	7.50	7.88	8.00	8.13	-		8.50		8.75	9.75	10.13	10.38	10.75
Equitable Trust, Toronto	-	-	10,000	5.25	5.50	4.25	4.25	5.75	5.75	5,000	7.30	7.50	7.88	8.00	8.13					8.45				
Family Trust, Markham	-	1.25	5,000	r4.88	r5.38	r5.63	r5.63	r6.25	r6.50	1,000	6.63	7.50	7.88	8.00	8.13	7.25	8.38	7.25	9.25	8.45	9.50	9.88	10.13	10.75
FirstLine Trust, Toronto	-	-	5,000	4.50	4.63	4.88	4.88	5.38	5.50	1,000	6.75	7.38	7.88	8.13	8.38			7.49		8.19	9.95	10.09		10.19
Household Trust, North York	-	-	5,000	4.50	4.75	4.88	5.50	5.88	5.88	1,000	7.00	7.38	7.88	8.13	8.25			8.00	9.25	9.25	10.00	10.38	10.38	10.75
Income Trust, Hamilton	-	-	5,000	4.88	5.25	5.75	5.75	6.13	6.25	1,000	7.13	7.55	8.00	8.00	8.00		8.75	8.00	9.00	9.00	9.25	9.63	9.88	10.00
Investors Group Trust, Winnipeg	-	0.25	5,000	4.50	4.63	4.63	4.63	5.38	5.38	1,000	6.38	7.25	7.63	7.88	8.00	7.50	8.38	8.00	9.75	8.25	9.25	9.63	9.88	10.00
Metropolitan Trust, Edmonton	-	-	5,000	4.50	4.75	5.25	5.25	5.50	5.75	1,000	6.38	7.50	7.63	7.88	8.00	-	8.38	7.25	9.25	8.45	9.50	9.88	10.13	10.25
Montreal Trust, Montreal	1.50	-	5,000	r4.25	r4.38	r4.63	r4.63	r5.13	r5.38	500	6.25	7.25	7.63	7.88	8.00	-	8.38	7.25	9.25	8.50	9.50	9.88	10.13	10.25
Municipal Trust, Barrie	1.25	0.75	5,000	r4.50	r4.63	r4.88	r5.00	r5.38	r5.63	500	6.75	7.25	7.50	7.75	8.00	-	8.50	7.25		8.50	9.75	10.38	10.50	10.50
Mutual Trust, Toronto	-	-	5,000	r3.75	r3.90	r4.20	r4.20	r4.75	r5.05	5,000	r6.30	r7.15	r7.65	r7.90	r8.05	7.50		7.25	9.25	8.45	9.38	9.88	10.00	10.00
National Trust, Toronto	0.25	0.75	5,000	4.50	4.63	4.88	4.88	5.38	5.63	500	6.50	7.25	7.63	7.88	8.00	-	8.38	7.25	9.25	8.45	9.38	9.88	10.13	10.25
North American Trust, Toronto	-	0.50	5,000	4.75	4.75	5.00	5.00	5.50	5.75	500	6.65	7.65	8.00	8.15	8.15	7.50	8.25	7.25	9.25	8.40	9.50	9.75	10.00	10.00
North West Trust, Edmonton	2.25	1.25	5,000	r4.25	4.50	4.88	4.88	5.25	5.50	500	6.25	7.00	7.50	7.88	7.88	-	8.38	7.25		8.50	9.50	10.13	10.38	10.50
Peace Hills Trust, Edmonton	-	3.75	5,000	5.00	4.00	5.50	4.25	6.00	5.50	5,000	6.25	7.25	7.50	7.75	8.00	-	8.50	8.00		8.50	9.50	10.00	10.25	10.50
Peoples Trust, Vancouver	0.50	0.50	5,000	5.00	5.00	5.50	5.50	6.00	6.00	5,000	7.38	7.25	7.63	7.75	7.75	7.25			9.25	8.45	9.50	9.88		
Royal Trust, Toronto	0.50	0.50	5,000	r4.25	r4.38	r4.63	r4.63	r5.13	r5.38	1,000	6.25	7.25	7.63	7.88	8.00	7.25	8.38	7.25	9.25	8.45	9.50	9.88	10.13	10.25
Sun Life Trust, Toronto	-	-	1,000	4.25	4.38	4.63	4.63	5.13	5.38	1,000	6.38	7.25	7.63	7.88	8.00	-	8.63	7.25	9.45	8.45	9.50	9.88	10.13	10.25
Trust General, Montreal	0.25	0.10	1,000	r4.25	r4.38	r4.63	r4.63	r5.13	5.38	1,000	6.25	7.25	7.63	7.88	8.25	-	8.38	7.25	9.25	8.45	9.50	9.88	10.13	10.25

TABLE IV

CANADIAN INDEXES

TORONTO STOCK EXCHANGE

52-week high	low	Index	Open	High	Low	Close	Chg	Vol (100s)	Div yield	Avg P/E	Tot. Ret.
4609.93	3918.07	TSE 300	4252.25	4268.48	4249.28	4257.00	-6.73	378922	2.30	32.28	8211.07
233.58	194.92	TSE 35	222.57	224.22	222.24	222.90	-0.73	182312	2.81	32.07	349.51
277.47	235.95	TSE 100	258.35	259.80	258.34	258.82	-0.49	298455	2.49	33.54	265.41
289.30	246.95	TSE 200	254.76	255.32	253.98	254.98	-0.04	80467	1.47	27.65	258.71

TSE 300 SUBGROUPS

Index	High	Low	Close	Chg	Vol
Metals & minerals	3991.88	3951.32	3953.90	-26.07	1380517
Integrated mines	4199.43	4146.99	4150.68	-27.18	853162
Mining	1938.72	1927.95	1937.42	-13.26	527355
Gold & Prec Mtls	9376.97	9298.41	9352.20	-9.70	7768714
Oil and gas	4546.49	4533.83	4546.49	-1.36	5232524
Integrated Oils	3999.71	3961.55	3979.29	-1.63	245322
Oil & gas prdcr	4736.17	4719.41	4735.75	-0.89	4629627
Oil & gas services	977.62	966.78	966.78	-3.05	357575
Paper & forest	4396.87	4330.08	4378.36	+68.05	4081660
Consumer products	6548.15	6499.62	6506.66	-14.27	1613277
Food processing	4857.08	4812.94	4825.56	-12.86	85277
Tobacco	9783.17	9625.91	9733.05	+44.24	402555
Distilleries	10767.07	10582.48	10613.24	-61.14	240625
Breweries/bev	4602.70	4516.34	4541.56	-6.69	510768
Household goods	1088.28	1070.57	1088.28	+13.77	155920
Autos & parts	8879.80	8825.42	8843.55	-22.81	181290
Biotech/pharm	469.00	462.95	463.93	-0.81	36842
Industrial products	2748.85	2732.17	2742.11	-2.55	5949857

Index	High	Low	Close	Chg	Vol
Steel	1288.31	1261.13	1267.17	-21.14	1231448
Fabricating & eng	3164.54	3138.25	3156.54	-8.00	159755
Transport equip	18041.31	17831.95	17933.06	-122.54	641650
Tech hardware	6554.26	6497.75	6546.93	+21.27	566378
Building materials	4649.00	4595.48	4618.48	+14.14	203780
Chem & fertilizer	4836.40	4790.47	4831.12	+6.66	2578909
Bus serv	1472.09	1461.03	1469.38	+9.95	289191
Tech software	977.04	960.27	960.27	-12.08	278746
Real estate & const	2454.95	2428.22	2433.50	-17.37	272356
Transport & envir	4756.72	4659.31	4737.22	+43.99	629492
Pipelines	3865.33	3807.29	3849.69	+18.56	1338343
Utilities	3528.29	3503.89	3507.74	-15.12	1660978
Telephone utils	3412.08	3385.57	3390.48	-16.81	1378959
Gas & Electrical	3617.25	3583.66	3596.83	-6.24	282019
Comm & media	8712.91	8657.21	8680.46	-21.78	1225320
Broadcasting	4479.58	4442.20	4442.20	-44.35	14300
Cable & ent	24701.19	24408.31	24683.60	-54.92	636305
Publishing	8122.91	8074.24	8074.24	-10.72	574715
Merchandising	3630.21	3604.60	3610.42	-9.14	691035
Wholesale	6297.45	6183.90	6269.06	+85.16	107769
Food stores	5898.71	5856.22	5856.86	-26.07	66556
Dept stores	1145.14	1133.00	1137.91	+0.65	173140
Specialty stores	1418.26	1403.76	1414.11	-6.11	209122
Hospitality	46781.18	46329.44	46329.44	-398.75	134448
Financial services	3157.14	3118.77	3134.05	-21.90	5018322
Banks & trusts	3574.47	3527.16	3547.35	-29.20	4539260
Invest co & fund	5494.94	5428.94	5449.41	-46.70	303448
Insurance	2524.14	2478.38	2505.13	+32.03	60050
Fin mangmt cos	993.74	987.22	987.72	+2.93	115564
Conglomerates	5278.21	5205.31	5245.19	+17.10	1029781

MONTREAL

Index	High	Low	Close	Chg	Vol
Market portfolio	2048.84	2037.66	2040.41	-6.27	3962264
Banking	2474.73	2438.74	2447.21	-29.63	1530660
Forest products	2685.76	2629.31	2681.42	+67.31	278758
Industrial products	1944.39	1936.10	1936.10	-5.53	1538327
Mining & minerals	2671.02	2660.02	2660.67	-5.82	1417076
Oil and gas	1522.90	1517.69	1520.66	+3.34	139380
Utilities	1997.05	1983.49	1992.12	+5.55	933145

THE DAY'S TSE 300

The TSE 300 composite index through the day yesterday, showing the change each hour from the previous day's close:

9:45 a.m.	4252.25	-11.48	1 p.m. 4262.00	-1.73
10 a.m.	4262.23	-1.50	2 p.m. 4255.83	-7.90
11 a.m.	4262.02	-1.71	3 p.m. 4250.77	-12.96
Noon	4261.63	-2.10	4 p.m. 4257.00	-6.73

VANCOUVER

Index	High	Low	Close	Chg	Vol
Composite	864.06	860.47	862.53	+2.06	15828783
Comm/Industrial	852.55	846.69	849.83	+3.14	816071
Resource	1359.22	1347.53	1354.73	+1.09	1540394

SOURCE: THE GLOBE AND MAIL

TABLE V

dividend payment that would be paid over the next twelve months, based on the latest dividend declared by the company. The dividend may be paid quarterly, semi-annually or annually, depending on company policy.

The Toronto and Montreal stock exchange tables included in the *The Globe And Mail Report on Business* give earnings information as well as financial ratios useful to investors. Two common ratios are yield and the price-earnings ratio. The yield is the dividend as a percentage of the stock price; the P/E ratio is the stock price divided by the latest twelve-month earnings. A P/E ratio of 12.7 means that an investor is paying $12.70 for each $1 of earnings.

The *Financial Times of Canada* uses technical analysis to compile its unique stock tables — Stock Trends. These tables are designed to provide investors with an indication of the long-term trend of individual stocks. Various different triangles and circles are used to indicate whether a stock is likely to increase or decrease in value in the coming weeks while lines, boldfaced type and stars are used to indicate significant increases or decreases in volume of shares traded or price. The tables also include each stock's P/E ratio, book value and cash-flow ratio.

Even if you don't follow individual stocks, you should keep an eye on the major stock market indexes. Virtually every major paper with a business section has a market summary graph and table as well as a commentary on the latest developments.

Mutual fund investors can find a daily table of fund prices in most major papers. The *Financial Times* monthly survey of investment funds groups funds according to investment objectives, so you can compare your funds' performance against funds with similar objectives.

If you are an active investor in the U.S. markets, you'll probably want a paper with extensive U.S. stock trading information. This information is available in *The Globe and Mail Report on Business*, *The Wall Street Journal* and *Barron's*, a U.S. financial weekly.

You'll also want a daily newspaper with complete tables if your investment interests extend to the options and futures markets. Because prices can be extremely volatile, you must remain well informed in order to make decisions quickly.

Corporate financial statements

Once you're adept at following business news and reading market tables, you should turn your attention to corporate financial statements. To do so, you don't have to become an expert investment analyst but if you're interested in getting better returns on your investments than you've earned up to now, it's essential that you learn the basics of financial statements.

Even if you plan to keep your money in the largest financial institutions or invest only in corporate bonds, you should learn to read a company's financial report. It is rare for an institution to get into trouble overnight and financial statements can offer valuable warnings of impending difficulties.

By law, every public company must issue an annual report covering financial results for its latest fiscal year. The company must also provide updates through quarterly reports, although these contain less detail. Companies selling securities to the public must issue a prospectus that includes all of the information a person needs to decide whether to invest.

Surprisingly, few people take the time to look at annual reports, which is a shame because the information contained can help investors understand the company. Even if you don't examine the financial statements, the management's discussion and financial review section of the report is helpful because of its description of the company's operations and its essential information about earnings and developments. It is this review that interprets the financial statements for the reader.

An annual report can generally be divided into a number of areas. The first is the report of the board of directors, chairman's or president's report. It usually reviews the company's operations during the year and often gives management's views of the outlook for the company and its industry. Of course, such reports try to show the company in a positive light.

Some investors ignore annual reports and financial statements because they expect their brokerage firm to deal with this information. In fact, the analysts employed by a brokerage house do watch for developments in companies whose shares have been recommended by the firm. Similarly, many people invest in mutual funds in order to have professional managers carry out this investment analysis for them. Even so, it makes sense to understand the basics so you can interpret results yourself – the experts aren't always right.

If you plan to invest in smaller companies you must learn to conduct your own analysis. While major brokerage houses follow major companies and provide detailed research reports, few provide studies of smaller firms. Sometimes the necessary information is not

ABC Ltd. Operating Statement
FOR THE YEAR ENDED DECEMBER 31

	1994 (000)	1993 (000)
REVENUE		
Sales of products, fees earned	$150,000	$125,000
EXPENSES		
Cost of sales and services	$125,000	$110,000
Depreciation	4,000	3,500
Interest on long-term debt	5,000	4,500
Other interest	2,000	1,500
TOTAL EXPENSES	136,000	119,500
Earnings before taxes	14,000	5,500
Taxes	6,000	3,000
NET EARNINGS	8,000	2,500
Earnings per share	$0.80	$0.25

TABLE VI

readily available, in which case it's best to stay away from the company – large or small – as an investment.

Although the financial statements are intimidating, they are not really that difficult to understand. Once you've made your way through the report from the president, chairman or board of directors you'll find four statements you shouldn't ignore. There is:
• the balance sheet;
• the statement of earnings, which shows revenues, expenses and earnings or losses;
• the consolidated statement of retained earnings, which shows the portion of earnings retained or reinvested in the business;
• and the statement of changes in financial position, which shows how the company financed its operations.

The financial statements of ABC Ltd. will help make the value of these statements clearer. The operating statement, corporate balance sheet and statement of retained earnings are fictitious and the statements are simplified. But by examining them you can see the basics that can be applied to analyzing genuine statements.

On the ABC Ltd. operating statement, the first line includes the revenue the company received from the sale of its goods or services. From this, you subtract the company's expenses. The cost of goods

ABC Ltd. Statement of Retained Earnings

AS AT DECEMBER 31

	1994 (000)	1993 (000)
Balance at beginning of year	$19,000	$17,000
Add net earnings	9,000	2,500
Less dividends paid	2,000	500
Balance at end of year	$26,000	$19,000

TABLE VII

and services includes the cost of goods sold, labour expenses, heat and light, rent and so on.

Depreciation is an expense that takes into consideration the declining value of equipment because of wear and tear on equipment – not a cash expense. For example, if a piece of machinery cost $1 million and has a life span of five years, it would be depreciated by $200,000 each year. That amount would be considered an expense, even though $200,000 wasn't spent. In our example, the total depreciation charged in 1993 is $4 million.

The company may have financed its operations by issuing a bond. The interest paid on this debt is shown separately from interest on short-term debt, usually money borrowed from a bank. Bank borrowings can be repaid at any time and consequently are considered short-term debt and would appear as "other interest."

Subtracting expenses from revenues results in pre-tax earnings. From these a company will pay taxes, leaving it with net earnings. Often a company will report current and deferred income taxes. Current taxes generally refer to taxes that are required for immediate tax purposes and deferred income taxes are generally segregated for accounting purposes. Earnings per share represents total earnings divided by the number of shares outstanding. In this case, we've assumed that the company has ten million shares outstanding.

There are a number of profitability ratios investors can apply to the income statement. You might look for trends of increased or decreased profitability by comparing the yearly change in the cost of goods sold as a percentage of revenues. Or you could compare this ratio with that of competing companies. Most important is the net profit margin – the percentage of earnings over revenues. Compare this ratio with previous years and with similar companies in

ABC Ltd. Balance Sheet
AS AT DECEMBER 31

	1994 (000)	1993 (000)
ASSETS		
Cash and investments	$20,000	$16,500
Inventory	30,000	10,000
Total current assets	50,000	26,500
Land	8,000	8,000
Buildings	40,500	42,500
Equipment	30,000	36,000
Less accumulated depreciation	12,000	8,000
Net fixed assets	66,500	78,500
Total assets	116,500	105,000
LIABILITIES		
Current liabilities	20,000	16,000
Bank loans	20,000	16,000
Total current liabilities	50,000	50,000
Long-term debt	70,000	66,000
SHAREHOLDERS' EQUITY		
Share capital	20,000	20,000
Retained earnings	26,000	19,000
Total shareholders' equity	46,000	39,000
Total liabilities and shareholders' equity	116,000	105,000

TABLE VIII

order to find trends. When looking at ratios, don't compare companies in different industries. Ratios vary widely from industry to industry.

A corporate balance sheet can also give you an insight into the health of the company. The balance sheet, a snapshot of the company's financial position, is broken into three sections:

• the company's assets, which are divided into liquid assets, cash and assets that can be quickly turned to cash; and fixed assets, such as buildings and machinery.

• liabilities, which is what the company owes. Current liabilities, such as bank loans, are liabilities that are due within one year.

Long-term liabilities, such as bonds and mortgages, refer to debts that are due at some date beyond one year.

• shareholders' equity, which is the difference between assets and liabilities. Shareholders' equity is made up of share capital – the value of shares sold to the public based on the price paid to the company rather than on market value – and retained earnings. Retained earnings are the profits which have been reinvested in the company. An example of a statement of retained earnings is shown in Table VII. This statement shows that of the $9 million profit, $2 million was paid out as dividends, leaving $7 million for reinvestment. Shareholders' equity generally grows by the amount of retained earnings.

Again, there are a number of financial ratios that should be examined. One of the most important is the current ratio, which is current assets divided by current liabilities. In the case of ABC Ltd., the current ratio is 1.5 to 1 – calculated by dividing $30 million by $20 million. The ratio indicates that the company has more than enough short-term assets available to pay off its current liabilities. Depending on the industry, a ratio of about one to one is reason for concern, although in some cyclical industries investors would require a much higher ratio in order to ensure liabilities are met and operations continue during down cycles.

Another important yardstick is the debt-to-equity ratio. In our example of ABC Ltd., the value of outstanding long-term debt exceeds the value of fixed assets, with the ratio being about 1.13 to one. This is acceptable in some industries, such as utilities, where earnings are assured. It is not healthy for a company in a cyclical industry.

Analysis of financial ratios is extremely important for people investing in debt such as corporate bonds or in guaranteed investment certificates in excess of what is covered by deposit insurance. If you are going to invest in corporate bonds, your broker will be able to provide you with the information you need to judge the quality of the issue. But if you are in doubt or cannot understand what you are being told, stick with investments that are backed by government guarantees.

The financial statements in an annual report also include the auditors' report to the shareholders, which states that the company's independent auditors examined the statements in the annual report and are satisfied that they are accurate. Rarely will auditors make a qualified statement indicating concern about a company's viability as an ongoing concern. When they do, it is a warning that should not be ignored. It is not the auditors' job to look for fraud. Instead, they review how the company prepared its statements and decide whether they are reasonable.

The statements also include a series of notes which give substantial information about the company's accounting policies, transactions involving officers and directors, important lawsuits, if any, and information on long-term commitments such as leases. Reading these helps build your understanding of the company.

After you've learned enough about statement analysis to enable you to ask the right questions, you are ready for the next step – learning about the different types of investments offered in Canada.

Debt versus equity

There are two major categories of investment. One is debt, the other is equity. In the case of debt, you lend your money to a government, corporation or individual. In return, you are promised the payment of interest and the return of your principal at the end of a set period. Common examples of debt investments are savings accounts, Canada Savings Bonds and guaranteed investment certificates.

The safety of your money depends on the financial strength of the issuer and whether your funds are insured or guaranteed by a third party. Money on deposit with a bank or trust company is insured up to $60,000 in principal and interest for each institution by the Canada Deposit Insurance Corporation. Credit unions have a similar arrangement. Canada Savings Bonds are guaranteed by the federal government. Some bonds are secured by specific assets, just like a mortgage is secured by property.

Some debt instruments, however, are a great deal safer than others. The subsidiaries of Principal Group that offered investment contracts may have guaranteed these instruments, but their guarantees were worthless when the parent company in Edmonton collapsed.

Here's a good rule to follow: If you aren't going to take the time to analyze the credit-worthiness of an issuer of debt, stick with deposits that are backed by a government guarantee or are insured. For amounts above those covered by deposit insurance, stick with the largest banks and trust companies.

Lenders invest in debt. If you invest in equity, such as common stocks, you become an owner and can share in the profits of enterprises. If you choose your investments carefully, you will profit through gains in their value and increased cash flow through dividend payments.

Historically, people who have invested for growth have earned returns of several percentage points a year more than those who have invested for income. That, of course, is a broad generalization. Many people have become wealthy through cautiously investing only in fixed-income securities, earning returns far in excess of what would have been earned with a portfolio invested in both equity and debt.

Conversely, many people who hoped to reap great profits by investing in equities have lost money because they failed to analyse, listened to bad investment tips or failed to monitor their holdings. Unfortunately, it's possible to lose on "safe investments" as well. And that brings us to the next part of this book – how the government taxes your investment income.

CHAPTER 3

Tax Rules: Increasing Your Take

IT IS ESSENTIAL THAT AS AN investor, you understand the income tax system and how it applies to investment income. Otherwise you could end up paying more tax than you should.

There are two key points to consider: how different types of investment income are taxed, and what you can and cannot do to split income among family members to reduce your family tax bill.

Since the introduction of tax reform in 1988, Canadians have three tax brackets, down from the previous ten. Federal income tax rates for 1994 are 17 percent on the first $29,590 of taxable income, 26 percent on taxable income from $29,591 to $59,180 and 29 percent on anything more than $59,180. These brackets increase each year based on a formula tied to inflation. Your federal tax is reduced by tax credits. All taxpayers receive a basic personal tax credit, which replaces the former basic personal deduction. Depending on your circumstances, you may be eligible for other credits, such as those for child support or spousal support.

Although personal tax rates were supposed to drop with the introduction of tax reform, the actual federal tax rates you pay are higher because of surtaxes. These are taxes paid on top of your base federal taxes — in 1994 they are 3 percent on the basic tax, 5 percent on tax over $12,500.

In addition to federal tax, you must pay provincial tax of a few points more than half the federal rate – provincial taxes vary from province to province. If your top marginal federal tax rate is 26 percent, your combined top federal-provincial rate will be about 41 percent, not including surtaxes. If your top federal rate is 29 percent, your combined federal-provincial rate will be about 49 percent. You will also face provincial surtaxes – taxes on taxes – which vary from province to province; these depend on your income level and can push your marginal tax rate as high as 54 percent.

Taxation of Interest and Dividends

	Interest	Dividend
Interest received	$100.00	–
Dividend received	–	$100.00
Dividend "gross up"	–	$25.00
Taxable dividend	–	$125.00
Federal tax (29%)	$29.00	$36.25
Less dividend tax credit	–	$16.67
Net federal tax + surtax	$29.87	$20.17
Add provincial tax*	$15.66	$10.57
Total tax paid	$44.66	$30.74
NET RETURN	**$55.34**	**$69.26**

*54% of basic federal tax. Provincial tax rates vary from province to province.

TABLE IX

The taxes you pay on money earned through investment depend not only on your marginal tax rate, but also on the source of the investment income. Interest from Canadian and foreign sources and dividends from foreign corporations are the most heavily taxed, followed by Canadian dividends and capital gains.

You'll pay your full marginal tax rate on interest income and on dividends from foreign companies, whether paid directly to you or through a mutual fund. If you have $1,000 of interest income and your marginal tax rate is 41 percent, the tax bill comes to $410. Until 1988, the first $1,000 of interest income was exempt from tax because of an investment income deduction that disappeared with tax reform. Interest is taxed in the year earned, whether you receive it or leave it to compound.

Dividends from Canadian corporations are treated differently. This treatment is designed to reflect the fact that dividends are paid from profits that in most cases have already been taxed, and to encourage investors to invest in common and preferred shares. If you receive dividends from Canadian corporations, your tax rate on those payments will be reduced by the federal dividend tax credit.

Calculating the tax on dividends can be complicated. The amount on which you base your federal tax calculation is 125 percent of the actual dividend received – known as the "grossed-up" figure. If you receive $100 in dividends, this $100 is increased by 25

Top Marginal Tax Rates

Province	Rate	Province	Rate
Alberta	46.1%	Nova Scotia	53.8%
British Columbia	54.2%	Ontario	53.2%
Manitoba	50.4%	Prince Edward Island	50.3%
New Brunswick	51.4%	Quebec	52.9%
Newfoundland	51.3%	Saskatchewan	52.0%
NWT	44.4%	Yukon Territory	46.6%

The table shows the maximum tax rate you would pay on salary income. The rate of tax which you pay depends on the province in which you live; provincial rates are a percentage of federal rates and vary widely. Moreover, provincial surtaxes, which have pushed top marginal tax rates higher in recent years, vary from province to province and kick in at different levels. For example, the top Ontario rate applies to income over $67,853 while the threshold for Prince Edward Island is $92,734.

TABLE X

percent to $125, against which you calculate federal tax. From this figure you subtract the dividend tax credit, which is 13.33 percent of the grossed-up dividend, or 16.67 percent of the dividend actually received. This amount is then subtracted from your federal tax.

Table IX compares the taxation of interest and dividend income. The calculation assumes the investor pays tax at the top marginal rate and has a provincial tax rate of 54 percent of the federal rate. Surtaxes are ignored.

In the end, the dividend tax credit reduces the tax you pay on dividends from Canadian corporations so that on a before-tax basis $1 of dividends is equal to about $1.26 of interest – a ratio that holds true no matter which federal tax bracket you're in. As a result, a 6.4 percent after-tax dividend is equal to an 8 percent interest-rate yield, an 8 percent dividend is equal to a 10 percent interest yield and a 12 percent dividend is equal to a 15 percent interest yield.

If you live in Quebec, you'll find some variance in your after-tax interest and dividend income because the province sets its own income tax rates, independent of federal rates. A Quebec resident paying the top federal and provincial tax rates would net about $47 from $100 of interest income, $61 from $100 of dividend income.

Capital gains are taxed differently. First, it is comforting to know that not all of the capital gains you earn are taxed. In fact, 25 percent of capital gains earned is untaxed, leaving only 75 percent unsheltered from the taxman's grasp. Therefore, if you have $100 of capital gains, $75 is taxable. If you're paying the top marginal tax rate, that will result in tax of $36.75 and net earnings of $63.25.

Until the February 22, 1994 federal budget, Ottawa allowed each taxpayer a lifetime capital gains exemption of $100,000. This applied to gross capital gains, as opposed to taxable capital gains, and affected just about any capital gain earned – including stock market profits and profits from selling precious metals. (Gains from the sale of a family's principal residence are exempt from tax and had no bearing on the lifetime exemption.) Ottawa changed the rules regarding real estate capital gains and lifetime capital gains in its February 1992 budget, excluding real estate gains from the lifetime exemption unless it was part of a business or a farm.

The change was intended to curb real estate speculation. However, it affected many people. For example, gains on the sale of a family cottage were no longer be eligible for the lifetime exemption (the taxation of a gain on the family cottage on death of the owner also affected many people's estate planning). Ottawa will determine the portion of capital gains taxable by the length of time the property is held. For instance, if your cottage has appreciated $50,000 in the ten years you owned it to February 1992 and you sold it in February 1994, one-twelfth of the gain will be taxable even though the cottage may have fallen in value in recent years because of recession. You might even consider sheltering any gains by transferring property to other members of the family at appraised value.

If you had unrealized capital gains on budget day you have the option of crystallizing them when you file your 1994 tax return. This could mean that you will not pay any tax on gains made up to and including February 22, 1994. The value at the close of business on February 22 will become your cost for reporting capital gains on any subsequent appreciation.

Borrowing to invest
Interest on money borrowed for investment can be deducted from your income when filing your tax return. If your marginal tax rate is 50 percent and you borrow money at 7.25 percent, your after-tax cost is only 3.625 percent; if your marginal tax rate is 41 percent

Borrowing to Invest – One-Year Holding Period
12% RETURN – 50% TAX RATE – 7.25% INTEREST

	Without Leverage	With Leverage
Equity	$100,000	$100,000
Loan	–	100,000
Total investment	100,000	200,000
Capital gain (12%)	12,000	24,000
Taxable gain (75%)	9,000	18,000
Tax (50% of taxable gain)	(4,500)	(9,000)
After-tax gain	7,500	15,000
Cash available for investment	3,625	0
Interest expense	0	(3,625)
Increase in equity after one year	$11,125	$11,375

TABLE XI

your after-tax cost of borrowing is 4.278 percent. Many people are attracted to leveraging — borrowing for investment — because of the relatively low after-tax cost of borrowing. However, it is important to realize that an individual who chooses not to borrow for investment has the use of the funds which would otherwise be paid as interest. Any comparisons of borrowing versus not borrowing to invest must include the use of this capital.

If you are approached to buy funds using borrowed money, make some projections. In these projections, use several rates of return and various different interest rates for your cost of borrowing. By doing this you will have a range of possible results and can understand your potential risks and rewards. You should also determine the cushion you must have to protect yourself against a rise in interest rates or a fall in the market. Before implementing your leverage program, ask yourself whether you could afford to continue with a leverage program if interest rates rose sharply. Similarly, determine the magnitude of a market correction your bank will tolerate before asking you to put up additional security. In fact, you might want to have a generous credit line available to provide additional security.

The following examples look at the results of leverage under certain circumstances and specific assumptions. In each case, the amount borrowed is $100,000. We've used two different interest rates — 7.25 percent and 10 percent and two different rates of re-

Borrowing to Invest – Five-Year Holding Period
12% RETURN – 50% TAX RATE – 7.25% INTEREST

	Without Leverage	With Leverage
Equity	$100,000	$100,000
Loan	–	100,000
Total investment	100,000	200,000
Capital gain (12%)	76,234	152,468
Taxable gain (75%)	57,176	114,351
Tax (50% of taxable gain)	(28,588)	(57,176)
After-tax gain	47,646	95,293
Gain from investing cash flow	3,065	0
Cash available for investment	18,125	0
Interest expense	0	(18,125)
Increase in equity after five years	$65,771	$77,168

TABLE XII

turn — 12 percent and 30 percent. A 50 percent marginal tax rate is assumed for all examples except the third, which assumes a 41 percent marginal tax rate.

The key assumption in the examples is that if the investor did not use his capital to pay the interest on a loan of $100,000, he or she would invest it. For example, at a 50 percent marginal tax rate and prime rate of 7.25 percent, the after-tax cost of the loan is $3,625. Our example therefore assumes that the investor would have invested $3,625 if he or she had not used a leverage program.

The examples look at the results of leverage in which an investor with $100,000 borrows another $100,000. In the first example (Table XI), we have assumed a rate of return of 12 percent, an interest rate of 7.25 percent and a marginal tax rate of 50 percent. In this case, our individual has a capital gain of $24,000 at the end of the first year using leverage. $6,000 is tax free and a 50 percent tax on the remaining $18,000 leaves her with an after-tax gain of $15,000. Although her bank charges her interest of 7.25 percent, her after-tax interest expense is only $3,625 because interest on money borrowed for investment purposes is deductible. This cost of borrowing reduces her profit to $11,375.

Without leverage she would have a capital gain of $12,000 at the end of a year — $7,500 after tax. But she would also have the $3,625

Borrowing to Invest – One-Year Holding Period

12% RETURN – 41% TAX RATE – 7.25% INTEREST

	Without Leverage	With Leverage
Equity	$100,000	$100,000
Loan	–	100,000
Total investment	100,000	200,000
Capital gain (12%)	12,000	24,000
Taxable gain (75%)	9,000	18,000
Tax (41% of taxable gain)	(3,690)	(7,380)
After-tax gain	8,310	16,620
Cash available for investment	4,278	0
Interest expense	0	(4,278)
Increase in equity after one year	$12,588	$12,343

TABLE XIII

which would otherwise have been her after-tax interest expense. Adding this to her capital gives her a total increase in equity of $11,125 over the 12 months. Using leverage would have given her only $250 more. The benefits of leverage are clearly marginal and the increased profit doesn't compensate for the risk she's taken.

If we take this example a step further and use a five-year holding period (Table XII), leverage seems a lot more appealing. The after-tax gain from leverage grows to $95,293 compared to $47,646 without leverage. In the leverage scenario we have to subtract interest of $3,625 a year for a total increase in equity of $77,168. Where leverage is not used, the $3,625 would have been available for investment. It would have produced a capital gain of $4,904 — $3,065 after tax. This provides the investor who has not leveraged with a total increase in equity of $65,771 — $11,397 less than with the leverage program. (We have ignored any taxes that would have been due on distributions during the five-year period. Taxes would have reduced the growth rate over the five years, and in this example, reduced the benefits of leverage somewhat.)

The third example (Table XIII) is similar to the first example but with one change in the assumption. We have lowered our investor's marginal tax rate to 41 percent. This means that she pays less tax on her capital gain. However, it also means that she gets to deduct less of her interest expense which means higher borrowing costs. Using

Borrowing to Invest – One-Year Holding Period
12% RETURN – 50% TAX RATE – 10% INTEREST

	Without Leverage	With Leverage
Equity	$100,000	$100,000
Loan	–	100,000
Total investment	100,000	200,000
Capital gain (12%)	12,000	24,000
Taxable gain (75%)	9,000	18,000
Tax (50% of taxable gain)	(4,500)	(9,000)
After-tax gain	7,500	15,000
Cash available for investment	5,000	0
Interest expense	0	(5,000)
Increase in equity after one year	$12,500	$10,000

TABLE XIV

leverage gives her an after-tax capital gain of $16,620 and after-tax interest expense of $4,278 for an increase in equity after one year of $12,343. If she had not used leverage she would have had an after-tax capital gain of $8,310 — plus the capital she would have had to pay her interest costs for a total increase in equity after one year of $12,588. Clearly, a lower tax bracket makes a substantial difference and our individual would have been better not to use leverage. In fact, leverage is best left for individuals who are in the top marginal tax brackets.

The next example (Table XIV) uses an interest rate of 10 percent. It demonstrates that leverage loses its lustre as the spread between the cost of funds and the expected rate of return narrows.

A more positive use of leverage is when you expect to earn a significant above-average return over a short period of time. For example, if you were able to earn a 30 percent return on your invested capital (Table XV) your increase in equity after one year would be $33,875 using leverage and $22,375 without leverage. (Indeed, this strategy would have generated huge returns over the twelve months ended June 30, 1993 with the purchase of many equity and resource funds. However, in the subsequent 12 months a leverage program would have given relatively poor results.)

Borrowing to Invest – One-Year Holding Period

30% RETURN – 50% TAX RATE – 7.25% INTEREST

	Without Leverage	With Leverage
Equity	$100,000	$100,000
Loan	–	100,000
Total investment	100,000	200,000
Capital gain (30%)	30,000	60,000
Taxable gain (75%)	22,500	45,000
Tax (50% of taxable gain)	(11,250)	(22,500)
After-tax gain	18,750	37,500
Cash available for investment	3,625	0
Interest expense	0	(3,625)
Increase in equity after one year	$22,375	$33,875

TABLE XV

Families and taxes

You should also be aware of how Ottawa treats income within a family. In most cases, income is taxed in the hands of the person who earns it, and income from investments is taxed in the hands of the person who provides the capital. In other words, you cannot give your husband or wife (including a common-law spouse after 1992) capital for investment and expect to have the income taxed at his or her marginal tax rate. Ottawa will consider the income yours and hold you responsible for the tax on it.

That's the simplest case. Things become more complicated if you provide your husband or wife with financial backing to open a business he or she will operate. In such a case, you should seek professional accounting and legal advice. If you give or lend funds to your children, grandchildren, nieces or nephews under the age of eighteen, the rules are again somewhat different. Interest and dividends are taxable in your hands, but capital gains are taxable in the hands of the children. Even more complicated is the fact that interest earned on interest, on which you have paid tax, is taxable in the children's hands.

If you invest child tax credit cheques on behalf of a child by depositing the payments directly to an account in the child's name, the interest earned is taxable in the child's hands. Because a child can earn several thousand dollars without affecting your ability to claim the child as a deduction, this income can be tax-free.

These income-attribution rules only affect spouses and children under eighteen. If you give funds to your adult children, the income will be taxed in their hands, but if you lend it to them, or any other non-arm's-length individual such as a parent, the income is taxable in your hands but any capital gains earned are not. However, the attribution rules won't apply if the loan is made at competitive interest rates. It was common in the past for parents to lend money to their adult children attending university, money which the children would invest to finance their educations. Usually, the children would not pay tax on the income. The attribution rules changed in 1988 and ended this strategy.

It is important to note that Ottawa began to recognize common-law marriages for tax purposes beginning in 1993. Under the old rules, if you gave or lent funds to a common-law spouse, any income would be taxed in their hands, not yours. This is no longer the case; any income is now taxed in your hands.

The attribution rules make it necessary for families to engage in long-term investment planning if they are to make wise use of their money. Ideally, each spouse should have approximately the same amount of investment assets. If a woman plans to leave the work force to have children, it might make sense for her to save her entire salary and for the couple to use the husband's income to pay expenses. Then, at a later date, he would build up his investment capital. This way, income earned by the wife will likely be taxed at a lower rate than if all the family investment income were taxed in the husband's hands.

Income-splitting was at one time a popular tax-saving strategy, but Ottawa has eliminated most opportunities to split income. However, there are still some ways of selling assets to a family member at fair market value to generate capital that can be invested. Again, if you are thinking about taking this route, you should seek professional advice.

Moreover, you should consider the impact of your province's family law on your strategy. For instance, in Ontario the matrimonial residence is considered family property regardless of who paid for it. A married man or woman who takes an inheritance and uses it to pay off the mortgage on the family residence has effectively gifted half the inheritance to the other spouse.

CHAPTER 4

First Things First

BEFORE STARTING YOUR investment program, there are some essential steps you should follow to ensure your financial well-being. One of the first is to dispose of all personal debts not used to purchase investment assets such as securities or real assets such as a home or cottage. Personal debts are the biggest barrier to building wealth.

Consumer credit is very expensive. The cost of carrying an unpaid balance on a credit card can be as much as 2 percent a month. On an average balance of $1,000 a month, that adds up to more than $240 a year in interest. Moreover, the interest on personal debt is not deductible from income, which means you must earn a great deal more than $240 to pay that interest. If your marginal tax rate is 41 percent, more than $400 of your gross income goes to paying the interest on that $1,000. It is easy to see, then, why the best investment you can make is to pay down that debt. You will not find a stock market investment that can give you a consistent rate of return that exceeds the cost of consumer debt.

Still, it is unrealistic to expect most people to stay out of debt completely. Credit is necessary in many cases, particularly for big-ticket items such as cars and houses. The trick is to keep debt costs to a minimum, and that means paying off your most expensive forms of credit first. You should, therefore, try to pay off your credit card debt as soon as possible, and then make a habit of paying off balances in full each month. Credit cards should never be used as a source of financing, but instead as a convenient alternative to carrying cash or a cheque book. If it is impossible to pay off the balance, it is better to borrow the necessary funds elsewhere at less cost. You are much better off using a bank personal line of credit, which offers substantially lower interest rates – generally, a percentage point or two above the prime lending rate. This could cut interest expenses by as much as one-half to two-thirds.

If you are in the market for a loan, shop around. The cost of credit varies widely, so if your own bank, trust company or financial institution is not the least expensive, ask it to match the best rate you can find. If it will not, consider going elsewhere. Similarly, mortgage rates can differ among institutions. Even a small fraction of a percentage point can make a significant difference in payments, especially on a large mortgage. Again, your best bet is to shop for the lowest rate possible, particularly if you are buying a new home. Changing mortgage companies to get a lower rate when it's time to renew a mortgage can be expensive because of legal costs (although some institutions will pick up these costs), so shopping at that time may not be so advantageous. In this case the best route may be to ask your current mortgage-holder to match the lowest available rate.

Invest now or pay off your debts?

Of course, you should strive to pay down your debts as quickly as possible. The quicker you do, the more money you'll have in your pocket for savings, investment or spending. However, many people feel they can do better by using their savings to play the stock market, rather than to eliminate debts.

Perhaps they can. But market performance figures suggest that the average investor certainly cannot. Even so, you may be confident you're a member of the minority that can realize a better return on stocks than you would get by paying down debt. Yet even in this case, it makes sense to structure your finances to cut your interest expenses.

First, use your savings or cash flow to pay off debts. Then borrow the funds back to buy stocks or other investments. You'll still owe the same amount but you'll reap additional gains at tax time. Because your loan is now for investments, the interest is deductible from income for tax purposes. But you must be prepared to show that the loan is, in fact, for investment – meaning you must have documentation to prove the money was borrowed to buy an investment and that it was used for an investment. And remember, if you want to deduct interest, your investment must be made with the expectation of producing income in the form of interest or dividends. So while stocks qualify – even if it is unlikely that some will pay dividends – gold bullion does not.

If you plan to restructure your affairs to make your interest deductible, you're probably best off reviewing the procedure with your financial advisor to ensure you have the proper documentation and that you will not run afoul of Ottawa's anti-avoidance tax rules.

Deciding whether you should borrow for investment is another matter. Certainly, fortunes have been made by those who invest with borrowed funds – and fortunes have been lost as well. Most real estate purchases are heavily leveraged, meaning investors provide some of their own capital, but borrow a great deal more. In the case of commercial real estate, deals are often financed 80 percent or more with borrowed capital.

Stock market purchases can also be leveraged, but stock exchange bylaws limit the portion of borrowed funds to 50 percent, or even less if you're investing in more risky junior securities. Many sellers of mutual funds also recommend purchasing funds with borrowed money, and a number of financial institutions have arrangements with mutual fund dealers to provide financing of up to $3 for every $1 the client invests.

But markets move down as well as up, and if you are heavily leveraged, a price drop could cause significant problems. If you buy securities with borrowed funds and the price of your investment declines you must come up with more capital so that the equity in your account meets the minimum under your purchase agreement. In the case of stocks, equity must at least equal the amount owed to your broker. In the case of real estate, the investor must come up with funds to pay interest on debt if the cash flow fails to cover costs.

So while leverage can make you a lot of money, it can also be a losing strategy. If you decide to use borrowed funds for investment, make sure you understand the risks and have the financial strength to keep yourself above water if your investment goes sour. It's best not to get in over your head when you borrow – if you must borrow at all.

Choosing an investment advisor

Choosing a stockbroker, mutual fund dealer or any other investment professional is one of the most important investment decisions you will make. Even the most sophisticated investors need brokers, if only to execute orders properly and pass on information. Novice investors, meanwhile, must depend heavily on brokers and other investment salespeople for advice, suggestions and guidance about specific securities and an overall investment strategy.

The choice of advisors has become more complicated in recent years with the introduction of specialized financial products such as options and futures on treasury bills, bonds, currencies and stock market indexes. Even traditional financial products such as stocks, bonds and mutual funds have become increasingly complex. As a result, an investor who diversifies – perhaps with a portfolio of stocks, mutual funds, bonds, and maybe even futures and options – can find himself dealing with several investment professionals.

Further complicating matters is the fact that since 1983 brokerage firms have been allowed to set their own commission rates, rather than adhering to a fixed-rate schedule set by major stock exchanges. A number of discount brokerage firms have opened up shop, charging commissions of as little as one-fifth of the old fixed schedule for large orders. But unlike traditional brokerage firms, they offer few services other than the execution of orders. The discounters are adding some services in the hopes of attracting additional business and improving profitability. Still, they appeal mostly to investors who conduct their own research and analysis and who don't want to pay for brokerage house research.

However, the majority of investors choose to deal with brokerage firms that can provide a variety of services and products, or with those that specialize in specific products. These firms should continually provide clients with essential information that affects their holdings, as well as keep them informed of new investment opportunities. In other words, brokerage houses should be more than simple order-takers.

Not all full-service firms are alike. Some are major underwriting firms, which raise capital for corporations by selling new securities to financial institutions and the public. Most of these firms are owned or controlled by major financial institutions and have large retail operations to handle trading for individuals. Within these retail operations are often found departments that specialize in mutual funds, commodities and options trading.

Other firms specialize in providing trading expertise and independent research to clients and do not get heavily involved in underwriting. Most of these firms deal almost exclusively with institutional investors such as pension funds, insurance companies, banks, mutual funds and trust companies. However, some actively pursue retail business and may even take part in some underwritings through what is called a selling group. While they are not involved in putting the underwriting together or in financing a major part of it, they are involved in the distribution of securities.

Mutual fund dealers are a somewhat different breed. Most call themselves financial planners and try to work out long-term investment programs aimed at meeting clients' financial goals. Financial planners often are licenced to sell insurance as well as mutual funds, while some also offer tax-shelter products. In addition, banks, trust companies and major insurance companies have been entering the mutual fund market in recent years.

There are two types of mutual fund dealers. The first includes those who are part of a direct selling force and sell only products belonging to one group of funds. Generally, commissions charged by these dealers are fixed although this may be changing. The second type is the independent dealer who sells funds offered by several fund management companies. In theory, such dealers can choose from among several hundred funds, but in practice they usually limit their selection to a handful. Commissions are negotiable, although many independent dealers, particularly those who offer detailed financial planning services, are unwilling to trim fees substantially. Most funds are sold without commissions but with redemption fees which decline with the length of time the fund is (or funds managed by the same company are) held. The latest twist involves dealers who charge a flat annual fee to clients and do not pay a commission when buying or selling funds.

Choosing a brokerage firm

Before choosing a brokerage firm you should decide on your main investment objectives. For example, people whose interests include substantial dealings in bonds are probably wise to consider large, integrated firms. Because of the underwriting business of these firms, they have major bond trading departments and are better equipped to buy and sell bonds than most small investment dealers.

If stocks are your priority, it's wise to make sure the firm you deal with is a member of the Toronto Stock Exchange or, in Quebec, the Montreal Exchange. Such memberships indicate the firm has direct access to the most important Canadian securities markets.

TSE members dealing with retail investors range in size from small firms with a handful of personnel in one office to large firms with offices in major centres across the country. Large firms usually provide a wide variety of research products, ranging from economic analysis to detailed reports on individual industry groups and stocks. However, they cannot be expected to follow many of the smaller publicly traded companies because it would not be a cost-effective use of their analysts' time. They may follow smaller companies as part of an industry group or as a special situation. But their emphasis is almost always on larger, more heavily traded stocks that are more likely to be of interest to clients.

Possible conflicts of interest

The salespeople at large firms are often not allowed to recommend stocks not followed closely by their analysts. As a result, their clients probably will not hear of many investment opportunities. In addition, because these dealers tend to track the same companies, information they distribute is rarely unique and is usually reflected in the price of a stock before clients have access to the research reports.

A second area of concern for investors is the possible conflict between the underwriting and sales departments of major firms. Dealers deny there is a problem, yet it is rare that a brokerage house will issue a negative report on a company that is an important underwriting client of the firm.

Investors should also realize that not all clients get information at the same time. A firm will be in contact more often with a client who generates $25,000 in yearly commissions than with one whose small portfolio results in $100 in revenues. Large clients, especially portfolio managers with financial institutions, are constantly in touch with brokerage house analysts and often benefit from analysts' views long before they are in print. Most firms have designed ways to pass on analysts' opinions to retail sales representatives quickly, but small clients still get the last phone call – if they are called at all.

For that reason, small investors who have only a few thousand dollars to invest in stocks and who are not likely to have large portfolios down the road are probably better off in a mutual fund. On the other hand, if you're capable of doing your own analysis and are assertive enough to pester your broker for information, you might consider individual investments. Even then, you should look at the economics of being a small investor in the stock market. If you have only $1,000 and want to split it between two stocks, you'll have to pay two minimum commission fees, which are likely to be at least $50 each. And you'll have to pay a commission when you sell, too.

Small brokerage houses usually follow the same pecking order when it comes to calling clients. The call made first is the one that is most likely to result in an order. But smaller houses usually have fewer underwriting ties, and as a result are more inclined to give impartial advice. Smaller dealers may also compensate for offering fewer services by following companies ignored by their larger competitors, bringing their clients superior opportunities for gains. Most firms offer research on individual stocks, but major integrated brokerage houses usually produce much more written information covering the economy, the bond market and preferred shares. Of course, if you do all your own analysis choose a discount broker to lower your trading costs.

The sales representative

There are thousands of people across Canada who are licenced to sell securities to the public. Some perform their duties superbly, while some are inept. But, as with most professions, most are adequate for the job.

You should, therefore, give much thought to selecting a broker or other investment advisor. If you know your investment objectives, your first step is to screen a number of dealers to find several that offer the services you require. A phone call to retail sales managers at most firms will get you much of the information you need for a preliminary screening. But face-to-face visits are best. You should be prepared to discuss your investment objectives and financial needs openly. If a firm appears able to provide the services you're looking for, its sales manager will usually try to introduce you to a sales representative with whom you seem compatible. If you have only a few thousand dollars you will likely be matched to the broker-of-the-day, the person selected to meet most walk-in clients on a particular day.

You should determine how much experience a sales representative has. There is no substitute for experience, so it is usually desirable to deal with someone who has several years of exposure to the markets, and who has worked in times of both rising and falling prices. Many less-experienced brokers were shellshocked when the market fell in October 1987. After five years of rising prices it was their first experience with a rapid decline.

You should ask for copies of past research reports sent to clients and study them carefully to determine whether the recommendations have helped clients' portfolios outperform the market. Ask the representative whether he or she sticks with the company list or conducts independent research. Find out how the firm deals with sell recommendations of shares of companies that are underwriting clients. In addition, ask the representative for the names of several clients you can contact for an assessment of the firm's and the sales representative's track records.

In your conversations with the representative determine his interests in the market. If he has expertise in junior speculative situations and you want a low-risk portfolio, find someone else. In addition, ask whether you can expect much in the way of personal service based on the size of your account. Some firms discourage their employees from taking on new, small accounts because the commissions hardly cover the cost of executing the transaction. No experienced broker can afford the time to service a small account that has little chance of growing.

Placing an order

Clients who understand basic stock market terminology stand a better chance of avoiding confusion when placing orders to buy or sell securities. It is, after all, of utmost importance that your sales representative fully understand your instructions. There should be no confusion about the number of shares being bought or sold.

Unless your order is "at the market" – the best price the broker can get at the time – the client should specify a buying or selling price. Furthermore, you must decide whether the order is a day order – one that must be resubmitted each day until the stock is bought or sold – or an open order that remains in effect until the transaction is complete. Many investors deal with more than one sales representative and it is essential that the order be placed with only one.

Sometimes disputes develop between a representative and a client over what was said. This breakdown of communications can usually be prevented by being explicit when placing an order. (Some brokerage houses tape-record all orders.) You should keep notes that contain the date and time the order was placed and the instructions given the broker – including whether the order was to buy or sell, the full name of the stock and the price. Make sure you receive progress reports on your orders during the day, particularly on volatile securities, and at the close of trading. If a problem develops, talk to your representative first. If a solution cannot be reached, speak with the office's retail sales manager. If that doesn't work, try the stock exchange involved or, as a last resort, your provincial securities commission. But remember, even though orders are not in writing, they are legally binding contracts.

Types of accounts

Brokerage firms offer clients several types of accounts, including cash accounts, delivery-against-payment accounts (DAP) and margin accounts. With cash accounts, clients pay for their shares on settlement date, which is five business days after a transaction is made. They can either take possession of their share certificates or leave them with the brokerage firm for safekeeping. Discount brokers offer fewer options. Generally, they require that clients have adequate cash in their accounts before placing an order to buy stock. Similarly, they require that shares be in the firm's possession before accepting an order to sell.

In the case of DAP accounts, a broker delivers the securities to the client's bank or trust company in exchange for payment. As a result, DAP accounts are mainly employed by institutional investors, but some individuals also use them. With margin accounts, part of the purchase price of the shares is made with funds borrowed from the brokerage firm. The purchased securities remain in the hands of the firm and can be used as collateral for loans used to finance the firm's operations. Fully paid securities are segregated from those that can be used as collateral.

Each type of account has its pros and cons. However, DAP accounts, although they are inconvenient for brokers and involve some extra expenses for clients, are the safest.

The question then becomes, how safe is safe? Clients, and potential customers, can take some solace in the fact that there have been few major financial disasters in the Canadian brokerage industry. The demise of Osler Inc. of Toronto in early 1988 caused some inconvenience and resulted in plenty of publicity, but individual clients didn't suffer any financial losses. Similarly, the collapse of Davidson Partners Ltd. in 1988 caused months of inconvenience for some clients before the exchanges and Investment Dealers Association decided to proceed with claims. The previous notable failure –

Malone Lynch in 1972 – also did not result in any losses to individuals. However, individuals with margined positions had their holdings liquidated and they were paid the resulting cash value.

Protection limited

Should a firm fail, investors are protected by the Canadian Investor Protection Fund, formerly the National Contingency Fund, established by the brokerage industry to protect clients against losses. It protects clients on up to $250,000 of assets in an account, including $60,000 cash.

If you worry about margin accounts, the only alternative is to use a bank line of credit. Investors who trade frequently on margin do not have an alternative to margin accounts unless they arrange their own bank financing and deliveries. Interest paid on money borrowed to buy shares is deductible for tax purposes, but it is important that detailed records be kept; otherwise, Ottawa may disallow the expense. If you choose a cash or DAP account and plan to keep your shares for some time, they should be fully registered in your name. This assures that you will get all company information and dividends directly, although investment dealers will collect these on your behalf and credit your account if the shares are in the brokerage firm's, or "street", name. Since early 1988, brokers have been required to send copies of company reports to clients whose holdings are in the broker's name.

Monitoring performance

Once an account has been established, it is important that the client monitor the broker's performance. As a client, you should ensure you are benefiting from the research you were promised and that you are getting personal service. You should also monitor the success of your broker's recommendations, and record whether you acted on them. Determine whether they brought higher returns than if you had left your portfolio alone. If you suspect your representative is making recommendations for your account for the sole purpose of generating commissions – known as churning – then it's time to move on. The alternative is to learn to make your own investment decisions or move into a mutual fund.

The funds alternative

If you're a smaller investor, your broker might recommend that you invest in mutual funds, which are also known as investment funds. If you decide funds are for you, and you intend to buy from your brokerage firm instead of a mutual fund dealer, make sure the sales representative you choose is a specialist.

Anyone can buy into a fund for clients, but it makes sense to use those who closely monitor the objectives and performance of fund management companies. An investment advisor should also help clients determine how funds can be used as part of a total savings and financial planning program and find funds that meet clients' objectives. The selection criteria for stockbrokers are just as applicable to those who sell mutual funds. Client names should be requested and references checked. It is important, too, that you determine what type of service you will receive. Will it be a once-a-year telephone call or a more involved relationship?

The cost in commissions

Until the beginning of 1990 most funds sold through brokers and mutual fund dealers were sold with a front-end commission or acquisition fee. These were and are negotiable, and virtually all funds have sliding commission schedules which vary according to the size of the order. When it is all added up, the commission rate you pay may be a lot less than the 9 percent maximum. Discount brokers, on the other hand, will generally charge half the maximum commission for a given order. If you do not require advice or service, most fund dealers or brokerage firms will match the discounter.

You can also buy most of these same funds with a redemption fee, rather than an acquisition fee. In fact, most mutual fund sales through dealers are on this basis. Many funds introduced these in 1990 to compete with funds sold without an acquisition fee by banks and trust companies. If you buy a fund with a redemption fee, all your money goes to work and the fund company pays a sales commission to the broker or dealer who sold you the fund.

You will pay a redemption fee when you sell your funds; however, this redemption fee declines over time and if you hold your funds for six or seven years you won't pay any fee at all. Moreover, many fund companies allow switching privileges which means you can move from one fund to another within a group − say from a stock fund to a bond fund − without triggering the redemption fee.

You can obtain a discount on an acquisition fee even if you require detailed advice. It depends largely on the circumstances and the policies of the company you deal with. Indeed, some firms advertise "zero" commission. Instead of receiving a load from you, the dealer is paid by the fund company through what is called a trailer – a portion of the management fee. It's best to discuss fees in advance so you won't face any surprises.

Financial planners

Some investment professionals call themselves financial planners. Rather than simply selling a financial product, they analyze their clients' financial situations, review their objectives and develop a plan aimed at fulfilling these objectives. A financial planner should look at debt management, life insurance, retirement savings and general investment.

Some financial planners operate on a fee-for-service basis and accept no commissions. However, most do not charge a fee but receive a commission if you buy a financial product through them and an ongoing trailer, or service fee, as long as you hold the fund. If you deal with a financial planner, make sure you understand the ground rules – especially how the planner is paid – so you can determine whether he'll give objective advice.

First, you should note that anyone can call himself a financial planner. This is a serious problem because it allows people who have no training or experience to hang a shingle suggesting some expertise in the area of finance. As a result, it is best to determine what qualifications a financial planner has. The Chartered Financial Planner designation after the planner's name means he has completed a series of industry courses leading to the CFP designation. The Canadian Association of Financial Planners also sets minimum standards for membership.

Preparing a will

It is essential that you have a will. Even if you already have one, you should not set it aside and ignore it. Your will should be reviewed periodically to ensure it continues to reflect your wishes and conforms to the laws of the province in which you live. For example, Ontario's Family Law Reform Act changed the rules dramatically for many people.

As well, Ottawa has changed the tax rules that apply to people in common-law marriages. These changes make it imperative that many Canadians review their wills. The objective of a will, and estate planning, is to make sure your assets are distributed according to your wishes after you die, while keeping the tax bite to a minimum. Even modest estates require the clarification a professionally prepared will can provide.

When preparing your will, make sure your lawyer has copies of important investment documents, such as a copy of the beneficiary form you may have signed when you opened an RRSP.

Life insurance

Life and disability insurance are also key planks in any financial strategy. As such, they should be taken care of before setting up an investment program. It is best to first determine how much insurance is necessary to maintain your family's standard of living should anything happen to you.

There are no hard-and-fast rules about adequate coverage, but many advisors suggest life insurance of ten times annual income, plus enough funds to pay off debts. In fact, many advisors have revised the ten times figure upward to reflect the decline in interest rates of the past few years.

Life insurance is a product offered by dozens of companies. Like any other financial product, quality and price vary widely so it makes sense to shop around and to ask agents for comparisons of companies and products. Some agents handle insurance products issued by only one company, others deal with several companies or provide computerized price comparisons of similar products.

You should also consider the differences between term insurance, insurance that covers you for a specific period, and whole life insurance, insurance that covers you for life and contains a so-called savings element.

A final note: Until recently few consumers thought about the financial health of an insurance company. However, the confusion following the demise of Confederation Life Insurance Company changed that. The Canadian Life and Health Insurance Compensation Corporation, an industry-owned protection fund honours life insurance claims up to a maximum of $200,000 (hardly adequate today), health insurance claims up to $60,000, disability and annuity income up to $2,000 a month; and RRSPs up to $60,000.

CHAPTER 5

Setting Your Investment Objectives

ONCE YOU'VE GOT YOUR financial house in order, you're ready for the next step – defining your investment objectives and meeting them. This means deciding how much money you'll need on a certain date for a particular purpose and structuring your financial affairs to meet that goal.

The most common investment objectives are building a retirement fund, saving for a child's education, a home or cottage, buying a business or simply building wealth. Some people might even want to speculate with some of their money in hopes of making gains quickly, although it is wise to ensure your more conservative investment programs are in place before you engage in speculative investing.

Investment objectives can often be divided into short-term and long-term objectives. The major difference, obviously, is the period of time the investment will cover. Someone saving $25,000 or $50,000 for the down payment on a house will probably want to use the money within a few years. Conversely, someone saving for a comfortable retirement might expect to wait twenty years or so before making use of the funds – a long-term proposition.

Meeting your goal of a down payment may not be easy. After all, you have to sock away the money. But it is more straightforward than making adequate provisions for retirement. What happens, for instance, if you decide you want to retire in twenty years with an income of $50,000 a year? Thanks to inflation, the major difficulty is determining how large a retirement pot you will need in twenty years to provide $50,000 with today's purchasing power. Even once you know how much you'll need, you'll have to predict the rates of return that you're likely to receive from your investments over the next two decades so you'll know how much to save each year.

What's more, you may have a number of goals in mind, not all of which are complementary. You may want to speed up your mortgage payments, contribute the maximum to your RRSP and set aside funds for children's education – only to find that doing all three would be an impossible drain on your finances. As a result, you must consider making some trade-offs and establishing priorities.

The level of risk

Timing leads to other important differences, the most crucial being the risk you can afford financially and emotionally. Different types of investments provide different returns. Guaranteed investments are safest because you know the rate of return in advance. If you put your money in a one-year term deposit, you are assured that at the end of the year you'll get all your money back along with the promised interest. But if you sink your money into a mutual fund that invests in Canadian stocks, you have no guarantee at all on what you will earn.

Historically, long-term investors in such funds, or in diversified portfolios of Canadian common stocks, have realized returns substantially higher than those for guaranteed investments. Some funds have long-term average annual compound rates of return in excess of 15 percent. But year-to-year rates vary widely and, in fact, the average ten-year annual compound rate of return for Canadian equity mutual funds is 9.7 percent for the period ended June 30, 1994. However, the one-year average is 2.4 percent, the three-year average is 10.2 percent and the five-year average is 6.0 percent. In most years they've exceeded the rates available from guaranteed returns, although in some years they've been lower.

It makes sense, then, that the person expecting to need money in a year or so is better off with a guaranteed investment. The person with a longer-term horizon, perhaps five to ten years or longer, is able to accept more risk and volatility in the rate of return each year and should consider investments with growth potential.

For long-term investors, higher compound rates of return make a significant difference in the pool of money created over time. If $1,000 is set aside each year for twenty years at an annual average interest rate of 5 percent, it will grow to $34,719. But a rate of 14 percent would result in $103,768 after twenty years. Even for a single investment of $1,000 the difference can be substantial. That single deposit earning 5 percent would be worth $2,653 after twenty years. At a 14 percent growth rate it would be worth $13,743.

If a guaranteed rate of return appeals to you, you can lock away your money for a relatively long period. You might buy government bonds for twenty years or longer. They pay significantly higher rates of return than term deposits or treasury bills, but the rate remains static for the entire period. That's good news if interest rates fall, but if they rise, investors may find themselves wishing they had taken another course of action.

When possible, investors should aim for growth. While growth investments are riskier because their returns are unpredictable, investors are usually compensated over time for this risk through greater gains. Conversely, investors without time on their side should play it safe.

No matter what route you choose, investment options are available to help you meet your goals. For safety, many people choose run-of-the-mill bank accounts. But why not consider alternatives that are just as secure? They include bank premium savings accounts, trust company and credit union accounts, term deposits, treasury bills and money market funds. All are reasonably risk-free but rates paid vary significantly.

Saving effectively can also involve a great deal more than investing for growth or income. You can make use of programs and tax breaks that can help increase returns without increasing risk. Saving for retirement and saving for children's education are two goals for which tax-assisted savings schemes are available.

Saving for retirement

Most people are eager to embark on a savings program that will allow them to live comfortably during retirement. This is recognized by the federal government through tax legislation that encourages companies to implement pension plans and allows individuals to save for retirement through registered retirement savings plans.

Because government pension benefits alone are inadequate for most people during retirement, private pension plans are an excellent way to ensure that the income you need will be available. The trouble is, many companies don't have pension plans. And if they do, the plans may prove woefully inadequate. So taking retirement savings into your own hands may be the best solution to financial freedom during your golden years.

If this is the case, there are three cardinal rules to remember: Save as much as you can, start as early as you can, and aim for growth. Starting early is the key, simply because it puts the power of compound interest at your command. The twenty-five-year-old who sets aside $1,000 a year at an 8 percent annual return will have $186,000 at age sixty. The forty-five-year-old who wants the same amount at age sixty will have to set aside more than $6,000 a year. Furthermore, if the twenty-five-year-old could earn 12 percent annually, he would accumulate $483,000 by age sixty – enough to provide an annual income of about $60,000.

It's never too late to start. If you haven't saved for retirement until now, you can still reap the benefits of an improving government regulatory climate for retirement savings. For one thing, pension plans are changing. Ottawa has improved the portability of pension plans and has enhanced survivor benefits.

Even so, this means nothing to those whose employers don't offer pension plans. There are no simple solutions to this dilemma, although the RRSP comes close. It is the most popular tax shelter available to Canadians, and its popularity has grown since the concept was introduced in 1957, especially among those who won't have the benefit of private pension plan payments when they retire.

With an RRSP you can set aside a portion of your earnings every year and it will not be taxed. Any income earned within an RRSP is allowed to grow untaxed until withdrawn from the plan. As a result, retirement savings through an RRSP grow much more quickly than those that are taxed. And when it comes time to withdraw funds from the plan, the taxman will likely take a smaller cut because your overall retirement income, and marginal tax rate, will be lower.

Most people invest in off-the-shelf RRSPs similar to guaranteed investment certificates or term deposits offered by banks, trust companies, credit unions, insurance companies and mutual fund distributors. Others use self-directed plans through which they choose their own investments. In fact, there are two types of plans: those that pay a guaranteed rate of return and those in which the returns can't be determined in advance because funds are invested in marketable securities with fluctuating prices.

But before you get carried away with plans to invest in RRSPs, make sure you are aware of the contribution limits.

Contribution Limits to Tax Shelters

Year	RRSP	DPSP	Money Purchase
1994	$13,500	$7,250	$14,500
1995	$14,500	$7,750	$15,500
1996	$15,500	indexed	indexed

TABLE XVI

The contribution limit for 1994 is 18 percent of your earned income in 1993 with a dollar limit of $13,500. It rises to $14,500 in 1995 and $15,500 in 1996. These limits will be reduced by what the federal government refers to as a "pension adjustment." This adjustment includes any contributions made to a pension plan or other tax-assisted retirement plan, such as a deferred profit-sharing plan. In addition, RRSP limits for those who have made past-service contributions to their pension plans will be subject to adjustments.

Calculations for RRSP contributions are more complicated than in the past. Employers will have to file pertinent information about pension contributions to the federal government, which will then calculate how much you can contribute to your RRSPs.

For the tax year 1994, you must make your contributions no later than March 1, 1995 to get a tax break for 1994. But starting with the 1991 tax year you have been allowed to carry unused contributions forward for seven years.

Cashing in your RRSP

You must dispose of your RRSPs by the end of the year in which you turn seventy-one. You have three basic options when that time comes – or before, if you wish. You can cash in your plan and pay tax on the entire amount, you can purchase an annuity, or you can put your money into a registered retirement income fund. Most people choose a RRIF, (pronounced riff), a life annuity or some combination of the two.

Life annuities, available from life insurance companies, provide monthly income for life. But there are variations on the standard annuity. A popular option is an annuity that pays for a guaranteed period of ten to fifteen years or until both husband and wife die, whichever is longer.

Annuities pay specified rates of return that depend on your age, or your spouse's age, when you purchase the annuity. Rates also depend on general interest rates at the time and on competition among insurance companies selling the products. Although you will receive a higher income if you take out an annuity when interest rates are high, you really have little control over timing.

Many people shy away from annuities because they involve surrendering control of their investments. RRIFs, on the other hand, allow you to hold the same types of investments that are allowed in RRSPs so investors never relinquish control. In fact, a RRIF is an RRSP in reverse – instead of making contributions, as you do with an RRSP, you withdraw funds from a RRIF.

You can withdraw as much from your RRIF each year as you want. The least you are allowed to withdraw is determined by your age. However, the rules changed in 1993. Under the rules for RRIFs started in 1992 or earlier, minimum RRIF withdrawals are based on the amount of money in a plan at the end of the previous year, divided by the difference between ninety and the RRIF owner's age or spouse's age, if it is lower. For example, someone who was seventy-one at the end of 1991 and had $100,000 in a RRIF would have been required to withdraw a minimum of 1/19 or $5,263 in 1992. Under the new rules, a RRIF can be structured to provide a lifetime income. The new rules require moderately higher minimum withdrawals for people less than seventy-one, the old fractions based on age or spouse's age ninety will continue to apply.

Saving for children's education

Many families decide that the best way to save for children's education is to start a savings plan at birth. Others decide the smartest course is to pay off the mortgage as quickly as possible and finance their children's education out of income.

Launching a savings plan when your children are very young makes a great deal of sense. But the way you do it has a significant bearing on how much money you'll have by the time you pack your kids off to university, college or technical school.

If the funds are being put aside by you, the child's grandparents or aunts and uncles, the taxation attribution rules apply and interest and dividends earned on the funds contributed will be taxed at the marginal tax rates of the donors. If structured carefully by keeping the interest separate, any interest earned on interest will be taxed in the child's hands. If the money is invested in stocks or equity mutual funds and capital gains are earned, the capital gains are taxable in the child's hands rather than donors.

For many families, Ottawa's decision to stop paying family allowance on a universal basis after 1992 ends one method of saving for children's education. However, the same strategy can be employed by those eligible to receive child tax credit cheques. Many people establish a separate bank or trust company account in their child's name and use the account only for child tax credit payments. These cheques are taxable in the parent's hands. However, if the money is invested directly on the child's behalf, any income earned on the original contribution is considered the child's. Because a child can have income of more than $2,500 a year before your ability to use the child as a tax deduction is diminished, there is little likelihood that taxes will be paid on income generated from child tax credit contributions. It may still make sense to open that separate account. It can be used for gifts to the child from people other than parents, grandparents, aunts and uncles or for inheritances.

And remember, there is no need to leave this money in a savings account. You can invest it in Canada Savings Bonds, GICs, stocks, mutual funds and other financial instruments as long as your purchases are made directly from the child's account. Most people tend to use interest-income investments because they are low-risk or risk-free.

Registered education savings plans

There are also tax-assisted plans in which you can save for children's education. Known as registered educational savings plans (RESPs), they allow tax-free growth of income from contributions to finance post-secondary education. The capital originally contributed is not deductible from income for tax purposes nor taxable when withdrawn, but income earned on that capital grows free of tax in the RESP until withdrawn to finance a child's education, at which time it is taxed in the child's hands. The advantage of a RESP is that students generally have low income, so the tax burden is either non-existent or negligible.

There are two variations of the RESP, both of which have distinct advantages and disadvantages. There are the "scholarship plans" in which your money is pooled with the funds contributed by other parents. The income earned in the plan is then distributed to the children who embark on a post-secondary education. If your child decides against continuing his or her education, you get back the money you put in the plan, but you lose the income earned over the years. In other words, you are gambling that your child will attend a post-secondary institution. Scholarship plans are available only from the firms that sponsor them.

Self-directed RESPs allow you to choose your own investments. Offered by some brokerage houses, mutual fund companies and insurance companies, these RESPs allow parents and others to invest up to $1,500 a year for each child, to a maximum of $31,500, with the freedom to withdraw this money at any time. (Prior to the February 1990 budget you were allowed lump-sum contributions to a maximum of about $32,000, but with the change in rules fewer brokerage houses now offer RESPs.)

The income earned on your contribution grows untaxed until withdrawn to finance post-secondary education. If the child does not go on to college or university, these plans usually allow you to change beneficiaries. The maximum life of the plan, however, is twenty-one years. You can even use the money yourself if you decide to return to school. However, the rules require that the money be used by full-time students. Alternatively, you can donate the interest portion of the money to a recognized post-secondary institution, although the donation will not be deductible for income tax purposes.

One important point to consider about this type of RESP is the taxation of the proceeds in the beneficiary's hands. All income is taxable without the benefit of associated tax breaks for dividends or capital gains.

As an alternative to either of these strategies, you may want to set up a portfolio of growth stocks or growth mutual funds for your children using your capital. While any interest or dividend income earned would be taxable in your hands, any capital gains would be taxed in your children's hands (and interest earned on interest would be taxed in your children's hands).

CHAPTER 6

As Safe as Money in the Bank

WHILE HOUSING IS CLEARLY the favourite investment of Canadians, money in the bank – or trust company or credit union – is a close second, with hundreds of billions of dollars invested in savings accounts, chequing accounts, term deposits and guaranteed investment certificates.

The volatility of interest rates during the late 1970s and early 1980s and indeed, during the past four years, made most people sensitive to small differences in interest rates. As a result, competition among financial institutions for savings increased and an array of savings instruments became available. No longer do you have a simple choice of just two accounts – savings and chequing. Now you can choose accounts to meet your specific needs and cash flow.

Look at chequing accounts. Traditionally, a chequing account was used just for writing cheques. You transferred enough money into it each month to cover the cheques you wrote and you neither expected nor received interest. Now it's a different story. You can find chequing accounts that pay interest, provided you maintain a minimum monthly balance. You can find chequing accounts that charge no fees, provided you maintain a minimum monthly balance. You can even get accounts that allow you to pay your bills at the bank without charge, provided you've paid an annual fee. Generally, this last type of account is part of a package that includes a personal line of credit and a credit card named after a precious metal.

Savings accounts have also come a long way. Some pay a low interest rate on the minimum outstanding balance but allow chequing privileges. However, most people who use accounts strictly for savings opt for premium savings accounts that don't allow chequing but pay a higher interest rate.

The type of premium savings account you choose depends largely on your cash flow needs. Some accounts pay interest on the minimum monthly balance, so if you keep $1,000 in your account for twenty-nine days of one month and let the balance drop to $1 on the thirtieth day, you get interest for the month on only $1. Others base payments on the minimum daily balance, so if the balance in your account fluctuates widely, the premium daily interest account makes more sense.

You can also keep your money in money market mutual funds which are usually invested in treasury bills and other top-quality short-term debt instruments. The rates paid on these are often several points higher than rates paid on savings accounts.

In addition, you can keep your money in term deposits with a bank or in guaranteed investment certificates with a trust company. With these you tie up your money for a specified period, which can be from thirty, sixty, ninety or 180 days to as long as five years.

The rates paid on term deposits and GICs are generally, but not always, higher than the rates paid on savings accounts (for example, during 1990 short-term rates were several points higher than long-term rates). How much higher depends on the amount you deposit and the length of time you are willing to invest. With a term deposit or GIC you agree to commit your funds for a specific time period at a specific rate. If you need your money before the end of the term you will probably face interest penalties or be forced to sell your GIC at a price that will reflect current interest rates.

If you need the money you have tied up, the best arrangement for conserving interest may be to borrow against the term deposit, GIC or bank account. Let's assume it's close to the end of the month and you need the $15,000 you have in an account that pays a premium rate of interest on your minimum monthly balance. Instead of withdrawing the money, it will save you a few dollars if you borrow the necessary funds for several days. A prearranged personal line of credit is the easiest loan source, but if you don't have one see your bank or trust company manager about a loan. Because you're putting up your account as collateral you should have no difficulty. And if the bank is reluctant to give you the loan or wants to charge you fees, argue. Banks are in business to make money and branch managers are well aware that they lose if you move your money elsewhere.

When tying up your money for a long time, there are a few details you should watch. In most cases, the interest rate paid by an institution on a longer-term deposit applies to the principal only. Interest

Value of $1,000 in Ten Years

Interest Rate	Compounded			
	Annually	Semi-Annually	Quarterly	Monthly
8%	$2,159	$2,191	$2,208	$2,220
10%	2,594	2,653	2,685	2,707
12%	3,106	3,207	3,262	3,300
14%	3,707	3,870	3,959	4,022
16%	4,411	4,661	4,801	4,901

TABLE XVII

earned on interest may be at the institution's deposit rate. Also, when comparing interest rates make sure you are comparing apples with apples. As you can see in Table XVII, the frequency with which your interest is compounded will make a significant difference in the wealth you are able to build over the years.

A 10 percent rate compounded semi-annually means you are earning 5 percent interest on your money for the first six months but in the second six months you earn 5 percent interest on both the money you originally deposited and the interest you earned in the first six months. On a $1,000 deposit you would earn 5 percent of $1,000 or $50 in the first six months and 5 percent interest on $1,050, or $52.50, for the next six months. Over one year you would earn $102.50, or an effective interest rate of 10.25 percent. Invest $1,000 at 10 percent compounded annually and you'll have only $100 in interest at the end of a year. You should also realize that you are responsible for paying tax on the interest you have accrued even if you haven't received it as would be the case with some investments which automatically reinvest interest earned.

Deciding on terms
The major investment decision facing many people who keep money on deposit is what term to take. It's not an easy choice, given the volatility of interest rates. If you lock in your money for five years at 10 percent and rates move up to 17 percent two years later you're out of luck – you will continue to get 10 percent. Conversely, people who left their money in savings accounts at 19 percent in mid-1982, expecting rates to move higher, saw their returns drop below 10 percent within a year and to less than 7 percent within

two years. Indeed, with savings rates in mid-1990 at 12 percent to 14 percent, investors faced the same decision as they did almost a decade earlier. Rates in fact did decline and were around 2 percent in mid-1993.

When deciding on terms, you have to choose between buying something like a five-year certificate at the going rate or holding off and buying a three- or six-month certificate because you expect five-year rates to move higher. There is no reliable way to forecast such moves, particularly over the longer term. But there are some rules of thumb governing what constitutes a reasonable rate of return.

The risk-free rate – "risk free" meaning there is no risk to capital as is the case with an insured deposit or a government guarantee – usually hovers around 3 percent above the rate of inflation. So if you think inflation is going to be 5 percent over the next few years, then 8 percent is a reasonable rate of return. A greater or smaller spread than 3 percent is a reflection of expectations in the market-place. Five-year GIC rates in mid-1988 were about 10 percent when the inflation rate hovered around 4 percent, reflecting an expectation that inflation may move higher. In mid-1991 when inflation was running at more than 5 percent, savings rates were about 5.5 percent while five-year GIC rates were about 9.25 percent. In mid-1993, with inflation running at 2 percent, five-year GIC rates had declined to about 6.75 percent.

If GIC rates are less than 3 percent above the inflation rate, you are probably better off sticking to short-term deposits and waiting for higher rates. So, if five-year GICs are paying 10 percent and you expect 8 percent inflation, keep your money in thirty-day deposits until longer-term rates move higher or until you are satisfied that inflation is abating. Conversely, if five-year rates are at 6.75 percent and you expect another economic slowdown and a further drop in interest rates, you might want to lock in the longer-term rate.

Sometimes short-term rates move higher than long-term rates, creating what is called an inverted yield curve. This reflects the market's view that long-term interest rates will move lower. To attract short-term money and discourage investors from investing for the long term, deposit-taking institutions raise short-term rates.

If you move into the short end of the market because you expect rates to move up and intend to switch later to five-year deposits, remember that you are speculating. Central banks, such as the Bank of Canada, are responsible for setting interest-rate policies and their interest-rate policies can change overnight. You could find long-term rates moving lower than you expected.

If you prefer short-term savings instruments, don't overlook treasury bills or money market mutual funds. A money market fund is a mutual fund that invests primarily in treasury bills and wholesale bank deposits or top-quality commercial paper and you can expect to earn about two percentage points more than you would with a savings account. If a savings account is paying 2 percent, you would expect to earn 4 percent to 4.25 percent. Treasury bills pay even more and are at least as safe as deposits. However, the T-bills are usually acquired through securities dealers who charge a commission and require a minimum investment of at least $5,000 – often as much as $100,000. Therefore, you should compare the net interest you would receive after commissions with the savings rate or yield available on a money market fund. The net rate on a treasury bill is almost always higher than savings rates of comparable maturities.

Whether a treasury bill pays a superior yield to a money market fund depends on the amount of money you're investing and the commission rate charged by the investment dealer. Banks also sell treasury bills, although the commissions or service fees may prove a great deal higher than those charged by investment dealers. It pays to shop around.

Deposit insurance

Money kept on deposit with a bank or trust company is covered by the Canada Deposit Insurance Corp., while depositors at credit unions are protected by a national insurance system run by the credit unions themselves. The CDIC insures each depositor for up to $60,000 in principal and interest at a specific member institution, and it is compulsory for banks and trust companies that accept deposits to belong.

The $60,000 limit cannot be circumvented by having two accounts at different branches of the same bank. However, if you have one account for yourself and another joint account with your husband or wife, each account is insured up to $60,000. If you have several accounts in trust for each of your children, each account is insured separately because each has a different beneficiary. Your RRSP, if on deposit with a member institution, is insured separately.

Deposit insurance applies to accounts that mature within five years and are denominated in Canadian dollars. Principal and interest are insured up to the date of default. Therefore, if you have a five-year GIC with an institution that fails before the term is up, you get your money back, plus interest owed up to the date of default. The CDIC insures your deposit, but it does not guarantee interest for the term of the deposit.

To avoid difficulties, many people choose to invest only with the largest, strongest financial institutions. Large investors such as mutual funds and pension funds may place millions of dollars with a single institution, but they carefully monitor the financial statements of that institution. If you plan to invest more than the amount covered by deposit insurance with any institution other than the major chartered banks or the largest trust companies, do your homework. While the largest banks may have their problems with Third World debt and real estate loans, it is a fair assumption that the regulatory bodies would never allow them to fail under any circumstances.

Deposit insurance does not cover securities, such as mutual funds, which are sold by a bank or trust company. Similarly, deposit insurance doesn't cover the mortgage debentures issued by some of the largest chartered banks. They are fully guaranteed by the issuing bank, and that's generally good enough for even the most conservative investor. Otherwise, it's caveat emptor.

The whole area of investor protection is currently being studied by various regulatory bodies. In the years ahead we will likely see arrangements that raise the limits of deposit insurance, and a better system than currently exists for protecting clients of an investment dealer who runs into financial trouble. The life insurance industry has introduced a system to protect policyholders within limits if a life insurance company fails.

CHAPTER 7

Bonds, Bills and Debentures

MOST PERSONAL INVESTments are in debt securities. Virtually all the savings instruments discussed in the last chapter are debt obligations of trust companies, banks and other financial institutions. Most are insured up to the limit of deposit insurance or issued by the strongest financial institutions. As a result, most of them can be considered risk-free.

This chapter deals with a different kind of debt security – the type that is marketed through investment dealers and traded in the marketplace. These marketable debt securities are instruments such as treasury bills, bonds, debentures and mortgage-backed securities.

The major attraction of this type of debt security is its marketability. Given the volatility of interest rates over the past two decades, many investors have decided it is worth opting for a slightly lower rate of return than might be available from a GIC in order to have the ability to sell their investment at any time. If their investments remain liquid, they can move into shorter-term investments such as treasury bills if they feel interest rates will move higher. And if they see rates moving lower they can buy long-term bonds to lock in what they feel will prove to be a high return.

The performance of bonds

Bonds are generally safer than stocks. Government bonds have a strong guarantee and corporate bonds must pay interest on their debt before any dividends can be paid on stock. Even if the company goes broke, the investors in the corporation's bonds have first crack at the company assets before stockholders are paid anything – although some lenders get priority over others.

So, bonds should be dull plodders when it comes to generating a return, right? Wrong. At least, not in recent years.

The *Financial Times* survey of investment funds for periods ended June 30, 1994 indicates that mutual funds that invest primarily in bonds showed an 8.1 percent compound annual return over the last five years. The best returned 10.8 percent while the worst eked out 6.5 percent.

For the same time period, mutual funds that invest primarily in Canadian stocks showed an average return of only 6.0 percent. The best stock fund generated a 25.7 percent return while the worst limped in with an annual compound return of -0.4 percent.

The risk difference can be measured by the spread between the best and worst of each type of fund: 4.3 percentage points for bonds and 26.0 percentage points for stocks. By investing in stocks five years earlier you could at best earn 26 percent a year – an exception – or at worst lose a bit. With bonds you would almost certainly earn an acceptable return.

If the rewards of the stock game seem worth more than the risk, so be it. Meanwhile, however, the bonds offer a profitable and safer choice for the long-term investor.

How will bonds perform in the future? No one knows the answer to that nor does anyone know whether stocks can continue their performance of the past. However, it is unlikely that the Canadian bond market will continue to generate double-digit returns over the next few years. Interest rates have declined substantially over the past few years because of the recession and declining inflation rates. With economic recovery, demand for funds by business, government and individuals will almost certainly increase which will cause rates to rise. That, in turn, would hurt bond prices. Indeed, most bond funds declined sharply in early 1994 as interest rates rose.

In the 1970s, the fixed rate per $1,000 of bond face value was quite low, about 5 percent for many issues. Most of the value of the bond was in its maturity value, normally $1,000, and that wasn't going to be paid for several years.

Bonds that will not mature for many years respond to interest rate changes much more violently than do bonds with less distant maturities. For example, a $1,000 bond that matures in five years would be worth $747 if the market interest rate is 6 percent. But if interest rates jumped to 10 percent, the bond's value would drop to $621, a decline of $126.

A $1,000 bond maturing in ten years would be worth $558 when the market interest rate is 6 percent, but would drop in value to

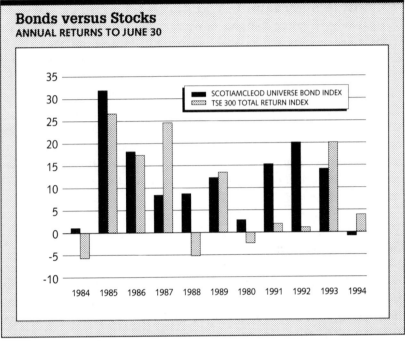

Bonds versus Stocks
ANNUAL RETURNS TO JUNE 30

- SCOTIAMCLEOD UNIVERSE BOND INDEX
- TSE 300 TOTAL RETURN INDEX

1984 1985 1986 1987 1988 1989 1980 1991 1992 1993 1994

CHART I

$386 if the interest rate rises to 10 percent. That is a decline of $172, a much steeper drop than the $126 decline for the five-year bond.

Today, most bonds have fixed coupon rates that are about 8 percent or more. This reflects the sharp rise in interest rates that occurred during the 1970s and early 1980s. Now, more of the value of the bond is tied to the interest payments and less to the maturity value. So, with more of the value coming earlier in the life of the bond, the bond's market price is less sensitive to interest rate fluctuations.

Further, bonds issued today usually have shorter maturities than was the case ten years ago. Ottawa's debt, excluding Canada Savings Bonds, has an average maturity of about 4.5 years. In 1979, the average maturity was 7.2 years. This makes all of the bond payments – interest and maturity value – less sensitive to market interest rate fluctuations.

Finally, many corporate bonds issued today have floating, rather than fixed, coupon rates. A fixed coupon rate means that a fixed amount of interest is paid each year. If that fixed coupon rate is

9 percent, then $90 a year will be paid on a bond with a face value of $1,000. A floating coupon is usually tied to some interest rate barometer, such as the federal treasury bill rate or the bank prime rate. As these rates move, so does the coupon rate. If interest rates move up, the interest paid on the bond also increases, making the price of the bond more stable.

The bond game is more interesting than it has been in many years. In 1992 inflation plunged and interest rates fell to the levels of the early 1970s. Consequently, the value of bonds soared and bond investors made excellent returns. On the other hand, rates soared in early 1994 and bond prices plummeted, except for those with floating rates.

Your guarantee

Before investing in marketable debt securities you should be familiar with the two basic types: those guaranteed by the federal government and those that are not. Individual investors should generally stick to Government of Canada bonds for two reasons. First and most important, they are backed by Ottawa, so your money is not at risk. Second, they are the most marketable bonds available in Canada. That means that Government of Canada bonds have very narrow spreads between the buying price and selling price. The difference between the bid and ask for $1,000 Government of Canada bonds might be as little as $5. In contrast, if you hold a corporate issue that is not actively traded, the spread could be as much as $50 per $1,000.

Provincial bonds can be considered risk-free as well, as can any other bonds guaranteed by the federal or provincial governments. However, the spreads on these can be wider than those on Government of Canada bonds.

Corporate bonds

Corporate bonds also carry little risk at the time they are issued but a lot can happen to a company over twenty years. Unless you have a large, diversified bond portfolio and are willing to monitor the quality of your holdings frequently, stick to Government of Canada bonds. If you decide to invest in corporate bonds because of their higher interest rates, try to stick to larger issues. The difference in the interest rates on corporate bonds reflects the bonds' quality –

lower-quality, higher-risk bonds pay more interest. As with any investment, the higher the promised return the greater the risk.

Also, the price of thinly traded bonds is usually more volatile than that of larger, broadly traded issues. You may pay less for thinly traded bonds when buying, and you may get more when selling if someone wants them desperately enough. But with a thinly traded bond issue, the selling price is often low.

Within the corporate debt market, investors can also find debentures. Corporate bonds are generally secured by specific assets, while debentures are often secured only by the general credit of the issuer. When buying either bonds or debentures, you risk having problems in the future if the company runs into financial difficulty, even if your debt is secured. Your money could be tied up indefinitely, and the eventual settlement may not be to your liking.

Aside from the risk of default, which you can eliminate by sticking to Government of Canada bonds, there is interest rate risk. When rates rise, bond prices fall because an investor who wants to buy a bond at current rates will consider an older bond with a lower rate only if the bond's price is discounted to make its yield comparable.

Government bonds

The federal government raises funds by issuing three types of instruments: Canada Savings Bonds, treasury bills and marketable bonds.

A Canada Savings Bond is actually a flexible term deposit with the government rather than a true bond. They often have a term of seven years, but the period and the interest rate are based on market conditions and can vary. The rate is adjusted each year, although a minimum is guaranteed for the full term. The bonds can be cashed at any time at full face value plus interest earned to the end of the previous month, with the exception of the first two months.

There are two types of Canada Savings Bonds: those that pay interest annually and compound interest bonds on which the interest is reinvested. Even if you buy compound bonds, you must declare the earned interest on your income tax return even if you haven't received it. You must declare interest in the year accrued.

Treasury bills and marketable bonds differ from savings bonds in that they are not redeemable on demand. But they can be sold through an investment dealer or bank in the bond market. Treasury bills are short-term instruments that mature in ninety to 180 days. They are denominated in amounts of $1,000 and sold at a discount to face value. For example, an investor purchasing a $1,000 treasury bill with sixty days left to maturity earning an annual interest rate of 6 percent would pay about $990 for the bill. Not only the federal government issues treasury bills. There are also provincial bills that sell at slightly higher yields, reflecting a moderately larger risk.

The commercial paper chase

Major corporations and finance companies issue commercial paper similar to treasury bills in that they mature within one year and are sold at a discount to face value. Yields on commercial paper, even for very sound companies, are higher than for either federal or provincial treasury bills. For instance, ninety-day treasury bills were yielding 5.50 percent in mid-1994, while top-quality ninety-day commercial paper was yielding 5.65 percent. The higher yields may appeal to large investors who monitor the financial strength of borrowers, but most individuals should stay out of this market. Commercial paper is usually subordinated debt, which means that if the company goes belly up, holders of the notes are paid only after secured creditors get their share.

Some companies issue commercial paper that is guaranteed by a bank. This allows small firms to tap this market for short-term funds. The rates paid reflect the quality of the guarantor.

Lower-quality, high-yielding commercial paper is also available. But be careful. Hundreds of millions of dollars were lost in the 1960s, when Atlantic Acceptance collapsed and its short-term paper became worthless.

Many issues of commercial paper and long-term bonds are rated by Canada's two bond rating services, Dominion Bond Rating Service of Toronto and Canadian Bond Rating Service of Montreal. Also, Moody's Investor Service Inc. and Standard and Poor's Corp., both of the U.S., rate Canadian bond issues that are of interest to U.S. investors. If you want to invest in commercial paper, stick to top quality issues only – those in the top two or three grades of rating classification. All major investment dealers selling commercial paper can supply information on ratings.

Bonds and coupon rates

Bonds issued by governments and corporations have coupon interest rates, which when multiplied by $1,000, the usual maturity value of a bond, tell you the amount of interest paid each year. Payments are usually made semi-annually. For example, the Government of Canada bond maturing June 1, 2010, has a 9.5 percent coupon, which means it pays $95 interest annually with two payments of $47.50 each. However, the coupon rate does not necessarily indicate the actual return an investor will receive. In mid-1990 this bond was trading at $927.50. Because of this discount, a buyer would earn a return if the bond were held to maturity of almost 10.4 percent, a return that is made up of interest and capital appreciation of $72.50, which represents the difference between the price paid and the maturity value. Three years later, in mid-1993, this bond was trading at $1,156.50, reflecting the sharp decline in interest rates over the previous two years, and yielding about 7.2 percent. Now the return a buyer would receive would represent interest, which would be reduced by capital depreciation of $156.60, to maturity.

There are a number of subtle differences in the rates of return an investor would earn on two bonds issued by the same source and with identical maturity dates but different coupon rates. For example, a government bond with a 6.50 percent coupon and maturing in 2004 traded in mid-1994 at about $836 to yield 9.02 percent. A 10.25 percent bond due in 2004 was trading at about $1,072 to yield 9.10 percent. The buyer of the discount bond would accept a lower yield because of the future capital gain. Remember, he will get back $1,000 and while interest income is fully taxable, capital gains are only partially taxed. Therefore, the lower-coupon bond is more valuable, which makes its yield lower and its price higher.

Investors who expect interest rates to decline will often invest in discount bonds. Someone who bought an 8.75 percent bond when interest rates were 10 percent and then saw market rates decline from 10 percent to 8.75 percent would make a capital gain of $110 on each bond. This capital gain on low-coupon bonds tends to make their prices more volatile than those of bonds with higher coupons. When interest rates fall, all bond prices rise and when rates rise, bond prices fall. However, a low-coupon bond's price will rise more sharply on falling rates, and drop more precipitously on rising rates, than will the price of a high-coupon bond. The reason lies in the overall income stream of the bond.

A decline in rates increases the ultimate maturity value of the bond more than it increases the value of the interest payments. For example, $10 in interest next year is worth $9.09 today when the interest rate is 10 percent. And $1,000 of maturity value ten years from now is worth $385.54 today. If interest rates drop to 5 percent, the present value of the interest payment will rise to $9.52, an increase of about 4.8 percent. But the present value of the bond's worth at maturity will shoot up to $613.91, an increase of almost 60 percent. With a low-coupon bond, most of the present value is in the maturity value, so an increase in interest rates magnifies the value of the capital gain, which is taxed more lightly than interest income, and pushes up low-coupon bond prices sharply. The opposite occurs when interest rates fall and capital gains shrink.

For those who want to take the risky path of speculating on interest rates, choosing bonds by the size of coupon is one possibility. If you believe interest rates are going to fall sharply in a short period, the best bonds to buy are long-term, low-coupon bonds; they will appreciate most. If you want to hold bonds but are worried about an interest rate increase, choose high-coupon bonds with a short maturity.

Bond speculators should also be aware of the effect of the term to maturity on bond prices. Long-term bonds respond more strongly to interest rate changes than do short-term bonds. The reason stems from compound interest; interest rate changes have a greater impact on payments far in the future than on payments in the near future.

Government of Canada bonds provide a good example of this phenomenon, as shown in Table XVIII. The table looks at the change in price between two 10.25 percent bonds. One of the bonds matured on Feb. 1, 1994. The second matures March 15, 2014. Bond prices are quoted in points, so a bond quoted at 102.05 means it is trading at $102.05 per $1,000 of face value. As you can see, a drop in market interest rates caused the price on the short-term bond to rise by 0.1 percent while the price on the long-term bond rose by 18.9 percent. Just as longer-term bonds generally rise more than shorter-term bonds when interest rates fall, they fall more when interest rates rise.

Change in Price of Two 10.25% Bonds

Bond	Price Feb 20, 1991	Price July 30, 1993	% change
10.25% Feb. 1, 1994	102.05	102.80	+0.1
10.25% Mar. 15, 2014	103.91	123.50	+18.9

TABLE XVIII

One thing certain

One thing is certain – few investors can accurately predict interest rate movements. Those who are investing for the long haul should hold bonds with a mixture of coupon rates and terms to maturity, slanting the portfolio in the direction they believe will provide the greatest short-term returns. This reflects an investment portfolio approach to interest rate risk, with parts of the portfolio geared to generating satisfactory performance, no matter what happens to interest rates. If you choose not to create a diversified bond portfolio, you can invest in a bond mutual fund, which offers the advantages of professional management and a diversified portfolio.

If you prefer your own portfolio, there are other bond features to be considered. For example, government bonds are almost always non-callable, which means that when you buy a twenty-year bond, it will be outstanding for the full twenty years. That isn't the case with corporate bonds. Often a corporate bond has what is known as a call feature that gives the company issuing the bonds the right to buy them back at a specified price after a specific number of years. If you buy a bond with a call feature, the price you pay is often based on the call date, rather than the maturity date.

Similarly, many corporate bonds have a sinking fund provision that requires a portion of the bonds to be repurchased each year after a specified number of years. The purpose of a sinking fund is to retire a number of bonds each year to reflect the depreciated value of the asset originally financed by the bonds. A sinking fund provision protects investors, and the expected diminishing supply of bonds can lead to premium prices.

Redeemable and extendable bonds

In periods of rising interest rates, it is common to see issues of redeemable and extendable bonds. For example, a government might issue a twenty-year bond, redeemable after five years. If you bought one of these bonds you would have the option, just before the five-year period, of keeping the bond or redeeming it for the full face value. If interest rates were higher than the coupon rate, you would likely cash in the bond and reinvest your money elsewhere. The market price of a redeemable bond would be based on the redemption date if market interest rates were higher than the coupon rate, and on the maturity date if market rates were lower than the coupon rate. An extendible bond might be issued for five years with a feature extending it, at the holder's choice, to fifteen years.

Both redeemable and extendable bonds appeal to investors who are concerned that interest rates might skyrocket. Without such features governments would have difficulty attracting long-term money in periods of rising interest rates.

Convertible debentures

Some corporate debentures are convertible into common stock. The issuer may have one of two reasons for offering such debentures: to make the bonds more attractive or to use the bonds to issue equity in a period when the market is nervous about accepting new share issues.

Convertible debentures carry coupons like those of regular debentures, although the interest rates paid would likely be lower than those paid on regular debentures. The lower coupon rate is offset by the provision that allows investors to convert their bonds to common stock at a predetermined price for a specified time period – usually several years. This way the buyer knows that if the stock price goes up, he can convert the debenture and realize a capital gain. If the stock price doesn't rise, he continues to receive interest until maturity, at which time the principal will be repaid.

The price of a convertible debenture depends on the conversion price relative to the price of the underlying stock. If a $1,000 debenture is convertible into 100 shares and the stock is selling at $15, the debenture would likely trade around $1,500. If the stock fell to $8, the convertible debenture would either trade at $800, plus some premium to reflect the possibility that the stock price might rise, or the price of the debenture based on its coupon rate, whichever is higher. Most companies issuing convertible debentures, as well as the investors who buy them, hope that the price of the company's shares will rise so the debentures can be converted to stock.

Junk bonds

Another type of bond is the so-called "junk bond," which may yield several points more than other corporate issues. The ability of a company to make the interest payments on these bonds is often questionable and the assets involved often leave little cushion for safety. That's why a buyer may get several points of interest more than less risky bonds such as a utility bond. Investors buy junk bonds because of their high coupon rates and because the market will reduce the risk premium paid and the bonds will appreciate in value if the company's profitability improves.

Some junk bonds trade at deep discounts when the issuer is in financial trouble and cannot pay the interest. These, too, offer buyers a chance at making healthy gains. Normally, if a company defaults on interest, the trustee involved in the receivership will try to get its hands on company assets, and the firm is liquidated – making bonds worth much less than their original value. However, there often is another solution that benefits everyone involved, including the holders of junk bonds. All parties may agree to a settlement that will see creditors get more than they would if the company were liquidated. Bondholders speculating on this outcome between the company and its creditors find their bonds are suddenly worth a great deal more because their share of assets has increased.

Where do you buy bonds?

In Canada, bonds trade "over-the-counter" rather than on an exchange like the stock market. This means you buy and sell bonds through an investment dealer and banks. Most knowledgeable traders deal with investment dealers because the costs are less and the returns are higher. Both investment dealers and banks will sell new government issues at the issued price, without commission.

A dealer with a bond department is probably buying bonds as principal, which means the dealer will buy bonds at one price from you and then either sell them at a higher price to another investor or hold them in inventory. If a dealer buys bonds as principal, the fee is built into the price paid and no additional commission is payable. Alternatively, if you sell a bond, the price received from the dealer is reduced by the dealer's markup.

Some smaller investment dealers don't have bond departments. If you deal with this type of institution, it will likely purchase from or sell to another dealer. In this case, your dealer will tack on a com-

mission. It is best, however, to work with a dealer that has a specialized bond department with expert staff. But remember, bond trading
is a big business, so don't expect much service if you're trading only
a few thousand dollars worth of bonds.

Mortgage-backed securities

A relatively new instrument on the market is the mortgage-backed
security. Available in Canada since 1987, generally through investment dealers in denominations of $5,000, mortgage-backed securi-
ties are in effect part of a portfolio of mortgages with principal and
interest guaranteed by the Canada Mortgage and Housing Corporation. Rates paid are mortgage rates, less expenses. Consequently, the
rates paid will be better than those for government bonds and GICs.
A payment representing principal and interest is made each month.
Maturity terms vary with the pool issuing the security and terms of
up to five years are available. Monthly payments can vary because
borrowers can pre-pay principal.

CHAPTER 8

Preferred Shares: The "Bond Stock"

A PREFERRED SHARE CAN BE viewed as a bond that hasn't quite made it in terms of safety, or as a common stock without the profit potential. Investors buy preferred shares because they pay dividends that generally provide an after-tax rate of return greater than that of interest-paying investments such as bonds and GICs.

Because of the dividend income tax credit, $1 of dividend income from a Canadian corporation is equal on an after-tax basis to $1.26 of interest income. This is just a rule of thumb, but usually if your choice is between a bond with a yield of 8 percent and a preferred share yielding about 6.4 percent, the preferred share will return more. But there are other considerations, such as the safety of your investment. Many people would rather take a slightly lower return on a guaranteed investment and worry less. However, when properly chosen, preferreds have a definite advantage over interest-paying securities because of that higher after-tax return. You would not include preferred shares in your RRSP for income because an RRSP cannot take advantage of the dividend tax credit.

Preferred shareholders are, in fact, owners of the company. But they generally don't have a vote on company affairs – a privilege usually reserved for common shareholders. Still, preferred shares have more clout when it comes to dividends. Preferred shareholders get their share of company profits before common shareholders but after interest due on bonds and other debt securities is paid.

If a company fails, preferred shareholders are entitled to nothing until all creditors, including bondholders, are paid. But preferred shareholders take precedence over common shareholders when a company winds up. Yet this may be of little comfort because companies that go under usually have a liquidation value that is too low to repay even the creditors. In addition, preferred shareholders have somewhat less protection in the event of a takeover than do common shareholders.

Preferred dividends are usually fixed, either in dollars or as a percentage of par (nominal) value. For example, a glance at Toronto Stock Exchange stock tables shows several British Columbia Telephone Co. preferred issues, each paying different percentages. On the other hand, BCE Inc. preferred shares include annual dividends in dollars and cents.

When earnings are inadequate, the preferred dividend will be skipped. But most preferred share issues have a cumulative feature requiring that all preferred dividends be paid, including those in arrears, before any common stock dividend is declared.

Even though preferred stock issues are safer than common, company failure or dividend default should be a concern. If you are buying preferred shares for income, and wish to keep your portfolio as low-risk as possible, you should consider only those issued by the most financially solid companies. The same services that rate commercial paper and bonds also rate preferred shares, so inform your broker that the only preferreds you wish to consider are those with P1 and P2 ratings, the two highest classifications. And make sure your broker informs you of any changes in the ratings of your stock.

In addition to sticking to the strongest companies, diversify your holdings in case one of your investments turns sour. If the fortunes of a company in which you hold preferreds become clouded, you are probably better off selling. The adage that your first losses are your smallest often proves true.

Of course, higher yields are available from preferreds with lower rankings and from shares of companies which are not ranked by the services. These often appeal to sophisticated investors who are willing to assume increased risk as a trade-off for higher returns.

The preferred market can seem complicated for the novice because of the different types of shares available. What they have in common, at least when issued by major companies, is that they trade on stock exchanges just like common stocks. The following are some of the types of preferred shares available.

Straight preferreds: These do not carry a maturity date and are, in effect, a perpetual security. Prices of straight preferreds are most sensitive to changes in interest rates. They can be volatile in periods of sharply changing rates, but are extremely attractive in periods of high rates – particularly if it appears that rates will fall.

Retractable preferreds: These give the holder the right to redeem the shares at a specific date for par value. This is an attractive provision because it protects investors against a sharp increase in interest rates. Retractable preferreds are a good choice in periods when the direction of rates is uncertain.

Floating-rate preferreds: These have an interest rate that floats with changes in the prime rate. Floating-rate preferreds are the best bet during periods of rising interest rates.

Fixed floating-rate preferreds: These have a fixed rate for several years, then a floating rate. These give some protection to investors against rising rates.

Convertible preferreds: These are convertible into common stock. Convertibles, particularly those issued by utilities, are popular with those who invest for income. In the short term, the convertible preferred pays a higher dividend than the common share. But in the longer term, there is a high probability that the common dividend will increase to a point that exceeds the preferred dividend. At that point, investors would convert their convertible preferreds to common shares.

The fact that preferred dividends are more certain than common stock dividends is a big plus for investors who want to maximize after-tax income. Even so, not every investor holds preferreds for income. Some buy those with dividends in arrears as speculative investments, hoping for capital gains if the company pays past dividends. But whatever the reason for investing, don't lose sight of the fact that shares of any sort are not as safe as government bonds. As a result, you must monitor your holdings carefully. If you're not prepared to do this, consider investing in preferreds through a mutual fund whose professional manager will decide what stocks have the best potential.

CHAPTER 9

Common Stocks: The Inside Story

TO MANY PEOPLE IT ISN'T that important whether gambling is legalized in Canada. After all, they can always take a chance on the stock market.

But stocks don't have to be a gamble. Thousands of individual and institutional investors who play the stock markets are rewarded with long-term profits far above what they would earn in guaranteed investments and bonds. However, to be successful you must know how the markets work.

Stock price movements on organized Canadian exchanges – the Toronto Stock Exchange, the Montreal Exchange, the Vancouver Stock Exchange and the Alberta Stock Exchange – and on the major American exchanges are continuously reported and updated during each trading day. With the exception of the Alberta exchange, the exchanges publish indexes of price movements that chronicle the aggregate ups and downs of the market.

Common shares, which represent ownership of a company, constitute by far the largest portion of listed stocks. Prices of common shares may change throughout each trading day. Share prices reflect the general outlook for the stock market; investor expectations about a firm's profits, dividends and other developments that affect the company; and the prospects for the industry the firm is involved in. Common share prices are generally much more volatile than prices of bonds or preferred shares, and some stocks are more erratic than others. For example, shares of a telephone utility that pays a high dividend will be more stable than shares of a penny mine with unknown prospects and whose share price reflects speculators' expectations.

Stock markets move in cycles, with prices and investor expectations rising and falling in response to changes in the economic outlook, interest rates, exchange rates, the rate of inflation and other economic variables. At a somewhat less august level, rumours of

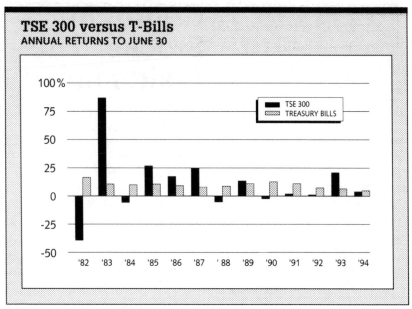

TSE 300 versus T-Bills
ANNUAL RETURNS TO JUNE 30

CHART II

takeover attempts or changes in the performance of large firms have been enough to cause at least short-run market fluctuations. However, if you have a diversified portfolio of stocks and hold them for some time, you can expect to earn a rate of return several percentage points higher than if you invest in guaranteed investments.

Some investors choose to invest in only a single stock or a small number of stocks in hopes of quickly making a substantial profit. Some succeed, but portfolios with only a few stocks tend to be more volatile than widely diversified portfolios. The Toronto Stock Exchange 300 composite index reflects the prices of the 300 TSE-listed stocks with the largest market capitalizations. Market capitalization is the value of the shares traded on the exchange, or the price of the shares multiplied by the number of shares outstanding. Therefore, a company with 10 million shares outstanding and a stock price of $25 has a market capitalization of $250 million.

Over the ten years ended June 30, 1994, the TSE total return index, which is the gain in the TSE 300 index plus stock dividends, recorded an average annual compound return of 9.7 percent, marginally more than you would have earned by holding treasury bills. Using a June 30, 1988 ending date, we see that the ten-year return was 16 percent – about five percentage points above the treasury

Market Cycles Since 1921
on the Toronto Stock Exchange

Bull Markets	No. of Months	% Gain	Bear Markets	No. of Months	% Loss
August 1921 to			September 1929 to		
September 1929	97	300	June 1932	33	80
June 1932 to			March 1937 to		
March 1937	57	201	April 1942	61	56
April 1942 to			May 1946 to		
May 1946	49	159	February 1948	21	25
February 1948 to			July 1956 to		
July 1956	101	273	December 1957	17	30
December 1957 to			May 1969 to		
May 1969	137	162	June 1970	13	28
June 1970 to			October 1973 to		
October 1973	40	64	December 1974	14	38
December 1974 to			November 1980 to		
November 1980	72	193	July 1982	20	44
July 1982 to			August 1987 to		
August 1987	61	202	October 1987	2	31
October 1987 to			October 1989 to		
October 1989	24	42	October 1990	12	25

Note: Changes in market sentiment reflect gains or declines of 20 percent or more. The market began climbing in October 1990, gaining more than 45 percent in the 45 months to June 1994.

TABLE XIX

bill return. For the ten years ended June 30, 1992, the return was 13.5 percent, more than three points above the treasury bill return. Chart II shows the year-by-year performance for periods ended June 30 of the Toronto Stock Exchange total return index and the rate of return on federal treasury bills. The total return index is a good representation of what you would have earned by holding a broadly based stock portfolio.

Market cycles vary in length. Rising periods are called bull markets and falling markets are known as bear markets. Table XIX, compiled by Toronto statistician Richard Anstett, shows market cycles of the TSE 300 from 1921 to the present. The October 1987 crash – when the Toronto market fell more than 22 percent – has to be looked at in its proper context. Between July 1982 and August 1987 the market gained 202 percent. In the subsequent three months it fell 31 percent. Investors who jumped in after the crash have done quite well, with the index gaining 42 percent to the end of October 1989. The index fell by about 25 percent over the next twelve months. It has risen more than 45 percent since October 1990.

Investment techniques

There are many different strategies and techniques for investing in the stock market. One that has proven consistently profitable over the years is creating a diversified portfolio of shares in senior companies with solid histories of earnings, strong balance sheets and good prospects for the future. Good prospects for earnings are very important and, indeed, many companies which were considered blue chip in the 1980s failed to participate in the stock market recovery of 1993 because their earnings prospects were poor. This kind of diversification spreads risk among many companies. You then constantly monitor your holdings, adding new investments that appear to have better than average prospects and selling those that no longer meet your expectations. You can do this by conducting your own analysis, by depending on your broker for advice or by using professional management through a mutual fund. Some brokerage houses, investment counselling firms and trust companies also have investment management divisions that will look after your portfolio.

Of course, it is impossible for small investors to purchase a diversified portfolio of shares of senior companies because of commission costs. Addressing this, the Toronto Stock Exchange has introduced a new investment product which will give investors diversification based on the TSE 35 Index. Called an Index Participation Unit, each unit will represent a fraction of one share of each of the 35 companies represented in the index. The shares of the companies themselves are held by a custodian. Dividends paid by the companies flow through to holders of Index Participation Units.

Another stock market investment technique, as we've already mentioned, is to hold only a few stocks in hopes of making gains far greater than those you would get from a diversified portfolio. This method suits some investors well, while others lose most of their capital. People who employ this technique specialize in trying to pick stocks before their prices start to rise and in unloading their dogs before they start to bark.

What separates the winners from the losers are their methods of picking stocks. Winners tend to use detailed analyses of companies, often confining their research to firms that are not widely followed by the investment industry in hopes of finding an undiscovered bargain. The share price of widely followed companies generally reflects all the known information, so it's difficult to stay ahead of the crowd when investing in these issues.

Benjamin Graham's legacy

The most successful method of investment analysis – perhaps at once the simplest and the most complicated – is the method developed by the American analyst Benjamin Graham more than sixty years ago. Simply put, it involves searching for value – the share price should be below the value of the company's assets as represented by each share, after deducting liabilities. Although there are many variations of the method, including careful consideration of earnings trends and developments that may enhance a company's earnings, it all comes down to buying value.

The Benjamin Graham method is not always the most exciting way of assessing stocks. It requires patience, but it usually proves profitable over the long term. And you won't get badly burned, particularly if you remember to sell when a stock's price rises above its underlying value. Other methods involve buying into a falling market and selling when prices are rising. However, most stock market investors find it emotionally difficult to move against the crowd. Indeed, this "contrarian" approach takes more discipline than the Graham approach. Even so, a follower of Graham is just as likely to be buying near the bottom and selling near the top.

Some investors play interest rate cycles. When interest rates move up sharply, stock prices usually move lower; declining interest rates are usually associated with rising stock markets. But playing interest rates can be extremely tricky. Rates can move higher because of demand for funds by growing companies, so selling on this basis can be costly in terms of potential profits.

Technical analysis is another way to predict market behaviour and to choose stocks. This technique looks not at balance sheets and income statements, but at charts of market and individual stock performance, trading volumes, various ratios of advancing stocks versus declining stocks and so on. Many people are sceptical about technical analysis, yet virtually every brokerage house has a highly paid technical analyst whose job is to produce observations that individuals and brokers can consider when making investment decisions.

Timing purchases

If you knew when the stock market has hit its peak or its bottom, you would not need this book. You could buy stocks when prices are at their lowest and sell when they are at their highest – and you'd be very wealthy. But you can't do it. Even the pros are not consistently accurate in calling the direction of markets. According to the American Statistical Association, which has been conducting an ongoing evaluation of forecasting accuracy, a 50 percent accuracy rating is par for the course – about the same as your chance of accurately calling heads or tails when flipping a coin.

Since it's not possible for you to buy at the bottom of the market and sell at the top, other rules have been developed. None of these work perfectly but at least two are better than buying in a hot market and selling when prices tumble, which is the apparent strategy of the emotional investor.

Buy-and-hold is one strategy. Simply put your money into a well-diversified portfolio consisting of fifteen or more stocks spread among different industry groups, and only make changes when the condition of one of the companies deteriorates. Otherwise, ignore the day-to-day twitches of the market. When the long-term market trend is bullish, as it has been for the past ten years or so, buy-and-hold pays off both in money returns and lack of anxiety.

Another strategy, somewhat more conservative, is to dollar average. To dollar average you must put the same amount of money into a diversified portfolio regularly, perhaps every month or every three months. When prices are rising, you will automatically buy fewer stocks. When the market is falling, and share prices are lower, you will be able to buy more stocks. As a result, when market prices are fluctuating, the average cost of your shares tends to be lower than with a buy-and-hold strategy.

Which strategy is better? When markets are strong, buy-and-hold appears better. When markets are fluctuating with either a few sharp down periods, as in October 1987, or many small down periods, dollar averaging is superior. Chart III compares the results of a buy-and-hold strategy with dollar averaging for four time periods, 1930 to 1934, 1977 to 1981, 1981 to 1985, and 1984 through mid-

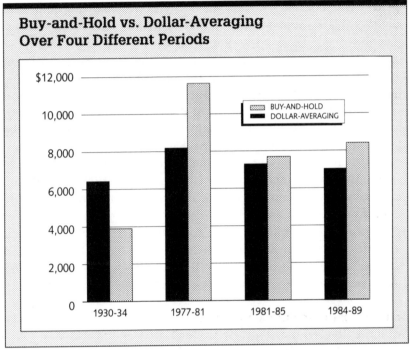

**Buy-and-Hold vs. Dollar-Averaging
Over Four Different Periods**

CHART III

June 1989. In each case, $5,000 was invested in the TSE composite 300. With the buy-and-hold strategy, the $5,000 was invested as a lump sum at the beginning of the first year. In the dollar averaging strategy, $1,000 was invested at the beginning of each of the five years. For each period, the first bar shows the amount of money you would have at the end of the period under buy-and-hold. The second bar shows the outcome with dollar averaging.

When TSE growth was slight, as in 1930 to 1934, dollar averaging generated over $2,000 more than the buy-and-hold strategy. From 1977 to 1981, TSE growth was substantial and the buy-and-hold strategy generated over $3,000 more than dollar averaging. Results were almost the same for the two strategies in 1981 to 1985 when TSE growth was moderate and there were few downturns. In 1984 to mid-1989, TSE growth was about the same but the market was strong in the early part of the period which made buy-and-hold generate about $1,000 more than dollar averaging. Monthly results show much the same. Compare two eighteen-month periods, July 1987 to December 1988 and November 1987 to April 1989. In each period, $18,000 was invested, all at once with buy-and-hold and $1,000 at the beginning of each month with dollar averaging.

In the first period – just four months before the October 1987 crash – the buy-and-hold strategy would have generated returns of only $17,075, a loss of $925, at the end of the eighteen months, thanks to Black Monday. Dollar averaging would have ended up with a value of $18,587, a gain of $587 over the eighteen-month period. In the second period, the ups were generally larger than the downs and buy-and-hold would have generated $22,059 at the end of the eighteen months, about $1,700 better than dollar averaging.

Which strategy do you choose? It depends on how averse you are to losing money. If you hate losing money, dollar averaging is better. In a bull market, it generates positive returns but they'll be smaller than with buy-and-hold. In a bear market, it will generate the smallest losses and, often, as in the 1930s, a gain. If you are more of a gambler, try buy-and-hold. It is still better than buying on hunches but it does expose you to sharp declines in the market.

Selling under dollar averaging

Adopting the right strategy for buying stocks is one trick to achieving a profitable portfolio. Selling strategies are even more obscure. But the time comes when an investor needs the proceeds from the portfolio for retirement expenses, tuition needs for children or just to spend on something else.

Selling at the top of the market or just when prices are beginning to slide is optimal. The trouble is that, at the top, most investors fail to recognize they're sitting on a peak. Even when prices begin to slide, there is always hope that the slide is a temporary "technical" adjustment, and that prices will recover in the near future. So, the investor holds onto his stocks and doesn't sell until the decline becomes precipitous and pessimism dominates the market. This kind of emotional selling is the other side of the coin to emotional buying: It leads to selling at lower prices than necessary.

Dollar averaging techniques also work for selling. However, they require some modification. If one simply sold a constant dollar amount of shares over the cycle, most shares would be sold when stocks are cheap and the fewest number would be sold when prices are high – not an ideal outcome.

Instead, the seller should sell those shares where the difference between market price and average cost of the shares is largest. If share A was bought at $100 and now has a selling price of $150, while share B was bought at $80 and now sells at $120, the investor would sell share A before selling share B because the gain spread on A is $50 while it is only $40 on B. The selling program can continue even if the price falls below average cost and the stocks are sold at a loss, as long as the stocks sold first are those where the loss is least – where the difference between acquisition cost and selling price is smallest. However, the regularity of the sales should persist: In other words, there should be no wholesale dumping. Sales should continue on a constant dollar of sales each month according to acquisition cost.

This rule is based on the assumption that the inherent quality of the stock has not changed. Stocks issued by companies which have deteriorated should be sold immediately if the investor believes that the weakness is permanent and will lead to further weaknesses.

This selling policy will probably result in the portfolio losing its diversification. At the bottom of the cycle, the remaining stocks will be what are called cyclical stocks, stocks that are very sensitive to economic and market conditions. However, as the market turns up, it is these stocks which usually show the strongest recovery and the investor will realize better gains than if the cyclicals had been dumped during the downswing of the cycle. Further, the disinvestment process will unload the "concept" or "trendy" stocks early in the game when their prices are highest, which is just when everyone is becoming emotionally high on the stocks.

Beating the market

As many stock pros have known for years, it is possible to beat the market. Still, for many years, there was a strong argument made that it was impossible to buy an undervalued stock. All stocks, the story went, reflect all the available information so that they are properly priced. This is called the efficient markets hypothesis. What made it work, the argument goes, is arbitrage, where a knowledgeable investor would sell a stock when its market price was above its true value, and buy a stock selling at a price below value. The sales would push the stock price down and the purchase of "cheap" stocks would push prices up. All of this supposedly happens so fast that no one could make an abnormally high profit on a stock.

A second and related argument was called the perfect capital markets theory. Under this theory, a stock's price was determined by its riskiness. If a stock seemed cheap, based on price and earnings, it probably was riskier than other similar stocks. An expensive stock was probably safer.

These arguments, which started among academic finance experts, became pervasive. Indeed, market index funds, where the composition of the portfolio mimicked the TSE 300, for instance, is a reflection of the theories. An index fund makes no attempt at stock selection: It simply holds stocks which follow the stock market index and the returns are then supposed to be as good as you can get without taking unnecessary risks. According to these arguments, fund managers who spend money on securities analysis were wasting both money and time. The market tells all.

In the last several years, empirical investigations, often done by the same people who erected the two theories originally, have called the effectiveness of the theories into question. There are just too many exceptions to the theory to support its original claims of supremacy.

However, there are a number of indicators investors can use to find bargains. Several of these indicators such as the price to earnings ratio, price to book value ratio and intrinsic value are thoroughly studied and often used; others do not have a rational explanation, at least not yet. Where there is no rational explanation, the investor using the indicators is acting on the historic repetition alone. There's nothing wrong with that except that, while financial history does repeat itself sometimes, it does not do so all of the time. Here's a look at a few of these bargain indicators.

The price to earnings ratio: Buy stocks with low ratios of market price to earnings per share and, according to the studies, you should do far better than the market. This is part of Benjamin Graham's formula for picking undervalued stocks. The notion has been around a long time and it makes some sense.

If a company is making high earnings and its price is still low, the chances are that the market will eventually recognize it. Meanwhile, a company with a high price to earnings ratio is likely to be a favourite, but an increasingly expensive one. When the trendiness of the high P/E stocks fade, so do the prices. At the very least, this strategy should keep you out of overvalued stocks.

The price to book value ratio: Sometimes this is called the Value Line effect, after the investment service which popularized it. Pick stocks with a low ratio of price to book value per share. Book value per share is the total of assets less liabilities and preferred shares, all divided by the number of shares outstanding. Low price to book value ratio stocks do significantly better than stocks selling at a high ratio of price to book value.

This effect has been borne out by many studies. It has nothing to do with risk. However, it may be related to the size of the firm and low price-to-earnings ratio. Once your stock's price starts rising faster than its book value, it becomes a candidate for sale.

Intrinsic value and mean reversion: For most of us, finding a value for a stock different from the market price is no simple matter. But this value, called the stock's intrinsic value, is significant. Intrinsic value is based on such things as expected earnings growth, industry growth and the hidden value of such things as real estate that may be worth far more than the value shown on the balance sheet. Press your broker and he is likely to be able to get some estimate of intrinsic value from his research team.

If he tells you that the intrinsic value equals the market price, don't bother buying it unless you want to do no better than average. But if he convinces you that the intrinsic value of the stock exceeds its price, give it some thought. While you are thinking, check to see whether the price has been at or above the intrinsic value over the past year or so. If it has, it becomes an excellent buy candidate. The reason for this is that stocks tend to move toward their intrinsic value.

A stock that has lost favour in the market but retains a high intrinsic value is likely to show superior price appreciation as its price reverts to the mean. There is a substantial amount of evidence supporting this argument and in markets where investors tend to buy trendy stocks only to move on to other stock trendies, it is a great way to avoid the crowd and make money at the same time.

Find a stock priced well above its intrinsic value and you have a strong candidate for sale. If all goes well, many of your intrinsic value bargains will become selling candidates as price rises toward intrinsic value.

Small is beautiful: In comparing firms that involve the same degree of risk, it has been found that the returns tend to be significantly higher for firms that have a small total value of equity than for firms that have a large equity capitalization.

In Canadian stock markets, there is evidence that portfolios of small firms show a 35% better monthly return than do portfolios of large firms of equal risk. Similar results have been found in Australia, Japan, the United Kingdom and the United States.

While it is an effect that works most of the time, it doesn't work always. Between 1969 and 1973, for example, small-firm portfolios underperformed portfolios with large companies. Again, there is no convincing evidence explaining this effect. It may have something to do with the growing dominance of large institutional investors who tend to overlook small companies. On the other hand, the effect has been recorded for nearly fifty years and the institutional investors were less dominant in the stock market in the 1950s than they are today.

The January effect: This is a dominant seasonal effect. Firms whose shares drop in December tend to rebound strongly in January. Therefore, buying a portfolio of these cheap stocks in December should generate above-average returns in January and maybe longer.

Some claim that this is a tax effect: Investors sell to establish losses at the end of the year and then buy back into their positions during January. In Canada, however, the January effect is discernable prior to 1972, when there was no capital gains tax on stock sales. Another argument against the tax sell-off explanation is that some studies have shown that January effect stocks can continue to outperform the market for as long as three years.

There have been some suggestions that the January effect reflects the effect of year-end bonuses or pension contributions made at the end of the year and invested by pension funds in January. Still, the January effect is not fully understood but it is persistent.

Day of the week effect: Sell on Tuesday through Friday, but buy on Monday. Studies going back to 1928 indicate that this is a way to improve the rate of return on your portfolio. There isn't an explanation for this but it is pervasive.

The monthly effect: Buy toward the end of the month and sell during the first half of the month. Studies have shown that from the last day of the preceding month into the first half of the next month, stocks tend to register most of their gains. In the second half of the month, returns are lower and even negative. So buy when stocks are cheap – in the second half of the month – and do your selling during the first half of the month when prices tend to rise.

The reasons behind this monthly swing are even more obscure. Still, it seems to work.

All shares are not equal

Investors should also be aware that there are different types of common stock, especially when it comes to voting privileges. At one time, common shareholders had one vote for each share held. This has changed in recent years and a number of companies now have two classes of common shares, one of which is a subordinated share for voting. The regular common shares generally carry more votes per share than the subordinated common shares. As a result, control of the company's affairs often lies with a group of investors who have substantial voting power but less than a majority of the equity in the company.

This normally isn't a problem for investors, except when a takeover offer is made. Securities law requires that when a premium price of 15 percent or more is paid for a control block of shares, a comparable offer must be made to all holders of that class of shares. This means that a takeover offer at a substantial premium to the market price will be made to the common shareholders, but not to the holders of subordinated common shares. Some companies with subordinated shares have what are called "coattail" provisions that are designed to protect holders of these shares in the event of a takeover. However, the market tends to discount the price of subordinated shares, even when there is a coattail.

There have been a number of cases over the past few years in which companies have been bought out, or offers made, with the common shareholders who control the company getting a better deal than other shareholders. As a result, some institutional investors have a policy of buying only shares that control the vote, even though it means paying a premium. If you decide to invest in a company that has two classes of common shares, check how the coattail, if there is one, protects you. If you're not sure, play it safe and go for the shares that will benefit from a takeover offer.

In the end, consistent profits are made by being careful, avoiding excessive greed and doing a lot of homework. Certainly, the investor who buys a stock simply because he believes there exists a greater fool who will pay more for the stock, is often the greater – and poorer – fool himself.

Unfortunately, many people get their first taste of the stock market by buying the penny dreadfuls – over-the-counter stocks only sold over the telephone by dealers who are not members of any exchange and make a living peddling paper and preying on people's greed and dreams.

If you are determined to try to get rich quickly, you must develop expertise in a specific area of the market, most likely in natural resources, and be prepared for massive ups and downs. Big money can be made, but luck is as much a part of it as is skill. And don't forget the adage about not putting all your eggs in one basket. Speculate with only those savings you can afford to lose without affecting your lifestyle and long-term goals.

Employee purchase plans

Many companies offer stock-purchase plans to encourage employees to become owners in their enterprises. Some plans are good, others are much better. When investing in your company stock always remember that your investment portfolio should be diversified. You shouldn't put everything in one stock, particularly if your industry is cyclical and you may need to cash out when the industry is in the dumps. Remember, too, that such stocks are long-term investments. If you think you'll need your money in a year or so, stay out of the plan.

There are several variations. Many companies have a matching program in which a percentage of the employee's income is used to purchase shares issued by the company's treasury. The purchase is matched by the company so, in effect, you are getting shares at half price. However, the purchases the company makes on your behalf are a taxable benefit.

Some companies give employees interest-free loans to buy shares. If you are offered shares at $20 each and the stock doubles you could make a lot of money. But what happens if the company's fortunes turn and the stock goes to 10 cents? You will owe the company the value of the loan. And even if the company forgives the loan, Revenue Canada will consider it a taxable benefit and you will have to pay tax on the value of the loan even though the stock is worth only a fraction of your purchase price.

Other companies give employees options to buy stock at a specific price for a specific time period. The advantage of the option is that you exercise it only if the stock goes up. Twenty-five percent of the gain is tax free. The remainder is taxed as income.

Another variation is the option loan plan. The option is granted at some price higher than the market price of the stock. Once the share price rises above the exercise price, the option is exercised and financed by a loan from the company. Any subsequent profits are capital gains.

CHAPTER 10

Mutual Funds: Suitable for Everyone

FOR MANY PEOPLE, MUTUAL funds are the best way to invest whether the investment is in stocks, bonds, mortgages, treasury bills or a combination of investment vehicles.

A mutual fund is a pool of investments that is owned by many people and managed by professional portfolio managers. Investors become part of these pools, which are also known as investment funds, by buying shares or units of the funds. The value of each share or unit represents the total value of the fund's investment portfolio divided by the number of shares outstanding. Most Canadian funds are open-ended, which means that the number of outstanding shares changes as people buy and sell shares.

There is also a handful of "closed-end" funds which have a fixed number of shares. These shares generally trade on a stock exchange. While the value of an open-end fund share or unit is based on the underlying value of the portfolio divided by the number of shares, the value of a closed-end fund share reflects whatever the market is willing to pay for it. In other words, the market value of a closed-end fund share may be lower or higher than the value of its underlying assets.

The pools of capital are invested by professional fund managers in a portfolio of securities, with the types of securities purchased reflecting the fund's objectives. For example, a fund with the goal of long-term growth within the framework of the Canadian economy would invest in common shares of Canadian companies. A fund whose objective is to earn current income might hold bonds or mortgages.

Mutual funds are extremely popular, with an estimated two million Canadians holding about $150 billion in the country's more than 900 mutual funds. There are several reasons for this popularity. First, mutual funds provide investors with an opportunity to diversify their investments. Because money is spread among many securities, investors are unlikely to suffer great financial losses if one investment goes sour. Most mutual funds invested in stocks usually own shares of at least twenty companies.

A second important reason for the popularity of mutual funds is professional management. In a mutual fund, investors' money is under the management of a full-time investment professional whose job is to select and maintain a portfolio of securities that meets the fund's objectives. Professional management often gives investors higher returns than they could earn on their own.

In addition, mutual funds offer a selection of investment opportunities that is not generally available to individuals. For example, some funds hold bonds payable in foreign currencies but issued by Canadian government agencies or corporations – instruments most individual investors simply don't have the capital to buy. Even investors who usually invest directly in securities can benefit from mutual funds, particularly if they want to invest a portion of their money in specific markets, such as Japan or Europe, and reap the rewards of global diversification and professional management.

Another big plus for mutual funds is liquidity. Investors can redeem shares of most funds on any business day, and the proceeds will be in their hands within a week.

Types of funds
Mutual funds fall into two main categories: growth and income. Within each of these categories are a variety of types, ranging from those that invest in a wide range of securities to those that concentrate on sectors such as precious metals or energy stocks. Some of these funds meet Revenue Canada's Canadian content requirements for registered retirement savings plans, while others invest internationally.

Most growth funds that are eligible for RRSPs invest in a broad spectrum of Canadian common shares covering many industries. But there are also RRSP-eligible specialty funds that focus on smaller sectors of the Canadian economy. Even within the international group of funds, investors can choose specialty funds such as health funds or funds that concentrate their holdings in a single geographical area.

Fixed income funds include bond funds, mortgage funds, preferred share funds, money market funds and funds that combine two or more of these investments. Almost all the bond, mortgage and money market funds – about 250 – are RRSP-eligible.

Preferred share funds invest primarily in dividend-paying preferred shares, and are usually purchased by investors who want high after-tax returns outside the shelter of an RRSP. Proceeds from such funds are eligible for the federal dividend tax credit, which effectively reduces the tax rate on dividends so that after-tax rates of return from preferred shares are competitive with those for bonds. However, the dividend tax credit cannot be used within an RRSP.

Money market funds invest in short-term debt securities such as government treasury bills, in deposits with major financial institutions and in corporate debt. Consequently, their rates of return are stable.

Of course, some funds are involved in a number of areas. There are several dozen balanced funds, or "managed-asset-mix" funds, that combine growth and income investments, with the mix of these vehicles changing according to market conditions. These have been growing in popularity since the October 1987 stock market decline, when such funds performed better than pure equity funds.

Mutual funds are available through a number of sources. Some are offered through independent mutual fund dealers and stockbrokers who deal in funds offered by several fund management groups. Others are offered directly by their managers through affiliates or direct sales forces. Most major banks and trust companies also offer families of funds, while major insurance companies offer mutual funds or segregated funds that are similar to mutual funds.

Funds sold through a sales force are generally sold one of two ways: with an acquisition fee or commission that is paid to either a dealer or salesperson and which reduces the amount of capital available for investment; or with a redemption fee which declines with the time the investment is held.

Given the choice, most investors choose the redemption fee alternative because it is often less expensive and because all of an investor's money is invested in the fund. Front-end loads or acquisition fees usually range up to 9 percent, with a sliding scale of reductions for larger purchases. For example, the maximum commission on a $50,000 purchase might be 5 percent. In addition, virtually every fund allows commissions to be negotiated, which gives brokers the latitude to adjust fees to be competitive and to reflect the level of service provided.

With the widespread introduction of redemption fees as an alternative – a response to competition from banks and trust companies which sell funds without any commissions – most fund buyers choose the redemption fee option if available. If you buy a fund with a redemption fee, the fund company pays the broker or dealer who sold you the fund a sales commission. The redemption fee declines over time. For example, if you redeem within a year of purchase you will be charged a fee of about 5 percent; different funds have different schedules. If you redeem in the second year, you could be charged 4.5 percent or 5 percent, again depending on the fund. If you redeem after, say, seven years, you might not be subject to any redemption fee. Some fund groups allow you to switch from fund to fund within the group without triggering redemption fees. You only pay redemption fees if you withdraw your money out of the fund group.

If you invest $1,000 in a fund that charges a front-end commission and you require a lot of advice, don't expect a reduction in the commission. But if you invest $50,000 and require little service or information from a financial advisor, you should be able to negotiate a lower fee. Indeed, a number of companies will handle the transaction at zero commission, receiving a small quarterly fee from the fund company for as long as you remain an investor.

Funds sold directly by fund management companies, as well as those sold by banks and trust companies, are generally "no-load" funds, meaning they are sold without a commission. With no-load funds, all your money goes to work for you.

Some no-load funds have staff members who offer limited advice on funds while trust companies and banks have improved the quality of information they provide to investors. Of course, don't expect an employee of a no-load organization to provide you with information on funds offered by competitors.

The rate of return you can earn from a fund depends on the type of fund, market conditions, the length of time you hold the fund and the skills of the fund manager.

Generally speaking, funds that invest for growth provide the highest long-term rates of return – often exceeding 12 percent annually or more over a period of ten to twenty years. In the short term, however, there is no way of predicting rates of return for a growth fund. Consequently, they should not be purchased with the view of making money over a very short period.

The *Financial Times of Canada, The Financial Post, The Globe And Mail* and several other papers publish surveys of investment fund performance every month. Twice a year the *Times* publishes the year-over-year performance for mutual funds for the past thirteen years. (The *Times'* survey for June 30, 1994 and its annual performance survey are in appendices three and four.) In addition, all of the monthly surveys track the volatility of funds.

The volatility refers to the stability of a fund's monthly rate of return. The least volatile funds are money market funds. Their monthly rates of return are the most stable and rarely vary widely on a month-to-month basis. In contrast, specialty funds such as energy funds, gold funds, resource funds or funds that invest in specific markets, such as Japan, tend to have monthly rates of return that can vary widely. Broad spectrum Canadian equity funds tend to be less volatile than specialty funds. Balanced or asset-allocation funds which combine stocks and bonds tend to be less volatile than equity funds but more volatile than bond funds. Bond funds are generally more volatile than money market funds but less volatile than those holding stocks.

If you want a stable rate of return, you will often have to settle for lower overall performance. If you want certainty, the only option is a money market fund. Because money market funds invest only in short-term instruments, you can redeem shares at any time and collect everything you invested, plus interest. Money market funds have historically paid about two percentage points more than premium savings accounts, but that rate of return is dwarfed by the long-term performance of growth funds. Still, money market funds offer excellent investment potential for those with short-term savings objectives – such as a down payment on a home.

Bond funds and other income funds usually provide medium- and long-term rates of return that fall between those of money market and growth funds. They are more volatile than money market funds but less volatile than growth funds because the income generated by the underlying assets stabilizes returns. They are best suited to people who want current income in their portfolios or who want more stability than they would have with growth funds.

Even though growth funds offer the best long-term returns, you should consider market conditions before making a purchase. If conditions suggest that stock prices are expensive, you may want to put your money elsewhere. Most equity fund managers will protect investors by building up cash reserves when stock prices seem high. But if you are nervous about market conditions you may want to choose a more conservative fund or a mixture of fund types. You might also consider funds with a mixture of asset types – balanced or managed-asset-mix funds – that make these decisions for you. These funds are designed to invest in growth assets when they are expected to perform best and in income assets when that is prudent.

Most investors buy funds entirely on past performance. Undoubtedly, historical performance is important because it shows how a manager has performed relative to competitors under identical market conditions. But there is a pitfall: you should make sure the person responsible for that stellar past performance is still running the fund. If not, past performance may be misleading. A fund's volatility ranking can also provide valuable performance clues. Top-performing funds with high volatility ratings often perform poorly in down markets.

When judging funds, look at various time periods. It is surprising how investors' conclusions can change when judging the performance of funds over different periods.

CHAPTER 11

Real Estate: Perils, Problems and Promise

IF YOU'RE LIKE MOST Canadians, the largest single investment you'll ever make will be in real estate – your family home. Following close behind, your next largest financial venture will probably be another property, either for vacations or as an investment.

Real estate has been a financial winner for thousands of Canadians in many parts of the country over the past few decades. But the road has not always been smooth. In most parts of the country, real estate prices have been volatile. A few years ago prices plunged in Alberta when the bottom fell out of oil prices. Some people walked away from their mortgages because they owed more than their homes were worth. High interest rates in 1990 triggered sharp declines in some markets, such as Toronto, where prices had soared beyond the reach of even affluent buyers.

Even with regional ups and downs, the forces that have pushed prices higher in many markets remain intact. These forces include a sharp shift in demographics that has increased the number of young families and singles reaching home-purchasing age along with speculative and inflationary forces and, until recently, relatively low interest rates.

Yet even with this history as a profitable investment, many people choose to be renters – and for good reason. Despite price increases, renting is still one of the best bargains in town. Monthly rents across Canada run at 50 percent to 75 percent of the cost of owning.

The better paid, and presumably more financially sophisticated, Canadians are the homeowners. Indeed, the vast majority of high-income Canadian families own their own homes. Are these people crazy to own instead of saving money by paying rent? More to the point, should you buy a house? Or if you are already an owner, should you sell your house and rent instead?

You must never ignore the emotional and lifestyle influences in this decision, but financially at least part of the answer lies in where rents are headed. The vacancy rate in rental housing in most urban areas is low, which means there are few rental apartments or houses available.

High mortgage rates, inflated maintenance costs and soaring purchase prices have combined with rent controls to make the building of new rental units both unprofitable and risky. Once a building is constructed, there isn't any difficulty renting it if rates are competitive with existing rent-controlled structures, except in markets with low vacancy rates, where new units rent at much higher prices. However, it is just about impossible to keep rents moving up as quickly as maintenance and financing costs.

As a result, it seems unlikely that the existing rental structure will prevail. Within the next few years, unless there is general price deflation, the existing rental structure may fall apart. Alternatively, buildings will deteriorate to the point that even fewer acceptable rental units will be available and new units put on the market will carry much higher rents.

Yet soaring rents do not automatically mean it will be better to own than to rent. The reason is that, as rents rise, many renters will find home ownership attractive, and the subsequent demand will push up housing prices.

Where are housing prices headed?

Both housing prices and rental rates have declined sharply in many markets because of the recession. Has the market hit bottom? Answer correctly and you'll be rich. When monthly rental costs are lower than ownership costs, the only economic justification for owning rather than renting is the expectation that housing prices will rise. The expected price increase promises a tax-free capital gain for the homeowner but the value of that gain must offset the higher monthly ownership costs.

Two factors suggest that the future rise in housing prices will be significantly smaller than it has been in the past. These factors are demographic patterns and the fact that the average weekly wage paid in all industries has been rising less rapidly than have housing prices.

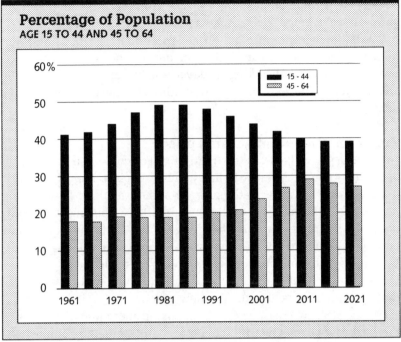

Percentage of Population
AGE 15 TO 44 AND 45 TO 64

Legend: ■ 15 - 44   ▨ 45 - 64

CHART IV

The impact of demographics

Most families have been having fewer children since the middle 1960s. The drop in family size has been so marked that, despite immigration, government officials believe that Canada is approaching zero population growth. This isn't a guess. The number of births per family has been dropping and shows no sign of increasing. This isn't a short-term fluke either. Except for the post-World War II baby boom, family size has been gradually decreasing since the turn of the twentieth century.

The early fruits of these smaller families are now in their twenties and early thirties. They are the next generation of house buyers, but their numbers are small. Already, the number of single-person households is rising dramatically and, according to government statistics, these people are not good candidates for home ownership.

Gradually, the percentage of the population from which new homeowners have traditionally been drawn, those aged fifteen to forty-four, will diminish after peaking in 1986. Meanwhile, there is an increase in the middle-aged segment of the population who already own their homes and may be thinking of selling as their children leave home and retirement nears.

These demographic factors do not spell doom for housing price increases. But they do indicate that one of the major sources of housing demand is shrinking. Today's housing shortages will gradually diminish and perhaps turn into a housing surplus early in the next century.

Trends in wages and housing prices

Another negative factor is the trend in wages compared to the costs of shelter. When wages drop below housing costs then the cost of housing, whether rents or the price of homes, tends to flatten. This happened in the early 1970s. By the mid-1970s, housing costs again began to rise more rapidly than wages, and flattened once again between 1979 and 1982. Since then, a gap has again gradually developed between housing costs and wages. Over the next few years, it seems likely that house prices and rents will increase less rapidly than they have in the past few years.

So there are two reasons to be pessimistic about housing prices in the next few years. Over the long term, shifting demographics will cut into the growth of demand for housing. And, in the short term, it is unlikely that wages will be able to support a rapid rise in housing prices.

Does that mean that housing prices will drop dramatically? No. Even if inflation is totally abolished, housing prices are at worst likely to remain flat in the next few years. In the longer run, if inflation is flat and demand for housing shrinks, prices may gradually decline relative to the inflation rate.

It also does not mean that housing prices will not boom in specific areas as bubbles of demand appear. An influx of population in Toronto set house prices there soaring during the last few years, until surging interest rates and worries about the economy set prices tumbling from peak levels. Vancouver prices have risen sharply, reflecting, it is said, purchases by Hong Kong speculators. But these bursts of prices are hard to predict and, over all, the long-term rate of price appreciation may be less than the historic average of 8 percent.

One grim memory should deepen your appreciation of the fact that housing prices do not always rise. In 1958, the price of a home was about the same as it had been in 1928.

Should you buy or rent?

With today's low inflation rates, it may be unreasonable to expect 8 percent appreciation in the long term. Of course, different locations can offer different rates of appreciation. On average, however, it is unlikely that prices will rise more rapidly than the inflation rate – and that may not be enough if mortgage rates return to the neighbourhood of 12 percent to 14 percent from current levels of 10 percent to 11 percent. Does it make much sense to pay 13 percent or 14 percent interest on an investment that appreciates by only 5 percent annually?

If mortgage rates stay some eight or so percentage points above inflation, the results could be disastrous for homeowners. The only factors keeping house prices from dropping sharply would be expectations of rising rents and the return of higher inflation rates.

There are three crucial variables in the economics of the decision to buy a home. The first is the amount of money needed to buy a home, including the down payment, financing and legal fees and renovation costs. The second is the monthly difference between ownership payments and rental payments. Ownership payments include mortgage costs, taxes, property insurance and maintenance. If you are a tenant, don't forget to include heat and other utilities as part of your rental costs if they are paid separately. The third variable is the expected price of the home at the time you expect to sell, less the mortgage outstanding at that time.

Though an oversimplification, your profit from owning a home will be the difference between the cost of buying the house and the money you'll have in your pocket after you've sold it and paid off the mortgage. On average, Canadians stay in a home for nine years, so let's look at whether it would be more profitable to buy or rent over that length of time. Over those nine years, all of the money that went into buying the home – the down payment, fees and taxes – could have been invested had you decided to rent instead of buy. A down payment of $100,000 invested at an annual after-tax interest rate of 5 percent, with all the interest reinvested, would be worth over $155,000 in nine years.

You must add to your $155,000 the value of investing the monthly difference in ownership payments and rent payments. At today's mortgage rates and tax rates, that could easily amount to $200 a month. If we use the 5 percent after-tax interest rate, that $200 a month could be worth about $28,000 in nine years.

All together, you could have had $183,000 in investment funds – the $155,000 value of the down payment plus the $28,000 from the difference between the monthly payments when renting and buying – at the end of nine years if you rent instead of buy.

The question then is: Will the value of the house increase by $183,000 or more in nine years? If you think so, then buy the house. If you think not, rent.

If the house's original price was $350,000, it would have to be worth at least $533,000 in nine years to make it a reasonable investment. That is an annual rate of appreciation of 4.8 percent compared to the historic average rate of increase of 8 percent. As interest rates rise, the decision tends to shift against buying for two reasons. The monthly cost of buying rises, and the return on invested funds if you rent also tends to rise. That means that the rate of appreciation on the house has to be higher than if interest rates were lower.

To have a truer picture of the financial advantages of buying over renting you must look at the present value of your gains in nine years. The calculations involved in adjusting dollars today to dollars in nine years is not difficult. Relatively inexpensive calculators can make the job quite easy. It's a calculation you must make. If you ignored it in the example above, you would combine the $100,000 down payment with the extra $200 monthly ownership cost to get $121,600, which you would add to the $350,000 price. You could be misled, thinking the house would only have to be worth $471,600 in nine years instead of the $533,000 price it really must rise to in order to be the better financial choice.

Should you sell your home?

Suppose you already own your home and it has risen dramatically in value since you bought it. Should you sell it and rent? Or is it better to hold on to the house and hope for even greater gain?

Deciding whether or not to sell requires exactly the same analysis as was used to determine whether you should buy. The cost of holding on to your home equals the net proceeds you would receive if you sold it. Remember, net proceeds are the selling price less sales commission and the cost of paying off your mortgage. You should also subtract from the price any legal fees involved in the sale and any renovation costs that would be needed beyond what might have to be done in a rented home.

The remainder of the analysis is identical to that followed by a home buyer. You combine the future value of the expected net receipts from selling the house with the future value of the monthly savings by renting instead of keeping your home. The total is the minimum amount by which your home must increase in value if you are to keep it.

You can use Table XX to determine the annual rate of appreciation at which your house must increase in value by dividing the value of the house in five years by its original cost. Once you determine how quickly your house must

How Quickly Will Your House Increase in Value?

Value of house in 5 years divided by original cost	Annual growth rate
$1.05101	1%
1.10408	2
1.15927	3
1.21665	4
1.27628	5
1.3382	6
1.4026	7
1.4693	8
1.5386	9
1.6105	10
1.6851	11
1.7623	12
1.842	13
1.925	14

TABLE XX

rise in value, you have to decide if this is reasonable considering historic patterns and current conditions, including the probable path of inflation. Finally, you must consider local market conditions. For instance, a market that has seen huge increases recently may stabilize or even turn down.

Buying a home

After pondering the question of renting versus buying and considering your personal desires, you may decide that you do want to buy. The next questions you must answer are when and how. Do you buy a home now or wait and risk the possibility that inflation – even at a moderate rate – will push the value of homes up at a faster pace than your savings?

There are no easy answers. Housing prices fluctuate like the prices of other goods and services. And while the general trend of housing prices is upward, they have fallen in some areas.

Before taking the plunge, consider your career path and, if you are married, your desire to have children and whether you will remain a household with two incomes. All of these have a bearing on whether a family can afford to carry a home without suffering a serious change in lifestyle. A person whose income is likely to grow by leaps and bounds in future years can probably risk assuming a large mortgage to buy a home. As a young working couple, you should include both incomes in your calculations but don't neglect to consider whether you could carry the home on one income if you decide to have a family. If you can't, are you better off buying a less expensive home?

There are various ways of financing the purchase of a home. Because a large down payment results in smaller mortgage payments, it usually makes sense to make as large a down payment as possible. In some cases, this also allows a repayment schedule that will increase your equity more rapidly.

Some people buy their homes with moderate down payments, choosing to keep as much of their savings in bank and trust company deposits or in certificates and stocks as possible. This makes little sense because mortgage rates exceed deposit rates. Also, because interest is taxed as income, the after-tax return from fixed income investments is dwarfed by the mortgage rate.

Mortgage interest is generally not tax-deductible. Therefore, you should consider paying off your mortgage as a risk-free investment. In fact, you probably couldn't get an after-tax rate of return exceeding your mortgage rate from any investment. If you have investments and a mortgage and feel you want both, consider selling your investments and paying off your mortgage. Then borrow against the equity in your home and buy a similar investment portfolio back. You'll still own a comparable portfolio and owe the same amount of money as before. But now your loan is for investment purposes and the interest is deductible from income for tax purposes.

How much money will the bank lend you?

Lenders look at two figures when considering a mortgage: your down payment relative to the value of the home and your income. Institutions usually won't lend more than 75 percent of a property's value unless the amount above 75 percent is insured.

With mortgage insurance, an institution will lend up to 95 percent of the property's value. High-ratio mortgages, as they are called, are more expensive with the additional cost of the insurance premium. An alternative to a high-ratio mortgage is a second mortgage, which makes sense if you are buying a home and assuming an existing mortgage with favourable terms or getting a first mortgage from the vendor at below market rates. While second mortgages are available from mortgage brokers, your bank or trust company is the first place you should try.

Many lenders have also put a ceiling on the values of properties against which they will lend 75 percent, especially in markets where house prices have skyrocketed in recent years. Lenders are concerned that if housing prices fall they might find the values of some properties falling below the values of their loans.

Shop for a mortgage

Lately, the mortgage market has been a strong area for lenders. As a result, financial institutions are competitive and will usually come up with terms to suit your needs. For instance, some will rewrite an existing mortgage when a house is sold, raising the loan amount and adjusting the payment to reflect a blend of current interest rates and the rate in effect when the mortgage was originally arranged.

New homes generally have financing in place when you buy. But if the home is a resale, the vendor will often take back a mortgage. However, you would probably be better off arranging your own financing before making an offer for a home if the existing financing is inadequate. By arranging your own funds, you can make an unconditional offer and possibly get the house at a lower price.

It's best to shop for financing before you make an offer on a house. See your bank, trust company or credit union manager to discuss your intentions and to determine the size of the loan for which you will qualify. The rule of thumb followed by some institutions is that mortgage payments, property taxes and heating expenses should not exceed 32 percent of your gross income. Those amounts, plus other consumer debt such as car payments, should not exceed 37 percent.

Your choice of term

Your mortgage will probably be amortized over twenty-five years. But the term over which interest rates are fixed will be less – one to five years in most cases, although some pundits expect to see twenty-five-year terms. People who feel rates will remain low or move lower usually go for short terms, while people who are nervous about the direction of rates usually go for longer terms.

Your choice of term should reflect not only your view on the direction of rates but your ability to take risk. Sometimes you might be better off locking in a rate for a longer term if only to have the peace of mind that your mortgage payments won't change for several years, no matter what happens to interest rates. If your mortgage comes up for renewal in a period of high rates and you think they might tumble, see if the mortgage holder will give you an open mortgage or a floating-rate mortgage. With these you'll be able to re-negotiate your mortgage to a longer-term fixed rate when rates fall.

If you need a mortgage or have one coming up for renewal, it pays to shop well in advance to find the best deals. It might not pay to move from one lender to another, especially since you are likely to incur legal fees and pay for an appraisal of your home. However, some institutions will pay a portion of the costs involved in moving a mortgage from another lender. If you find a rate lower than the one your lender has offered, see if your lender will match the competing bid.

Before buying a home, inspect it thoroughly so you're aware of any faults or potential repairs. Many people use inspection services, which for a few hundred dollars look over the house, reporting on the condition of its electrical system, plumbing, heating system and other features.

Selling a home, like selling any other investment, also incurs costs. But a house is one of the few investments you can sell on your own. However, it is a difficult, time-consuming task. Most people who decide to sell turn to a real estate broker. With dozens of firms to choose from in most cities, finding the real estate broker who's best for you can be wearisome.

The quest for competence

Finding a competent real estate broker and agent is extremely important. A poor choice could mean your home will sit on the market for months because it is listed at an unrealistically high price. Conversely, you don't want your home sold at a price substantially below its value.

When properly chosen, a broker will get you the best possible price quickly. The agent will screen out sightseers and show the house to more potential buyers than a homeowner can. A good broker can also come up with financing to help potential buyers make a deal. But, it's expensive to use a broker. Commissions range from 4 percent to 6 percent of the selling price for an exclusive listing, with the rate dependent on the value of the home and market conditions. Including the home under a multiple listing service costs another percentage point but it exposes your home to many brokers and their clients. Don't expect to negotiate the commission rate, even though technically it is negotiable. Despite growing pressures to change, in reality, rates in most markets are fixed.

When the time comes to choose a broker, talk with three or four before making your decision. Ask each to come to your home to appraise its value and discuss how he or she proposes to sell it. The brokers you invite should have plenty of experience in your neighbourhood. It doesn't matter whether the firms are national, independent franchise operations or a trust company. It does matter that they are successful at selling homes in your area.

If you're not familiar with a firm's roster of agents, call the owner or manager and insist that the agent sent to deal with you is experienced and has sold extensively in your neighbourhood. It is also important that the agent be experienced in selling your type of home. It makes little sense to have someone who specializes in rambling mansions if your home is a modest bungalow.

Agents should be prepared to suggest a selling price, backed by recent sales figures of homes in your area. You should be made aware of listing prices, selling prices and how long the homes were on the market. You should also be shown listings of homes that didn't sell because of high prices.

An agent who does not arrive properly prepared, or who cannot back up an evaluation with data, should be rejected. Similarly, reject any agent who does not ask about existing mortgages and who has no suggestions about financing. Financing arrangements can often make or break a sale.

Most homes have mortgages held by banks, trust companies or insurance companies. A good agent will first determine whether the holder would be willing to rewrite the mortgage for the purchaser. Many financial institutions will do this routinely, so be wary of any agent who suggests a financing alternative before checking to see what can be done with the existing mortgage.

The agent should also present a strategy for selling your home. Most will ask for an exclusive listing, which may be for ninety days. In return for this, the broker will spend some money advertising your home. Determine the firm's advertising policy and look at recent issues of the daily newspaper to determine if homes listed with the firm get good exposure. On any given day a firm may advertise only a few of the homes it has listed in a neighbourhood, but its agents would probably show several homes to anyone responding to an advertisement.

Once you make your choice, the agent will give you a listing agreement to sign. It is a binding contract appointing the firm as your agent for a limited time, so your lawyer should examine the agreement before you sign it. Many listing agreements state that a commission is payable for procuring an acceptable offer. In other words, the broker gets paid even if the deal doesn't close. Many lawyers insist that this clause be changed so the commissions are paid only if the actual sale takes place. If the deal doesn't close, the vendor should be entitled to keep the deposit made by the potential buyer. This compensates for lost time and legal expenses.

Do-it-yourself sale

Many people are capable of selling their own homes, but this can be a time-consuming task and individuals often make errors in assessing the values of their homes. However, the saving on commission is reason enough to consider acting as your own broker. Remember, however, that in private sales the buyer often thinks he should get the benefit of commission savings.

If you decide to bypass a broker, set a realistic price. This can be determined by checking recent sales in your neighbourhood. It makes sense to hire an independent appraiser, who for a fee of $200 to $300 will give you a written report on the value of your home. The appraisal itself can be an excellent sales tool. Check with the mortgage departments of several banks, trust companies and insurance companies for names of appraisers they use. Most institutions will accept an appraisal as proof of value for mortgage financing. You can then take the appraisal to the institution that holds the mortgage on your property to determine the amount it would lend to a purchaser who meets its requirements.

You should also advertise your home. A simple sign on your lawn is essential, but make sure it says "By Appointment Only" so you can control who comes in and when. Your newspaper advertisements – budget at least $500 for a long-term campaign – should list the location of your home, type of home, the number of rooms and outstanding features.

To leave room for haggling, the price you ask for should be about 5 percent higher than the price you expect to get. Make sure your lawyer knows what you're doing and show him every offer you are considering. Remember, once your signature appears on the offer, it becomes a binding contract. In addition, let your lawyer know about any outstanding liens against your property so arrangements can be made to deal with them before your home is sold. Any offer made to you for your home should be accompanied by a deposit, around 10 percent of the selling price. It will be held by your lawyer in trust until the sale closes.

A cottage as an investment

The economics of buying a cottage or a resort condominium as a vacation home involves an analysis identical to buying your residence, with one important difference – 75 percent of the capital gain on selling a second home will be taxable. You should also be aware that the increase in the value of vacation homes does not necessarily follow the same pattern as price movements on residences.

Again, demographics is a major factor in explaining the differences. Back in the 1950s and 1960s, Canada's population was surging and it moved beyond traditional city limits as city property values rose. Businesses were also moving from urban areas in search of less expensive land and lower taxes, so they pulled even more people in their wake as workers were tempted to move to the countryside to be closer to work.

In the past decade, explosive population growth has slowed, reducing the pressure on land values in some cities. Furthermore, urban areas have found themselves stuck with empty factory sites because of the combination of high land costs and high taxes. Cities are rapidly developing programs to keep and attract new businesses and jobs. These changes should result in a slowing of the movement to rural areas and a lower rate of price increase for vacation properties, if not a decrease.

Another factor has been the slow growth of real personal income. Traditional first-home buyers – those in their twenties and thirties – are having difficulty buying a first home, never mind a summer cottage or ski chalet. The blight on real income growth has also hit older families, impeding their ability to buy a second home.

All these factors combine to make the outlook for second-home price appreciation far less optimistic than it was a decade ago, although the lifetime exemption on capital gains has improved the attractiveness of a second home as an investment.

Commercial property

As a pure investment, commercial property is more interesting than a second home. Commercial income-producing property includes stores, office buildings, warehouses and residential rentals. Residential rental properties in provinces such as Ontario, where rent controls are in effect, are generally avoided by investors these days.

However, consider the advantages of commercial property. All expenses, including mortgage interest, real estate taxes and capital cost allowances are deductible for tax purposes from gross income.

If your major business is real estate management, losses incurred in conducting a commercial property business are deductible from other income in determining personal taxes. However, you should get advice from a tax professional before assuming you can integrate losses from real estate investment into other personal income. A retired person is likely to qualify, as might a spouse who has a source of personal income, such as that from a trust, and whose only work outside the home is managing the properties.

The value of commercial property

One long-standing rule for determining the value of commercial property dictates that the price should not be more than ten times net income from the property before financing charges and income taxes. Net income is gross income less all cash expenses, including maintenance and property taxes but excluding mortgage payments.

For example, an older property with a small store and a doctor's office upstairs might generate income of $1,000 a month, or $12,000 a year. Maintenance and other cash expenses, including real estate taxes, could be $9,000 annually. So a first approximation of the value of the property is $30,000 – ten times the $3,000 difference between gross income and cash expenses.

If we assume there is a $22,500 mortgage at 12 percent, the investment profile of the property for the first year would be as follows: $12,000 gross income less $9,000 cash expenses, $1,500 capital cost allowance and $2,629 for interest payments on the mortgage. At the end of the year, there would be a net loss of $860 before income taxes. But, this loss doesn't mean that the investor is out of pocket this money. It simply means that for tax purposes, no income tax is due.

In fact, the building has generated a positive cash inflow of $640. The capital cost allowance is simply a bookkeeping charge against income and does not reflect a cash outlay.

The capital cost allowance is 5 percent of the unamortized value of the building. A $30,000 building has a capital cost allowance of $1,500 in the first year. In the second year, capital costs would drop to 5 percent of the unamortized value, which is $30,000 less the first year's capital cost allowance, or $30,000 minus $1,500. Capital cost allowance in the second year amounts to 5 percent of $28,500, or $1,425. In the third year the capital cost allowance would be 5 percent of $27,075, or $1,353.75. Keep in mind that capital cost allowance is allowed only on the buildings and equipment, not on land. If the land were part of the investment, its cost would have to be deducted from the cost of the investment to find the depreciable asset investment base on which the 5 percent would be charged.

Investment analysis of commercial property

The analysis of commercial property is identical to that for home ownership. Legal and closing fees, as well as any renovation costs, must be added to the owner's investment. Let's assume in our $30,000 store and office property that these total $2,000, to which must be added the down payment of $7,500 for combined initial costs of $9,500.

These initial costs of $9,500 would be worth about $12,125 in five years at an after-tax interest rate of 5 percent. Suppose that the monthly flows total $640 a year with no income tax liability on building income over a five-year period.

At an after-tax interest rate of 5 percent, the cash flows would be worth about $3,714. Unlike the housing example, where the cash flow of owning versus renting was negative, this cash flow is positive since you would not have received the cash if you had not bought the commercial property. Therefore, the $3,714 should be deducted from the $12,125 initial costs. The property must appreciate by at least $8,411 to make the investment worthwhile. The price of the building after five years must be $38,411, an annual appreciation rate of 5.1 percent. The investment should be undertaken if, in your judgment, that rate of appreciation is the minimum rate of appreciation expected. It should be noted that as interest rates fall, the values of cash flows increase.

In the analysis, remember that the cash flows were assumed to be positive. If they were negative, instead of deducting the cash flow from the acquisition costs you must add them to your costs. If there had been a negative cash flow of $860 a month for five years on our store and doctor's office, the present value of $42,415.20 would be added to the $9,500 initial cost. The building now has to be worth $97,721.27 in five years, a jump of 325 percent or 26.6 percent a year, to make the investment acceptable. Unless there are special circumstances that might generate such extraordinary results, perhaps the opening of a subway station nearby, a reasonable investor would be justified in rejecting this investment. Negative cash flows do not necessarily mean the investment is bad. They do mean that the value of the property must increase over the investor's planning horizon, and the larger the negative numbers, the larger the required increase.

Of course, many people live in the small apartment buildings or duplexes which they own. Their investment analysis is essentially the same as for commercial property. The difference is that you cannot deduct the capital costs, real estate taxes or mortgage interest for that part of the home in which you live. In a duplex, for example, these deductible costs would be halved if the owner lived in half the house. On the other hand, only half of the capital gain would be taxable when the property is sold.

Should you be a landlord?

The answer to this depends on the price you pay for the property, the level of rent you can expect, expected capital appreciation and expected rent increases – in other words, can you expect to make a profit by being a landlord? The analysis is similar to the one for commercial property. However, many individuals apparently jump into the real estate game without doing proper analyses.

An example is the condominium market in Toronto in recent years. Individual investors were encouraged to put the minimum down payment on condominiums before constuction even began on the expectation that by the time the building was completed and they had to take possession, the condo's price would have risen 10 percent to 20 percent. These investors hoped to sell their properties and make a hefty profit. In reality, prices did not surge ahead. Moreover, there were many, many other investors in the same situation. To protect their investment and avoid losses the investors took possession and placed their units on the rental market. In many cases, the rental income covered only a fraction of the carrying costs. With rent increases restricted by rent control, it will be many years before these investments break even on a cash flow basis.

The situation can get even worse – the tenant could stop paying rent. It can take a landlord many months to evict a tenant, a period during which the landlord gets no income. When the tenant is finally evicted it is unlikely the landlord will recover lost income. The bottom line is that being a landlord has become a high-risk business, one in which the potential rewards do not compensate for the high risks.

Real estate syndicates

Small investors can participate in large real estate projects through real estate syndicates. Generally, these take the form of limited partnerships in which investors can purchase partnership units and own an interest in apartment buildings, hotels, office buildings and shopping plazas. Investors participate in the profits or losses of the partnership and get a portion of capital gains, if any, should the property be sold at some time in the future. Depending on the specific issue, the minimum investment ranges from $10,000 to $150,000.

The rule with real estate syndicates is caveat emptor. In many cases, the returns promised in early years consist of losses from the project which investors can use to reduce their taxable income. Often cash flow from the project is inadequate to cover mortgage payments and other expenses in the early years so the general partner guarantees any shortfalls for the first five years. Future profits are often based on expected rent increases and capital gains.

Before signing up for any real estate syndicate look at what you are getting for your money. Examine any appraisals critically to determine if the price you are paying for the property is inflated. Determine what portion of the price covers fees, including the cost of the cash flow guarantee. These can make a project very expensive. Read the fine print. In some cases, the cash flow guarantees are actually loans made by the general partner. These have to be repaid, generally when the project has to be refinanced. Look closely at the definition of cash flow so you fully understand what is included and what is excluded.

The prospectus will almost certainly include a table showing cash flow projections. Do the projections make sense? While real estate has been an excellent investment in recent years in many areas of the country, there is no way of knowing whether revenues will continue to climb. You should also determine whether you have any additional liability besides your initial investment. For example, projects may have to be refinanced after five years. If the cash flow is inadequate to cover the costs at that time, what liabilities do you face? You also have to look at the liquidity of your investment should you wish to sell it at some time in the future. Generally, there is no market for units of a specific project or at best a very limited market.

Actual liquidity often depends on the type of project. For example, some are offerings of specific suites in condominium projects. While cash flows to cover costs are guaranteed by the general partner who is responsible for renting and maintaining the units, you are the one who is really responsible for mortgage payments. If the building has not appreciated when the mortgage comes up for renewal and rents have not escalated substantially, you could find yourself having to subsidize the carrying costs. And if you and other investors in the complex decide to sell at the same time, you could drive down prices and suffer a capital loss.

If you are seriously considering an investment in a real estate syndicate, take the time to do some in-depth analysis. Play with the projections provided. Determine where you will stand if cash flows grow at a lower rate than the promoter projects or if the property appreciates at a moderate rate or not at all.

Look at the general partner's financial strength and how it has performed on other projects. The general partner's financial strength is very important because you are often dependent on it for cash-flow guarantees. If the guarantor fails, the guarantee is worthless. And make sure you know how much money you have at risk. You may be required to put only $10,000 up front. But you could be on the hook for $150,000. Read the fine print. Finally, never buy any property without inspecting it first yourself or having it inspected by someone who is independent. Brochures may provide illustrations of a building. But an inspection of the property and the surrounding area can tell you a lot about the quality of a neighbourhood and whether rents charged in the project are competitive.

CHAPTER 12

Options: Heaven or Hell in the Market

SO YOU'RE LOOKING FOR AN investment that will double your money overnight – or at least within a week.

It's rare for stocks to perform that well. But the doubling of investors' money is fairly common in the options markets. Options can be a speculator's paradise, or they can be a place to quickly lose your shirt in a few days. Ironically, options are also used by conservative investors as a vehicle to reduce risk. Indeed, some analysts blame the volatility of stock markets – particularly the sharp price declines of October 1987 – on institutional use of options and futures contracts to hedge exposure through a computer strategy called program trading.

Options are the right to buy or sell a specific security, currency or commodity at a given price until a set date. There are options on stocks, bonds, currencies, stock market indices, gold, silver and bonds. Much of the growth in options trading in Canada is a relatively recent development. Options were first introduced on the Toronto Stock Exchange in 1975 for blue-chip stocks such as Bell Canada. In 1987 the TSE introduced options on a new market index, the Toronto 35, giving institutional investors a new instrument for hedging their portfolios. Even so, the options market is still "thin", which means there isn't a massive amount of trading. However, it has been picking up.

There are two types of options – calls and puts. A call option on a stock gives the holder the right to buy 100 shares of a specific stock, the underlying security, at a fixed price until a given date. A put option gives the right to sell the shares at a specified price by a certain date. For example, an XYZ Ltd. February $17.50 call option gives the holder the right to buy 100 shares of XYZ Ltd. at $17.50 until the third Friday in February.

Maturity dates for options are standard. There are three maturity cycles:

- January, April, July and October;
- February, May, August and November;
- March, June, September and December.

Each option trades in one cycle only, and the longest option contract is nine months. Exercise prices are standard as well, but there can be several options available on the same stock with the same maturity date and with different exercise prices. This would happen if a stock price were to move sharply. New options would be created using $2.50 intervals for stocks selling below $50.

Since 1990 in the U.S. and 1992 in Canada, investors have been able to trade longer term options called LEAPS, which stands for long-term equity anticipation securities. These give holders the right to buy, in the case of calls, or sell, in the case of puts, the underlying shares for up to two years.

Options contracts are issued by a clearing corporation such as Trans Canada Options Inc., which is responsible for guaranteeing that all parties involved meet their obligations. You can trade options through any stockbroker registered to deal in options.

The option itself is liquid and marketable. Its value is called the premium, which consists of the difference between the stock price and the exercise price, plus the value the market places on the time remaining before the option expires. With our XYZ Ltd. example, if the stock trades at $19 and the $17.50 call option trades at $3, the option price, or premium, is made up of $1.50 in difference between the price of the stock and the exercise price plus $1.50 in time value placed on the option by the market. The time value can quickly disappear as the option approaches maturity.

If you buy an option at $3 and the stock price moves almost immediately to $22, you would expect the option to appreciate by about $3 as well, so you would double your money. Compare your potential return with what you would have gained by buying the stock. However, if you bought the stock and it failed to move, you would dispose of the option prior to the exercise date at $1.50 – the difference between the stock price and the exercise price. This means you would lose half your money, plus whatever commissions you must pay.

Playing the options market can be risky, and many people quickly lose all their capital. But the potential rewards are great, and that's what entices investors. A good rule of thumb is to not use more than 10 percent to 20 percent of your total investment capital when buying options. And if you're going to speculate in options on stocks, stick to options on securities that have historically been more volatile than the general market. For example, if you buy call options because you think the market is going higher, go for options on stocks that tend to do better than the market when it is rising. Conversely, if you are buying put options, go for options on underlying securities that tend to tumble hard when the general market moves lower.

Some people participate in the options market in a more conservative way. They "write" options to reduce the risk of losing money on their portfolios. In other words, they sell options against stocks they own.

For example, ABC Ltd. may trade at $20. An investor buying at this price might decide to sell an August $22 call option contract against the holding at $2. This investor has now reduced his cost by $2, which acts as a cushion if the stock declines. If the stock moves up, but doesn't exceed $22, the investor won't see the option exercised, so he will not only have the premium but will also keep the stock. If the stock moves above $22 at the exercise date, the option will be exercised and the investor's broker will turn over the shares to the options exchange or clearing corporation at $22, making the investor a profit of $4 before commissions.

You can, of course, purchase an option to cover your liability. For instance, if the stock price fell to $18, the premium would fall too. An investor might purchase the option back at a fraction of its previous sale price and then sell another option on it, exercisable at a lower price.

You shouldn't be too concerned if a call option is exercised against you. The price of the premium is usually great enough that the likelihood of your shares being called is slim. And if the shares are called, you will earn a significant return on your capital.

You can also sell options without owning the underlying security. However, this is extremely risky because your exposure is unlimited, while your maximum profit is the premium you've received. For example, you might sell an option that can be exercised at $20, only to find that a takeover offer is suddenly made at $60 a share. Your option could be called, forcing you to buy shares at $60 to satisfy your obligation. Few brokers recommend writing "naked calls" because it's a dangerous strategy for the client and the broker if something goes sour.

Options trading has become much more sophisticated in recent years with the development of computer programs that calculate potential profits using assumptions about where the markets might move. Options departments at most major brokerage firms have these programs in use for their retail and institutional clients.

Program trading is an extension of these facilities. With program trading, a large financial institution attempts to hedge against swings in the value of its portfolio by using futures contracts and general index options. For instance, a portfolio manager might sell an index option or futures contract against the value of the portfolio to lock in profits. If the index fell, the gain in the price of the futures or the premium from the option would offset any decline in the value of the portfolio.

In thin markets, the values of options and futures get out of line with the values of underlying securities. Picture a system where computers monitor portfolio, options and futures prices and trigger trades to take advantage of price differences. This trading activity is known as arbitrage. Now imagine what happens when a computer triggers trades in a thin, volatile market. Buying and selling pressures send prices even more out of line, thus increasing the volatility of the market. Some people in the investment business see program trading as a problem. In the U.S., measures have been taken to reduce the volatility by restricting the magnitude of price movements caused by program trading.

Individual investors can use options to stabilize their returns or as an alternative to holding stocks. For example, if you have realized substantial paper profits and are worried about the market moving lower, you might take your profits and use some of your gain to buy call options to participate in further price moves up that might occur in the near future. Alternatively, you might sell call options against your portfolio, giving you a cushion if prices decline.

You can play the same game with put options. Rather than selling your shares, paying a commission and possibly using up some of your lifetime capital gains exemption, you could continue to hold the stock and buy put options. If your shares continue to rise, your profits will grow and the put options you bought will be worthless when they expire. But if the stocks reverse, your put options will appreciate in value, offsetting any declines. When you use call and put options to lock in profits, consider your costs as insurance.

You can also sell put options. But by doing this, you commit yourself to buying a specific stock at a specific price, even if it is well below the market price. Selling put options is a strategy you might use if you want to buy a specific stock but feel it is too expensive. By selling a put option you can potentially get the stock at a lower price if it pulls back. And if it doesn't, you're still ahead of the game because you've received a premium for your efforts.

Buying put options is an alternative to "short selling," which involves borrowing shares from your broker, then selling them with the intention of buying them back at a later date at a lower price. In this case, the difference in price at which you borrow and the price at which you buy represents your profit. Selling short incurs unlimited liability, while buying puts limits your risk to the cost of the put.

Similarly, you can use index options to protect your entire portfolio. The TSE 35 Index was created specifically to allow the trading of options and futures based on a basket of liquid, widely held stocks found in many institutional portfolios.

Options can also be used for some fairly conservative strategies. You could, for instance, put 95 percent of your money in treasury bills and 5 percent in call or put options. If properly used, this strategy will protect your capital while giving you an opportunity to participate in market movements. You don't have to tie this type of strategy to stock options; you can also use bond options if your objective is to profit from moves in interest rates.

There are numerous strategies that employ more than one option in order to limit potential losses in options trading. The thing to remember is that any strategy that limits losses usually puts a ceiling on profits. For example, you might write one call and one put against the same security. You would earn two premiums, thereby reducing your cost and earning a profit if the price increases. You could lose, however, if the stock fell sharply and you were "put," meaning you would have to buy more shares as the puts were exercised.

Options strategies are quite complex and many investors make the mistake of ignoring commissions when they calculate their potential returns. Commissions can be significant and should be included in any calculation, although they will vary, depending on what type of dealer you chose. You can do business with a full-service dealer or a discounter with low commissions. If you need advice, information and the use of a dealer's option expertise, the full-service dealer will prove good value. Just make sure the broker you choose has extensive experience in options and the firm has the latest technical equipment to give you the information you need to make the best decision.

You should also familiarize yourself with the language of options and learn some of the terms involved. Most dealers can provide you with literature on options, and some offer seminars on the topic.

You'll encounter phrases such as in-the-money options, intrinsic value, opening-purchase transaction, opening-sale transaction and straddles. Here are some explanations of terms used in options trading:

In-the-money option: In the case of a call option, this is an option for which the stock price is higher than the exercise price. In the case of a put option, the stock price is lower.

Out-of-the-money option: In the case of a call option, this is an option for which the stock price is lower than the exercise price. For a put option, the stock price is higher than the exercise price.

Intrinsic value: The difference between the stock and exercise prices when an option is in the money.

Opening-purchase transaction: A transaction in which an investor buys an option.

Opening-sale transaction: A transaction in which an investor writes an option. The writer is the seller of an option contract.

Straddle: A strategy that involves buying or selling both puts and calls. A straddle is an order to buy or sell the same number of put and call options on the same underlying stock for the same exercise price and expiration date.

Time spread: Also known as calendar spread and horizontal spread, this refers to the practice of holding options with the same exercise price but with different expiration dates.

Price spread: This involves the holding of options with different exercise prices but with the same expiration date.

Diagonal spread: A combination of time spread and price spread.

CHAPTER 13

Commodities, Currencies and Futures

STORIES ABOUND OF PEOPLE starting off with next to nothing and becoming millionaires in a matter of days by playing the futures markets. There are also plenty of stories about people losing everything in the futures markets. They're true, too. They just aren't as popular as the tales of success.

Depending on whom you listen to, the futures markets are either one of the few places where huge fortunes can be made overnight or they're a path to financial disaster where you can lose your shirt in minutes. In fact, both can happen. But many novices jump into commodities without fully considering how risky they can be. When things go wrong, you can lose not only your investment money, but just about everything you own. If you want to dabble in the futures markets, it is imperative that you understand what futures are and the purpose of the markets.

Special delivery

A futures contract is an obligation that covers the delivery of a specific amount of a commodity, currency or security at a specified future date at a specific price. The amounts are standard, such as 112,000 pounds of sugar, 100 ounces of gold or 12.5 million Japanese yen.

You can also invest in stock index futures that involve a cash settlement, rather than delivery of a stock portfolio. One type of futures contract is based on the Toronto Futures Exchange's index of thirty-five stocks. You aren't required to deliver a basket of thirty-five stocks, but you must settle with an amount of cash based on the index's closing value on the third Friday of the month.

Even if you buy commodity futures, you needn't worry about having 112,000 pounds of sugar dumped on your lawn – unless you really want delivery. Instead, your broker would automatically buy or sell an offsetting contract prior to the delivery date.

The original hedge

Futures markets were established to allow commodity producers, such as farmers, mining companies and lumber companies among them, and commodity purchasers, such as food processing companies, metal fabricators and lumber dealers, to hedge against price swings. The major North American commodity exchanges are in Winnipeg, Chicago and New York, and they deal with a variety of commodities, including grains, meats, cotton, lumber, coffee, sugar, livestock and metals such as gold and silver. In addition, exchanges trade in currencies and interest-rate futures as well as stock market futures. In Canada, the Toronto Futures Exchange and the Montreal Exchange specialize in contracts tied to securities and precious metals.

The large players in the markets are hedgers. A farmer who is worried that the price of wheat might be lower at harvest time might decide to sell some of his anticipated production in the futures market. But he will not necessarily deliver wheat on the contract date; instead, he is likely to buy another contract to cancel the one he sold. If his prediction of lower prices is correct, he will buy a contract at a price lower than that for which he sold a contract. The difference, his profit, will help offset the low prices received for his crop.

However, if he's wrong and prices move higher at harvest time, he'll take a loss in the futures market. But he'll still get more for his crop, so in the long term hedging allows him to stabilize his income. Similarly, users of commodities may want to lock in a price months or even a year in advance of taking delivery by buying futures contracts to hedge against wide price swings.

Something for everyone

Who uses futures markets to hedge? Everyone from major gold producers to the operators of small businesses who want protection against changing currency values. A Canadian retailer who buys merchandise in New York may worry that the Canadian dollar will tumble before the goods are delivered. He could lock in an exchange rate using the futures market. Importers can also deal with their banks in what is known as the forward market, whereby a bank will specify an exchange rate for a specific amount and a specific date.

But to be efficient, the market requires a large number of participants. There aren't enough farmers and food processors to give the market liquidity, but there are enough speculators. They trade in futures not because they want to hedge, but because they are trying to make a financial killing.

A matter of leverage

Futures markets are risky because of the leverage involved. Unlike stock markets, where investors have to put up at least half the value of a stock when they make a purchase, futures markets require only a small portion of the total value of a contract. It is possible to buy a contract valued at about U.S.$100,000 – most contracts are quoted in U.S. funds, including some traded in Canada – with only $2,000 tied up as margin or good faith money.

If the value of a $100,000 futures contract tumbles by, for instance, 5 percent in a given day, a trader who is "long," or obligated to buy, would have to come up with an additional $5,000 to maintain his margin position. If the trader doesn't have the necessary funds, the position will be sold out by the broker and the trader will lose his initial investment and be responsible for the difference.

How do people make millions? They do it by pyramiding their positions. If a commodity goes up in price by 5 percent, a trader would then buy additional contracts with his new equity and continue to add more as the price rises. But if the trend reverses, watch out. Equity will quickly evaporate, leaving the trader responsible for additional losses.

The risks inherent in commodities futures markets are underlined by the fact that a broker will allow you to open a trading account only after you've read and signed some detailed forms that spell out the risks. That doesn't mean everybody reads the forms carefully before signing. Many investors begin to understand the risks only when they face substantial losses.

Beginner's luck

The biggest pitfall facing beginners in the futures markets is lack of experience. Although individuals with beginner's luck may make money in the beginning, they don't always hang on to it. At the end of 1979 it was possible to buy a gold contract for about U.S.$500 an ounce. A few weeks later, gold peaked at U.S.$850. As prices rose, some investors used their growing equity to finance additional purchases. When the trend reversed, they lost heavily.

Even the experts get burned. Take the rapid price decline of silver, which tumbled in early 1980 from U.S.$50 an ounce to about U.S.$12. Brokers and players, including the legendary Hunt brothers of Texas, lost hundreds of millions of dollars.

Both silver and gold fell sharply – gold to below U.S.$300 an ounce in early 1985 and silver to less than U.S.$6. However, fortunes were made by those who were able to ride the downtrend.

Many beginners think they can protect themselves by issuing stop-loss orders. These are orders to liquidate positions if the price reaches a certain level with the aim of limiting losses. While stop-loss orders are something speculators should consider, they must also realize that such orders don't always limit risk. A commodity price can decline for a number of days without any futures trading taking place. When the stop-loss is finally executed, the loss may greatly exceed the amount originally projected.

Because of the potential volatility of commodities markets – for example, the sharp rise in orange juice futures on news of a heavy, unexpected frost – mechanisms have been put in place to restrict price movements, including limits on how far a price is allowed to move up or down in a day.

Who should play?
If you intend to play the futures markets, make sure you understand the risks, that you can live with them and, most important, that you can afford them. There are no hard and fast rules about who should or should not get involved with commodities or other futures. But anyone interested should first realize that for every winner there is a loser, and in some cases the person on the other side of the trade is a lot more knowledgeable about the factors affecting the price of a specific commodity. If you want to trade in coffee or sugar, for example, odds are that the trader for a food processing company who may be on the other side of the trade will almost certainly know more about the relevant markets than you do.

Then there's the matter of cost. Most brokers want only clients who can afford the risks. Some won't take clients who have a net worth of less than $250,000, excluding their homes and cars. These people should probably restrict the futures portion of their holdings to 10 percent, and they should be prepared to lose that 10 percent. Many experienced futures brokers will also refuse to accept as clients people who seem unable to handle the stress that trading commodities futures produces. And if you have a history of losing money in the stock market, stay out of futures; you'd probably end up losing even more – possibly everything you own.

Many beginners make the same errors, which explains why most investors lose money on commodities. Using the pyramiding strategy unsuccessfully is one of those errors. There is a tendency among traders and brokers to pyramid positions, which increases the trader's risk. A minor setback puts the trader in a major loss position. Another common error is holding too large a position in one area of the market. The markets are simply too volatile for investors to put all their eggs in one basket.

The key decision

If you decide to invest in commodities, your key decision will be your choice of broker. With a good broker you might make money – possibly a great deal of money. More important, a good broker won't let you get into a position where you could lose everything.

Most brokerage houses will check your credit rating. Don't withhold information about other commodity accounts because you are embarrassed about your previous losses. The industry is small enough that your omission will be discovered. And remember, you make the decisions, not your broker. His or her job is to advise and guide you, and to try to keep you out of trouble. But you're the one who places the order and accepts the consequences.

Of course, you should check out your broker thoroughly. Deal only with an established firm. Most are affiliated with major stock brokerage houses or are members of futures exchanges, including the Toronto Futures Exchange.

The research provided by brokers to their clients is fairly standard and consists of industry studies, technical analysis of trends and news reports of developments that affect prices. Some firms have computerized trading models that can be used to provide trading discipline with the objective of cutting losses and letting profits ride.

Some people may want to consider buying units, or shares, of one of the commodity funds offered from time to time by major brokerage houses. They offer the advantages of professional management, diversification and limited risk. With these funds you can't lose more than you put in.

Before launching a futures program, ask yourself, "How much can I lose?" not "How much can I make?" Of course, you can lower your risk by putting up more margin in the form of U.S. government treasury bills. But most people who play the commodities futures markets are interested in speculating rather than limiting risk.

As with options, there are numerous trading strategies you can follow to limit your risk. Most futures dealers can provide detailed information on how such trading strategies can be used to your advantage.

CHAPTER 14

Gold and Silver: Money That Is Real

IT'S DIFFICULT FOR SOME people to understand why gold, silver and other precious metals are considered investments. After all, gold doesn't pay dividends or interest.

On the other hand, there are many people who can't understand why anyone would sink all his money into securities issued or guaranteed by governments, given the history of paper money around the world. Indeed, inflation has eroded the value of paper money in most countries over the years.

The fact is that precious metals have proven to be a store of value through periods of inflation, political upheaval, war and social unrest. Also, gold is a historical and universal medium of exchange. But putting everything you own into precious metals can be risky if the prices that people are willing to pay for those metals get out of whack with reality.

Take the events of late 1979 and early 1980. People were lining up at banks, coin dealers and precious metals dealers to buy gold and silver. Inflation was higher than interest rates, so people who put their money in banks to earn interest were losing, even before taxes. As a result, people flocked to buy tangibles. In less than a decade, gold moved from about U.S.$40 an ounce to its early 1980 high of U.S.$850. Silver followed a similar pattern, peaking at U.S.$50 an ounce. (Gold and silver prices are quoted worldwide in U.S. dollars in both troy ounces and metric weights.)

Then the bubble burst and prices plunged. In mid-1992, gold was trading at about U.S.$340 an ounce. Silver was trading at around U.S.$4. One year later, gold was at U.S.$400 an ounce and silver was at U.S.$5. Undoubtedly, fortunes have been made by traders who have caught the many swings in precious metals since the early 1970s, when the U.S. government decided to stop selling gold at U.S.$35 an ounce and no longer redeem its silver certificate

U.S.$1 bills for silver dollars. But fortunes have been lost by people who misunderstood the markets and allowed greed to rule their decisions.

If you put everything you own into gold and silver, you become a gambler, betting that currencies and securities that pay interest are going to lose much of their value – like the German mark did in the 1920s. However, if you put 5 percent to 15 percent of your assets in precious metals, you can classify yourself as a hedger, holding precious metals as a hedge against a sharp increase in inflation or political turbulence.

Gold, silver and other tangible investments, such as diamonds, rise in inflationary periods when people are worried that the purchasing power of their money is being eroded. They rise most when the spread between nominal interest rates and inflation is shrinking or when inflation exceeds nominal interest rates. They do poorly when people can do better by putting their money in interest-bearing securities.

Sometimes politics helps gold and silver. Worries about political unrest in different parts of the world often send money looking for havens. Sometimes that haven is the U.S. dollar, at other times it's gold.

Inflation hasn't been a big problem lately, so gold and silver have been in the doldrums. But many investors continue to hold a portion of their assets in precious metals as a hedge against inflation.

Shopping for gold

There are several ways to buy gold. You can buy the metal itself in the form of wafers and bars, or in coins such as the Canadian Maple Leaf. You can also buy gold certificates, which are backed by the assets of the issuer but not necessarily by gold itself. You can buy the shares of gold mining companies and you can even invest in gold through mutual funds that hold the metal itself, shares in gold mining companies or both.

Gold shares tend to outperform gold bullion when prices are rising. But bullion tends to fall less than gold shares when bullion prices decline. Many people prefer bullion because it is a tangible investment.

Bullion is sold in bars and wafers in a wide range of weights from five grams to standard bars of 400 ounces. The gold prices quoted in newspapers generally apply to 400-ounce purchases and sales.

Bullion has a number of advantages for the investor. It is easily marketable worldwide and it is probably the least expensive way of buying gold because commissions and other charges are small. Also, it can be purchased in some provinces without paying sales tax. The disadvantages of holding gold bullion include storage and insurance fees, and possible assay charges if you sell after the gold has been in your possession.

Banks and dealers that sell gold to the public quote prices based on 400-ounce bars. On a given day they may bid for gold at one price, perhaps U.S.$378 an ounce and sell it at another, maybe U.S.$381.50. But few people have the resources to buy 400-ounce bars. Instead, they purchase smaller amounts and pay a bit more per ounce to cover manufacturing charges. These bar charges range from about $1.10 an ounce for a 100-ounce bar to $3.35 for a one-ounce wafer to $15 an ounce for a five-gram wafer, or 0.161 ounces. You do not pay a premium when you sell.

Poor man's gold

Silver is sometimes described as poor man's gold. Its price tends to be more volatile and, because of the metal's widespread industrial use, it may not always move with gold. Silver can also be more susceptible than gold to movement by groups of buyers. That was the case in 1979 and early 1980, when a group tried to corner the silver market and its value increased fivefold before crashing.

Like gold, silver can be bought as wafers, bars, coins and certificates. Also, most precious metals funds invest in silver as well as gold. The prices quoted for silver by dealers are for 1,000-ounce bars, but you can buy smaller sizes, ranging from one ounce to 100 ounces. A one-kilogram bar, which contains 32.150 fine ounces of silver, is also available. The premium for a one-ounce wafer is about U.S.$3, which makes a small purchase proportionately expensive.

Commissions and fees

Besides the premiums and assay charges on gold and silver, you have to consider other possible charges. There may be delivery fees, and even a small commission. One bank recently quoted a commission of 0.25 percent on transactions of less than $5,000 and 0.125 percent on transactions beyond that. Storage charges are about 0.375 percent on the first $50,000 of gold bullion held and

0.125 percent on the balance. For silver, charges are fractionally higher.

Bullion is available from bullion dealers, a handful of stock brokerage houses and some banks and trust companies. You should choose your dealer with care, and the novice is best off dealing with a bank or trust company. Remember, however, that they are dealers and it isn't their responsibility to dispense advice on price trends.

Certificates and coins

If you don't want to take delivery of your gold or silver, you can buy certificates. They can be converted into bullion, with delivery usually taking place within thirty days. They are also negotiable outside of Canada at certain institutions. However, they aren't always backed by bullion. Instead, they are backed by the general assets of the institution from which the certificates are purchased. That's why you should buy certificates only from stable institutions, such as the major Canadian chartered banks which have precious metals departments.

Certificates are usually sold in minimum amounts of ten ounces of gold and fifty ounces of silver. Storage and administration charges are minor – only a few cents a day for each 100 ounces. However, you could face manufacturing charges if you trade your certificate for the real thing.

One advantage of certificates is that you can buy them in frac-tional weights, calculated to three decimal places. This means that you can purchase $1,000 of gold, which at the time of writing would entitle you to a certificate for 2.941 ounces.

Coins and certificates for coins are also popular. Until the mid-1980s, the South African Krugerrand one-ounce gold coin was the favourite of goldbugs worldwide. But its popularity has waned at the hands of the Canadian Maple Leaf and coins issued by the U.S., Mexico, China and Australia. Few major dealers still sell the kruger-rand. But people holding them have no trouble getting full value if they sell. After all, gold is gold, no matter what is stamped on it.

The Canadian Maple Leaf gold coins are available in one-ounce, half-ounce, quarter-ounce and one-tenth ounce sizes and are readily marketable anywhere in the world. The coins trade at a premium above the price of bullion. For example, you would be able to buy a one-ounce Maple Leaf coin for about $393.50 if bullion is trading at $381.50. That's a premium of about 3 percent. You could sell a

Maple Leaf for about $386 when bullion is selling at about $377 an ounce, a premium of about 2 percent. If you live in certain provinces, you will also have to pay sales taxes on gold coins (but not GST, as gold and silver bullion are exempt). For example, Ontario and British Columbia charge 8 percent and Quebec charges 9 percent. There is no sales tax on coins in Alberta.

You can also buy what are known as numismatic coins. They sell at prices above the value of the bullion they contain, and appeal to collectors. Their price reflects their scarcity as well as their gold content, but they are less marketable than bullion coins.

Playing gold stocks

Gold share prices reflect gold price expectations as well as companies' production, profits, dividend payments and the outlook for new discoveries. The gold stocks market is highly specialized, but it can be divided into three major categories:

- Senior companies, which are major producers and generally have large market capitalizations;
- Intermediate companies, which are medium producers of about 200,000 ounces annually;
- Junior companies, which are exploration plays that have yet to produce gold. There are also those companies that have yet to discover gold, but which have promising properties.

The prices of shares in companies that produce and pay dividends tend to be less volatile than those of junior exploration companies. Yet they are still more volatile than the prices of most other stocks, with the junior stocks extremely volatile. If you want to invest in the junior gold stocks, you should first decide whether you can afford the risks. If you can't, stay away.

Much of the recent action in gold has been in North American stocks, particularly those involved in gold plays in South America and West Africa. But Canadian investors can also buy shares of South African and Australian gold mining companies through any broker. Some investors find them attractive because their dividend yields are higher than those of Canadian gold mining shares.

Gold mutual funds make sense for investors who want a diversified precious metals portfolio. As with other mutual funds, the advantage is professional management.

Precious stones

In the past decade or so, diamonds and other gemstones have grown increasingly appealing to investors, particularly during periods of high inflation. However, their prices can be very volatile and, just like gold and silver, plunged sharply during early 1980. Diamonds are a highly specialized area of investment, and are definitely not for the beginner.

There are two key points to remember. First, no two diamonds are alike, even if they are in the same class and are of the same weight. And, unlike commodities, gold and stocks, diamonds are not sold in an auction market.

Diamonds differ from gold in that you cannot obtain a price quote over the telephone or buy and sell at the same price throughout the world. To determine a diamond price, you must obtain an appraisal. Moreover, the spreads between the bid price and ask price are substantial. Unlike gold, where the markup is usually less than 1 percent, the markup on diamonds can be 100 percent to 200 percent. In other words, the price has to double for you to break even, unless you can buy at cost. On top of that, unless you're buying smuggled diamonds, you're paying a hefty federal tax and duty.

Diamonds do have their uses as investments, particularly in parts of the world where people are looking for hedges against political upheaval. After all, it's easier to flee a country with $100,000 of diamonds than with $100,000 of gold.

If you want to invest in diamonds, stick to top-quality stones of about one carat. Larger ones may prove difficult to sell because the market is thin. Buy only from reputable dealers. More than one person has purchased industrial-grade stones thinking they were jewelry quality. Others have been fooled into buying synthetic stones, believing them to be the real thing. Some experts suggest that investors buy and store their stones outside Canada to avoid paying duties and sales taxes.

You can also invest in coloured stones, such as emeralds, rubies or sapphires, but the market for these gems is more fragmented than the diamond market, and there are no standard grading systems.

CHAPTER 15

The Art of Investing in Art

THE 1980s WERE A BONANZA for astute art investors as prices soared. In early 1989, the Getty Museum paid U.S.$35.2 million, almost $43 million Canadian dollars, for a portrait of a Florentine duke painted by Jacopo Pontormo, an old master, more than 450 years ago. The sale broke the previous old master record price of $10.5 million that had been set in 1985 by Andrea Mantegna's *Adoration of the Magi.*

In 1990 the highest price ever paid for an art object was set when Christie's sold Vincent van Gogh's *Portrait of Dr. Gachet* for U.S.$82.5 million; Sotheby's set a new high for paintings by Auguste Renoir when it sold *Au Moulin de la Gallett* for U.S.$78.1 million. The recession has temporarily ended the art boom. More attention, though, is being paid to paintings that don't sell at an auction.

But how did the seller fare?

During booms auction houses profit. The normal auction house toll is 10 percent charged to both buyer and seller. If neither buyer nor seller were given a concession by Christie's, the auction house pocketed over U.S.$7 million just for marketing the sale of Pontormo's painting. And market it they did, with plenty of press releases speculating on whether or not the Getty would go for it.

The painting was sold to the Getty Museum by the estate of Chauncey D. Stillman, a New York investor and philanthropist. Stillman had bought the painting in 1937 for U.S.$37,000. If we ignore the auction house fee, the Stillman estate pocketed a pre-tax gain of over U.S.$35 million.

That impressive sum shrinks to something mere mortals can understand when we calculate the rate of return earned over the fifty-two years that elapsed between the 1937 purchase and the 1989 sale. Stillman earned 11.7 percent annually on his

U.S.$37,000 investment – good, but not much better than the 11.1 percent performance of the TSE 300 for the same period. And remember, the 11.7 percent was earned with a record-breaking painting while the 11.1 percent was earned on a basket of typical stocks.

But who computes compound rates of return? Certainly not the throngs that once filled the New York auction halls of Christie's and Sotheby's in November 1988. They paid U.S.$433 million for impressionist, modern and contemporary art, twice the take from auctions a year earlier.

Jasper Johns, a fifty-nine-year-old American painter, saw his *False Start* bring U.S.$17.1 million. In 1960, it sold for U.S.$3,150. In fact, that was a startling rate of appreciation – almost 36 percent compounded annually. And Johns is a contemporary painter whose name may not even be in the art history books 400 years from now.

But the Johns price, and the oversized compound rate, reflected art fever, a fever that reached such an unprecedented pitch because two well-heeled collectors, S. I. Newhouse, the American publishing tycoon, and Hans Thulin, a Swedish property developer, were both determined to have *False Start*. It was their battle of bids that caused the price to soar.

In the end, Newhouse won. Thulin had to console himself with a $7 million all-American white flag by Johns and a $6.3 million giant collage by Rauschenberg, another contemporary painter.

Question: Will either Newhouse or Thulin achieve an 11 percent return on the swollen prices they paid? The record suggests they will not. These days even the auction houses have problems.

The Canadian experience

Canadians are not immune to art fever. In mid-1993, the National Gallery of Canada unveiled seven recent purchases and a selection of 244 pieces purchased for $3.4 million. The number of purchases, their significance and their average price of just under $14,000 were overshadowed by the $1.9 million paid for Mark Rothko's *No. 16*. In fact, the seven pieces, which included Lawren Harris's $410,000 *Decorative Landscape*, represented the bulk of the $3.4 million.

In November 1989, Clarence Gagnon's *Ice Harvest* sold for $495,000, the record auction price for a piece of art in Canada; in May 1990, Jean Paul Riopelle's *Composition* fetched $420,000.

In the same auction, *Lynn Valley* by Group of Seven painter Frederick Varley sold for $363,000. Just four years earlier, the painting had sold for $85,000. The annual return of almost 44 percent was extraordinary.

Rules for buying

You'd be foolish to expect that kind of return on your art investments – they're much like winning a lottery. There's little anyone can do to ensure a high return on art. It's said you can never go wrong buying high quality – this might be true esthetically but it's not true financially.

If your aim is high returns, you're better off timing your art purchases. Art prices move in cycles much as do stock prices. Unfortunately, just as with stock market investing, when prices are falling, we wait for them to go lower; when prices are rising, we all climb on the bandwagon.

Salomon Brothers, the investment banking house, compiles the rates of return for different investments including art and collectibles. Over the past few years the price of art has been on the boil. Robert Salomon, a managing director of Salomon Brothers, says of the contemporary art scene: "Conspicuous consumption by people who want to flaunt their wealth . . . why does someone pay $40 million for a picture when you can buy one for $20? I assume the people who buy such things are trying to make a statement."

Of course, most of us are not in the league of art buyers able to pay millions for a painting. Neither do we have to come up against the tycoons in bidding wars. But do we have a chance at making a reasonable return on an art investment?

The hype artists

Art as an investment is pushed by art auction houses and fancy dealers. Without high art prices, art sellers could not afford expensive rented premises and the good things in life. So, although good dealers and auction house people usually know a fair amount about art, they clearly have a vested interest. But art is what counts, not money. So the suave dealer peddling a $10,000 piece of art can become downright contemptuous if you ask what the investment prospects are for his treasure. He may well reply: "If you are interested in money, buy bonds." For some reason, he will seldom refer to the stock market, where the risks more closely reflect the art market.

The world of art is in many ways like the world of stocks. Just as there are established artists and new artists, there are established stocks and new issues. There are stocks for which there are always buyers, although not always at the best price, and there are stocks for which the market disappears at the first sign of a cloud.

What the art dealer wants to do, as does the auctioneer who wears formal dress to peddle paintings, is to intimidate you. Your $10,000 is as real to the dealer as it is to you. But the major difference is this: Until you have bought the painting, the $10,000 is yours, not his. You could like the painting but feel that unless the price of the piece will appreciate by at least the rate paid by your friendly bank, it is beyond your means.

Of course, dealers don't have the slightest notion of how fast the price will rise, or if it will rise at all. So they take the noble posture of being above mere money. Still, the dealer and everyone involved in selling art has to rely on hype that implies fast returns if they are to make sales.

One of the schemes used by art dealers is announcements of record prices. The art auction season, which traditionally runs from late October through late May, but actually extends as long as the major art auction companies think they can attract enough money to make an auction profitable, has become the focus of the announcements.

Dealers often view auction houses as competition, even though their relationship is symbiotic with auction houses providing at least some degree of liquidity to the art market. If there were no auction houses, it would be even more difficult for collectors to unload their treasures. Dealers would have to provide liquidity themselves or sell less at lower prices. Auction houses also serve as a means through which dealers can efficiently adjust inventories.

Auction houses and dealers both benefit from announcements of record prices, even though the announcements are made by auction houses. The most potent announcement is the establishment of the highest price ever achieved for a painting widely viewed as a masterpiece, or the highest price for a work painted by a particular master. The news media report the record price, and dealers and auction houses let their clients know.

The problem with the record announcement approach is that to get a world record price you need a very unusual and beautiful piece of art. These, by definition, are rare. So the auction houses often lack items of rarity and beauty.

Trying to create gold from dross

Caught in a booming art market, some greedy dealers and auction houses work rapidly to bring new artists to the $100,000 range and more. They also attempt to revive the fortunes of long-dead artists whose work has fallen out of favour. They even work to make a market for the work of long-dead artists who never were in favor.

The arguments used by some dealers to sell old works that are now of small value, never were of value, and probably never will be of value should have a familiar ring to investors in penny stocks.

To keep the ball rolling, living artists, even relatively young ones, may form the subject of an announcement of a record price. Despite the fact that the auction tradition and the tradition at the grander art galleries favour dead artists, there are often announcements on the works of some living artists for whom there are enough well-heeled enthusiasts.

Buying a living artist's work as an investment is like grubstaking a prospector. Either is risky but acceptable if you don't overspend. Neither the artist nor the prospector is likely to have any real success.

Crass causes

What is usually ignored is the fact that one needs more than a masterpiece to generate an announcement of a record price. Inflation, particularly if combined with low interest rates, is a big help.

It also helps if the record-setting bidder's personal currency, such as a Japanese buyer's yen, has appreciated compared to the currency in which the art is being sold. It really isn't a big deal if a Japanese art buyer, whose currency may have appreciated 100 percent against the U.S. dollar, ends up paying 10 percent more in dollars than the last time the painting sold.

Art is an international commodity of global appeal and it is not an accident that Europeans dominate the art markets when the Euro-currencies are strong. Japanese dominate, despite cultural differences, when the yen rises. And Americans buy everything in sight if the U.S. dollar is strong.

Currency movements can be a major factor in record prices. If an auction is held in yen instead of dollars, after the yen has appreciated, prices might fall. As a result, as an investor you should try to make purchases when the Canadian dollar is strong, and let others buy when the dollar is in the doldrums.

The penny paintings

Most new artists will not make rewarding financial investments even if you like their work. Of course, if the promoter – the art dealer in this case – has a good track record, you may buy a few more so-called penny paintings or pay a bit more than you might otherwise. But unless you have good connections, it may be hard to buy into an attractive deal.

Otherwise, the pennies in art can be far more satisfying than the penny stocks issued in Vancouver. If you like the art and paid little for it, who really cares if it appreciates?

After the pennies come works by the juniors – local artists who have had a number of shows and who are usually represented by a reasonably prestigious dealer. The work of a junior can cost well in excess of $10,000, but some good ones are available for around $5,000. It would be encouraging to say that the prices of these works will certainly appreciate – and some dealers say exactly that. But the truth is that the worth of most will dwindle.

Better dead than alive

Even junior artists who should be seniors mess up the deal if they stay alive. They can paint junk and sell works they should have burned, as did Picasso. In time, if the junior's work becomes blue chip, the world will be willing to distinguish between the good and the bad. But few juniors make that jump.

Canada's Norval Morrisseau is an excellent example of a junior who may come to nothing. Morrisseau is to woodland Indian painting what Van Gogh was to impressionist painting. However, Van Gogh died young. Morrisseau has been awarded the Order of Canada and his works hang in every major museum in Canada as well as in many abroad. Yet one can buy Morrisseau oils of good quality for much less than $10,000.

The trouble is that Morrisseau also shares Van Gogh's instability. He is extraordinarily self-destructive. He has fallen into schemes that cheapen his art by too many poor reproductions of his work.

Except for these tragic weaknesses, Morrisseau could be a painter of blue chip calibre. Will he be in any event? Who knows? Those who think so spend all they can on what they view as undervalued examples of his art. Others scratch their heads in wonder.

The risky blue chips

The blue chips – particularly Canadian blue chips – are generally bad investments. Even if you bought a painting by Tom Thomson, the father of the Group of Seven, for $20 in 1918 and sold it for $35,000 in 1988, your rather handsome gain is a lot less impressive than it sounds. When translated into a compound rate of return, the annual yield on the investment is 11.125 percent. Although it is somewhat better than the yield on most financial investments, it is a lot riskier.

Who in 1918, or even 1928, would have recognized the commanding position painters like A. Y. Jackson, A. J. Casson and the other members of the Group of Seven would hold in Canada over the past two decades? Few investors did. Furthermore, converting a Thomson into cash during the Great Depression of the 1930s, when you might well have preferred cash to art, was virtually impossible. The return was not only risky, the investment was highly illiquid.

That's all behind us, so perhaps an investor should buy a Thomson today. Indeed, many investors are doing exactly that. The argument is that, even if we ignore the problem with fakes that grows in parallel with the price of the artist's work, there won't be any more Thomsons painted. Furthermore, many of the holders, such as museums, will keep their Thomsons off the market. Thus, we really are dealing with a shrinking number of Thomsons. Still, it is not impossible to imagine a time when Thomson or the Group of Seven are viewed as simply regional examples of post-impressionism. Such a view could bring prices down appreciably.

Indeed, the only art that is truly of investment quality, comparable to government bonds or stocks of blue-chip companies, are the best examples of the international masters. Their value is not distorted by regionalism because the works are well known and have been heavily reviewed. They have stood the test of time. If you cannot get top examples from the work of the eighteenth-century masters, settle for those top-drawer artists of the nineteenth century. But be careful of the twentieth century, there is too much chance of trendiness that pushes prices above value. Who knows how Picasso's works will stand the test of real time?

Of course, most of us cannot afford the hundreds of thousands of dollars involved in buying a single example of such work. We may be decorating by buying works of imitators or preening ourselves by buying inferior examples of the work of first-class artists in a kind of autograph hunting. We may be showing off as art collectors. We may even really be collectors.

All of these things may be great fun but they are not investing. Someone with limited dollars can get much better returns, albeit with less pleasure, in the securities markets.

CHAPTER 16

Tax Shelters: Easing the Pain

EVERYONE LIKES TO KEEP their taxes to a minimum. Indeed, because of the way that taxation has increasingly bitten into incomes, cutting taxes has become a prime ambition for many Canadians.

Tax avoidance – as opposed to tax evasion – is legal and involves the use of a variety of measures allowed by Ottawa to reduce taxes. For instance, RRSPs and pension plans are popular tax shelters. Investing in Canadian dividend-paying shares to get the dividend tax credit is another widely used method of cutting the amount you pay to Revenue Canada.

There are other ways people can shelter income, although some tax shelters are quite complex and not suitable for most families of moderate means. Moreover, the federal government has been cutting back on tax shelters. In 1985 it virtually ended income-splitting plans between spouses and between parents and minor children. The most common strategy involved low-interest or no-interest loans between husbands and wives, whereby one spouse would lend funds to the other if the borrowing spouse had substantially lower income. The borrower would invest the funds and any interest earned would then be taxed at his or her marginal tax rate, which was usually much lower than that of the lending spouse.

With these spousal loans, families could circumvent Ottawa's attribution rules, which require that within a family, tax on investment income must be paid by the person who supplied the capital, not the person whose name is on the bank account or share certificates. Ottawa's February 1992 budget ended income splitting between common-law spouses effective 1993.

Although most income-splitting devices are gone, there are still some left. If one spouse makes a loan to the other to buy or invest in a business to be managed by the spouse to whom the money is lent, the profits are taxed in the hands of the spouse operating the business.

As a result of tax reform, you can no longer make low or no interest loans to children eighteen and over for investment purposes. People with such loans should consult their professional tax advisors. Until the change, these loans made sense for those with children at university because the children could earn investment income that was lightly taxed due to tuition deductions. In effect, you had shifted investment income to be taxed at your children's marginal rates from your higher one.

A shelter for education savings

As mentioned earlier, another shelter popular with parents who expect their children to attend university is the registered education savings plan (RESP). With a RESP, a parent or grandparent can shelter investment income from taxes, as long as the income is eventually used to finance full-time post-secondary education expenses. You are allowed to put up to $1,500 a year in a RESP to a maximum of $31,500 for each child but you aren't entitled to a deduction for that contribution.

However, the interest earned and capital appreciation grows untaxed as long as it remains in the plan. Earnings are then taxable in the hands of the recipient when they are withdrawn. Several investment dealers and mutual fund management companies offer RESPs. As well, there are RESP "scholarship" plans.

There are some distinct disadvantages to RESPs. First, beneficiaries must go on to some sort of post-secondary education. If they don't, matters can get complicated and you may even lose a substantial amount of money. What happens to the earnings if beneficiaries decide not to continue their education depends on the type of RESP you have. The dealer-sponsored plans allow you to change beneficiaries if those you originally named decide not to continue beyond high school. With the scholarship plans, you forfeit the income earned on your capital and it is paid out to students who do continue their education.

The risk is always there

Other types of shelters have allowed individuals to invest in specific industries to reduce taxes. Ottawa has reduced the attractiveness of this type of issue in recent years. Provincial legislation, however, may give rise to regional tax shelters.

Another method of sheltering money from taxes is to invest with borrowed funds through a limited partnership in a venture that is losing money. You can write off your share of the losses from the limited partnership against other income and deduct the interest you pay for tax purposes. You are, of course, at risk for the money that you've borrowed. Ideally, the venture will eventually be sold and you will recover your after-tax costs or, better still, make a handsome profit.

The truth of the matter is that shelters are usually risky. However, some are a lot riskier than others and there are ways to separate those with good investment potential from those without. First, use the investment's prospectus to determine your after-tax costs. In other words, if you put up $10,000 and get $6,000 back from Ottawa, your after-tax cost is $4,000. Then determine, also from the prospectus, the after-tax value of the investment. For example, if you sold the shelter at the earliest possible time that allowed you a full tax write-off, what would you get? If the value of your $4,000 investment is, say, $5,000 after taxes when sold, it would appear to be a good prospect.

It is important to understand what you own when you buy a shelter and what that holding is worth. Too many investors have used borrowed money to buy a shelter, and then spent the tax refund while under the impression that the value of their investment was equal to the value of their loan. They then find that when it comes time to repay the loan, on liquidation of the investment, that the amount borrowed exceeded the after-tax value of the investment.

If you're in the market for tax shelters, you should look at the investment aspects of any proposal before you look at the tax implications. If it doesn't look good from an investment perspective, it should be avoided. The tax-shelter benefits should be considered the icing on the cake.

Marketability is another important factor. It is often quite difficult to get out of a shelter once you're in because in many cases there is no secondary market. Moreover, few shelters provide a mechanism for liquidity after a set period. In the past, some flow-through limited partnerships rolled into mutual funds that could be redeemed for full market value at any time. Others distributed the shares in which the partnership invests and these can be sold like other stocks.

In addition, you should be careful about how you finance your purchase. Interest on funds borrowed for investment is deductible for tax purposes, so many people have in the past borrowed to buy shelters in the hope of increasing their tax deductions and sheltering a major portion of their income from taxes. Problems arose when their investments failed to bring the promised returns and they found themselves in debt. What's more, if the shelter is sold or goes under, and you still owe money on it, the interest you pay will not be deductible.

Provincial stock savings plans

Some provinces have provincially sponsored tax shelters, the most successful and best known being the Quebec Stock Savings Plan. Introduced in 1979, the plan allows Quebec residents a tax break for investing in Quebec-based public companies.

The plan encourages Quebec residents to become investors rather than savers. As with any other investment, the tax aspect is an added bonus. Any shares considered should be able to stand on their own as investments.

Labour-sponsored funds

Labour-sponsored venture funds are offered in some provinces. These invest in small business ventures and should be considered high-risk investments. They are heavily marketed during January and February when people are making RRSP decisions. Investors who buy these funds get a tax credit which reduces their costs. However, as with any investment, the tax break should be looked at as a bonus. If the investment can't stand scrutiny, it should be avoided.

CHAPTER 17

Strategies: Do What Works Well

YOU MIGHT HAVE HEARD A long-term investor described as "a short-term investor whose stock went down." There's some truth to this. Indeed, many people make the mistake of holding their losers indefinitely in hopes that they will rise in price. Sometimes the losers do recover, but people holding investments that have lost value should ask whether they can do better investing their money elsewhere.

That's what this chapter is about: demonstrating some of the strategies you can use to structure your investments to meet your objectives and make the most of your money.

It pays to diversify

Strategy number one is diversification – in other words, don't put all your eggs in one basket. It's a fact of financial life that if you put everything in one security and the company has difficulties, you will have serious problems as well. And putting all your money into a company you think is stable can also be a recipe for disaster; even blue-chip companies can have problems. You might recall when Royal Trustco was considered a blue-chip stock and paid handsome dividends – before it fell on hard times.

Of course, by diversifying you won't make the killing in the market that you would if you put everything in one stock that skyrockets. But steady growth is preferable to watching your fortune go down the tubes.

Just how much you diversify depends on how much risk you are willing to take. Even splitting your money between two growth investments significantly reduces risk, so try to introduce some variety into your holdings or at least place a limit on the portion of your assets with which you speculate.

Another point worthy of consideration is diversification across different classes of assets. Many people diversify within one asset group, such as the stock market. But not venturing outside that asset group can be a mistake; no single class of asset is best all the time.

Take the stock market as an example. Although it performed extremely well in the five years prior to the October 1987 crash, if you had all your money in the market during the crash you took a short-term beating. Similarly, there have been times when guaranteed investment certificates and long-term bonds have been poor investments, and periods when treasury bills have been a costly choice because of falling interest rates.

By spreading your investments among different types of assets, such as gold, interest- and dividend-producing instruments, stocks and real estate, your returns are likely to be more stable than if you put everything into growth investments.

Manage your investments

Another secret to success is managing your investments well. To achieve maximum returns, you must constantly re-evaluate your holdings in light of current and anticipated economic and market conditions. For example, long-term government bonds may be safe, but you don't want to hold them if it looks like interest rates are ready to skyrocket. And you don't want a heavy equity position when stocks are a poor value relative to other investments.

Be prepared to change the mix of assets you hold to take advantage of opportunities while preserving capital. You must constantly monitor your individual holdings within asset groups to ensure each security continues to meet your criteria for holding on to that investment.

Even if you've delegated the management of your assets to a professional – through mutual funds, for instance – you must be aware of their status so you can determine whether your manager's performance is satisfactory. However, don't be too quick to make changes. You may want to judge professional results over a few years, or even a full market cycle, rather than over a couple of months.

Taxes and speculation

To make the most of your investments, any strategy must take full advantage of government-approved methods of saving to meet specific objectives. Your RRSP, for instance, is the best way to save for retirement because of the generous tax breaks.

You should also keep the speculative portion of your portfolio within limits. There is nothing wrong with speculating, but it should only be done with money you can afford to lose. Don't, for example, gamble with your retirement prospects by speculating with your RRSP funds. Don't speculate at all if the loss of the funds involved will affect your lifestyle and destroy your chances of meeting other financial objectives.

The Future Value of an Annual Investment of $1,000

YEARS	1%	2%	3%	4%	5%	6%	7%	8%	9%	10%
1	1,010	1,020	1,030	1,040	1,050	1,060	1,070	1,080	1,090	1,100
2	2,030	2,060	2,091	2,122	2,153	2,184	2,215	2,246	2,278	2,310
3	3,060	3,122	3,184	3,246	3,310	3,375	3,440	3,506	3,573	3,641
4	4,101	4,204	4,309	4,416	4,526	4,637	4,751	4,867	4,985	5,105
5	5,152	5,308	5,468	5,633	5,802	5,975	6,153	6,336	6,523	6,716
6	6,214	6,434	6,662	6,898	7,142	7,394	7,654	7,923	8,200	8,487
7	7,286	7,583	7,892	8,214	8,549	8,897	9,260	9,637	10,028	10,436
8	8,369	8,755	9,159	9,583	10,027	10,491	10,978	11,488	12,021	12,579
9	9,462	9,950	10,464	11,006	11,578	12,181	12,816	13,487	14,193	14,937
10	10,567	11,169	11,808	12,486	13,207	13,972	14,784	15,645	16,560	17,531
11	11,683	12,412	13,192	14,026	14,917	15,870	16,888	17,977	19,141	20,384
12	12,809	13,680	14,618	15,627	16,713	17,882	19,141	20,495	21,953	23,523
13	13,947	14,974	16,086	17,292	18,599	20,015	21,550	23,215	25,019	26,975
14	15,097	16,293	17,599	19,024	20,579	22,276	24,129	26,152	28,361	30,772
15	16,258	17,639	19,157	20,825	22,657	24,673	26,888	29,324	32,003	34,950
16	17,430	19,012	20,762	22,698	24,840	27,213	29,840	32,750	35,974	39,545
17	18,615	20,412	22,414	24,645	27,132	29,906	32,999	36,450	40,301	44,599
18	19,811	21,841	24,117	26,671	29,539	32,760	36,379	40,446	45,018	50,159
19	21,019	23,297	25,870	28,778	32,066	35,786	39,995	44,762	50,160	56,275
20	22,239	24,783	27,676	30,969	34,719	38,993	43,865	49,423	55,765	63,002
21	23,472	26,299	29,537	33,248	37,505	42,392	48,006	54,457	61,873	70,403
22	24,716	27,845	31,453	35,618	40,430	45,996	52,436	59,893	68,532	78,543
23	25,973	29,422	33,426	38,083	43,502	49,816	57,177	65,765	75,790	87,497
24	27,243	31,030	35,459	40,646	46,727	53,865	62,249	72,106	83,701	97,347
25	28,526	32,671	37,553	43,312	50,113	58,156	67,676	78,954	92,324	108,182
26	29,821	34,344	39,710	46,084	53,669	62,706	73,484	86,351	101,723	120,100
27	31,129	36,051	41,931	48,968	57,403	67,528	79,698	94,339	111,968	133,210
28	32,450	37,792	44,219	51,966	61,323	72,640	86,347	102,966	123,135	147,631
29	33,785	39,568	46,575	55,085	65,439	78,058	93,461	112,283	135,308	163,494
30	35,133	41,379	49,003	58,328	69,761	83,802	101,073	122,346	148,575	180,943
31	36,494	43,227	51,503	61,701	74,299	89,890	109,218	133,214	163,037	200,138
32	37,869	45,112	54,078	65,210	79,064	96,343	117,933	144,951	178,800	221,252
33	39,258	47,034	56,730	68,858	84,067	103,184	127,259	157,627	195,982	244,477
34	40,660	48,994	59,462	72,652	89,320	110,435	137,237	171,317	214,711	270,024
35	42,077	50,994	62,276	76,598	94,836	118,121	147,913	186,102	235,125	298,127
36	43,508	53,034	65,174	80,702	100,628	126,268	159,337	202,070	257,376	329,039
37	44,953	55,115	68,159	84,970	106,710	134,904	171,561	219,316	281,630	363,043
38	46,412	57,237	71,234	89,409	113,095	144,058	184,640	237,941	308,066	400,448
39	47,886	59,402	74,401	94,026	119,800	153,762	198,635	258,057	336,882	441,593
40	49,375	61,610	77,663	98,827	126,840	164,048	213,610	279,781	368,292	486,852

YEARS	11%	12%	13%	14%	15%	16%	17%	18%	19%	20%
1	1,110	1,120	1,130	1,140	1,150	1,160	1,170	1,180	1,190	1,200
2	2,342	2,374	2,407	2,440	2,473	2,506	2,539	2,572	2,606	2,640
3	3,710	3,779	3,850	3,921	3,993	4,066	4,141	4,215	4,291	4,368
4	5,228	5,353	5,480	5,610	5,742	5,877	6,014	6,154	6,297	6,442
5	6,913	7,115	7,323	7,536	7,754	7,977	8,207	8,442	8,683	8,930
6	8,783	9,089	9,405	9,730	10,067	10,414	10,772	11,142	11,523	11,916
7	10,859	11,300	11,757	12,233	12,727	13,240	13,773	14,327	14,902	15,499
8	13,164	13,776	14,416	15,085	15,786	16,519	17,285	18,086	18,923	19,799
9	15,722	16,549	17,420	18,337	19,304	20,321	21,393	22,521	23,709	24,959
10	18,561	19,655	20,814	22,045	23,349	24,733	26,200	27,755	29,404	31,150
11	21,713	23,133	24,650	26,271	28,002	29,850	31,824	33,931	36,180	38,581
12	25,212	27,029	28,985	31,089	33,352	35,786	38,404	41,219	44,244	47,497
13	29,095	31,393	33,883	36,581	39,505	42,672	46,103	49,818	53,841	58,196
14	33,405	36,280	39,417	42,842	46,580	50,660	55,110	59,965	65,261	71,035
15	38,190	41,753	45,672	49,980	54,717	59,925	65,649	71,939	78,850	86,442
16	43,501	47,884	52,739	58,118	64,075	70,673	77,979	86,068	95,022	104,931
17	49,396	54,750	60,725	67,394	74,836	83,141	92,406	102,740	114,266	127,117
18	55,939	62,440	69,749	77,969	87,212	97,603	109,285	122,414	137,166	153,740
19	63,203	71,052	79,947	90,025	101,444	114,380	129,033	145,628	164,418	185,688
20	71,265	80,699	91,470	103,768	117,810	133,841	152,139	173,021	196,847	224,026
21	80,214	91,503	104,491	119,436	136,632	156,415	179,172	205,345	235,438	270,031
22	90,148	103,603	119,205	137,297	158,276	182,601	210,801	243,487	281,362	325,237
23	101,174	117,155	135,831	157,659	183,168	212,978	247,808	288,494	336,010	391,484
24	113,413	132,334	154,620	180,871	211,793	248,214	291,105	341,603	401,042	470,981
25	126,999	149,334	175,850	207,333	244,712	289,088	341,763	404,272	478,431	566,377
26	142,079	168,374	199,841	237,499	282,569	336,502	401,032	478,221	570,522	680,853
27	158,817	189,699	226,950	271,889	326,104	391,503	470,378	565,481	680,112	818,223
28	177,397	213,583	257,583	311,094	376,170	455,303	551,512	668,447	810,523	983,068
29	198,021	240,333	292,199	355,787	433,745	529,312	646,439	789,948	965,712	1,180,882
30	220,913	270,293	331,315	406,737	499,957	615,162	757,504	933,319	1,150,387	1,418,258
31	246,324	303,848	375,516	464,820	576,100	714,747	887,449	1,102,496	1,370,151	1,703,109
32	274,529	341,429	425,463	531,035	663,666	830,267	1,039,486	1,302,125	1,631,670	2,044,931
33	305,837	383,521	481,903	606,520	764,365	964,270	1,217,368	1,537,688	1,942,877	2,455,118
34	340,590	430,663	545,681	692,573	880,170	1,119,713	1,425,491	1,815,652	2,313,214	2,947,341
35	379,164	483,463	617,749	790,673	1,013,346	1,300,027	1,668,994	2,143,649	2,753,914	3,538,009
36	421,982	542,599	699,187	902,507	1,166,498	1,509,191	1,953,894	2,530,686	3,278,348	4,246,811
37	469,511	608,831	791,211	1,029,998	1,342,622	1,751,822	2,287,225	2,987,389	3,902,424	5,097,373
38	522,267	683,010	895,198	1,175,338	1,545,165	2,033,273	2,677,224	3,526,299	4,645,075	6,118,048
39	580,826	766,091	1,012,704	1,341,025	1,778,090	2,359,757	3,133,522	4,162,213	5,528,829	7,342,858
40	645,827	859,142	1,145,486	1,529,909	2,045,954	2,738,478	3,667,391	4,912,591	6,580,496	8,812,629

The Future Value of a Single Deposit of $1,000 Using Different Rates of Return

YEARS	1%	2%	3%	4%	5%	6%	7%	8%	9%	10%
1	1,010	1,020	1,030	1,040	1,050	1,060	1,070	1,080	1,090	1,100
2	1,020	1,040	1,061	1,082	1,103	1,124	1,145	1,166	1,188	1,210
3	1,030	1,061	1,093	1,125	1,158	1,191	1,225	1,260	1,295	1,331
4	1,041	1,082	1,126	1,170	1,216	1,262	1,311	1,360	1,412	1,464
5	1,051	1,104	1,159	1,217	1,276	1,338	1,403	1,469	1,539	1,611
6	1,062	1,126	1,194	1,265	1,340	1,419	1,501	1,587	1,677	1,772
7	1,072	1,149	1,230	1,316	1,407	1,504	1,606	1,714	1,828	1,949
8	1,083	1,172	1,267	1,369	1,477	1,594	1,718	1,851	1,993	2,144
9	1,094	1,195	1,305	1,423	1,551	1,689	1,838	1,999	2,172	2,358
10	1,105	1,219	1,344	1,480	1,629	1,791	1,967	2,159	2,367	2,594
11	1,116	1,243	1,384	1,539	1,710	1,898	2,105	2,332	2,580	2,853
12	1,127	1,268	1,426	1,601	1,796	2,012	2,252	2,518	2,813	3,138
13	1,138	1,294	1,469	1,665	1,886	2,133	2,410	2,720	3,066	3,452
14	1,149	1,319	1,513	1,732	1,980	2,261	2,579	2,937	3,342	3,797
15	1,161	1,346	1,558	1,801	2,079	2,397	2,759	3,172	3,642	4,177
16	1,173	1,373	1,605	1,873	2,183	2,540	2,952	3,426	3,970	4,595
17	1,184	1,400	1,653	1,948	2,292	2,693	3,159	3,700	4,328	5,054
18	1,196	1,428	1,702	2,026	2,407	2,854	3,380	3,996	4,717	5,560
19	1,208	1,457	1,754	2,107	2,527	3,026	3,617	4,316	5,142	6,116
20	1,220	1,486	1,806	2,191	2,653	3,207	3,870	4,661	5,604	6,727
21	1,232	1,516	1,860	2,279	2,786	3,400	4,141	5,034	6,109	7,400
22	1,245	1,546	1,916	2,370	2,925	3,604	4,430	5,437	6,659	8,140
23	1,257	1,577	1,974	2,465	3,072	3,820	4,741	5,871	7,258	8,954
24	1,270	1,608	2,033	2,563	3,225	4,049	5,072	6,341	7,911	9,850
25	1,282	1,641	2,094	2,666	3,386	4,292	5,427	6,848	8,623	10,835
26	1,295	1,673	2,157	2,772	3,556	4,549	5,807	7,396	9,399	11,918
27	1,308	1,707	2,221	2,883	3,733	4,822	6,214	7,988	10,245	13,110
28	1,321	1,741	2,288	2,999	3,920	5,112	6,649	8,627	11,167	14,421
29	1,335	1,776	2,357	3,119	4,116	5,418	7,114	9,317	12,172	15,863
30	1,348	1,811	2,427	3,243	4,322	5,743	7,612	10,063	13,268	17,449
31	1,361	1,848	2,500	3,373	4,538	6,088	8,145	10,868	14,462	19,194
32	1,375	1,885	2,575	3,508	4,765	6,453	8,715	11,737	15,763	21,114
33	1,389	1,922	2,652	3,648	5,003	6,841	9,325	12,676	17,182	23,225
34	1,403	1,961	2,732	3,794	5,253	7,251	9,978	13,690	18,728	25,548
35	1,417	2,000	2,814	3,946	5,516	7,686	10,677	14,785	20,414	28,102
36	1,431	2,040	2,898	4,104	5,792	8,147	11,424	15,968	22,251	30,913
37	1,445	2,081	2,985	4,268	6,081	8,636	12,224	17,246	24,254	34,004
38	1,460	2,122	3,075	4,439	6,385	9,154	13,079	18,625	26,437	37,404
39	1,474	2,165	3,167	4,616	6,705	9,704	13,995	20,115	28,816	41,145
40	1,489	2,208	3,262	4,801	7,040	10,286	14,974	21,725	31,409	45,259

YEARS	11%	12%	13%	14%	15%	16%	17%	18%	19%	20%
1	1,110	1,120	1,130	1,140	1,150	1,160	1,170	1,180	1,190	1,200
2	1,232	1,254	1,277	1,300	1,323	1,346	1,369	1,392	1,416	1,440
3	1,368	1,405	1,443	1,482	1,521	1,561	1,602	1,643	1,685	1,728
4	1,518	1,574	1,630	1,689	1,749	1,811	1,874	1,939	2,005	2,074
5	1,685	1,762	1,842	1,925	2,011	2,100	2,192	2,288	2,386	2,488
6	1,870	1,974	2,082	2,195	2,313	2,436	2,565	2,700	2,840	2,986
7	2,076	2,211	2,353	2,502	2,660	2,826	3,001	3,185	3,379	3,583
8	2,305	2,476	2,658	2,853	3,059	3,278	3,511	3,759	4,021	4,300
9	2,558	2,773	3,004	3,252	3,518	3,803	4,108	4,435	4,785	5,160
10	2,839	3,106	3,395	3,707	4,046	4,411	4,807	5,234	5,695	6,192
11	3,152	3,479	3,836	4,226	4,652	5,117	5,624	6,176	6,777	7,430
12	3,498	3,896	4,335	4,818	5,350	5,936	6,580	7,288	8,064	8,916
13	3,883	4,363	4,898	5,492	6,153	6,886	7,699	8,599	9,596	10,699
14	4,310	4,887	5,535	6,261	7,076	7,988	9,007	10,147	11,420	12,839
15	4,785	5,474	6,254	7,138	8,137	9,266	10,539	11,974	13,590	15,407
16	5,311	6,130	7,067	8,137	9,358	10,748	12,330	14,129	16,172	18,488
17	5,895	6,866	7,986	9,276	10,761	12,468	14,426	16,672	19,244	22,186
18	6,544	7,690	9,024	10,575	12,375	14,463	16,879	19,673	22,901	26,623
19	7,263	8,613	10,197	12,056	14,232	16,777	19,748	23,214	27,252	31,948
20	8,062	9,646	11,523	13,743	16,367	19,461	23,106	27,393	32,429	38,338
21	8,949	10,804	13,021	15,668	18,822	22,574	27,034	32,324	38,591	46,005
22	9,934	12,100	14,714	17,861	21,645	26,186	31,629	38,142	45,923	55,206
23	11,026	13,552	16,627	20,362	24,891	30,376	37,006	45,008	54,649	66,247
24	12,239	15,179	18,788	23,212	28,625	35,236	43,297	53,109	65,032	79,497
25	13,585	17,000	21,231	26,462	32,919	40,874	50,658	62,669	77,388	95,396
26	15,080	19,040	23,991	30,167	37,857	47,414	59,270	73,949	92,092	114,475
27	16,739	21,325	27,109	34,390	43,535	55,000	69,345	87,260	109,589	137,371
28	18,580	23,884	30,633	39,204	50,066	63,800	81,134	102,967	130,411	164,845
29	20,624	26,750	34,616	44,693	57,575	74,009	94,927	121,501	155,189	197,814
30	22,892	29,960	39,116	50,950	66,212	85,850	111,065	143,371	184,675	237,376
31	25,410	33,555	44,201	58,083	76,144	99,586	129,946	169,177	219,764	284,852
32	28,206	37,582	49,947	66,215	87,565	115,520	152,036	199,629	261,519	341,822
33	31,308	42,092	56,440	75,485	100,700	134,003	177,883	235,563	311,207	410,186
34	34,752	47,143	63,777	86,053	115,805	155,443	208,123	277,964	370,337	492,224
35	38,575	52,800	72,069	98,100	133,176	180,314	243,503	327,997	440,701	590,668
36	42,818	59,136	81,437	111,834	153,152	209,164	284,899	387,037	524,434	708,802
37	47,528	66,232	92,024	127,491	176,125	242,631	333,332	456,703	624,076	850,562
38	52,756	74,180	103,987	145,340	202,543	281,452	389,998	538,910	742,651	1,020,675
39	58,559	83,081	117,506	165,687	232,925	326,484	456,298	635,914	883,754	1,224,810
40	65,001	93,051	132,782	188,884	267,864	378,721	533,869	750,378	1,051,668	1,469,772

Survey of Annual Fund Performance

(for periods ending June 30)

Fund	1994	1993	1992	1991	1990	1989	1988	1987	1986	1985
Canadian Equity Funds										
Admax Cdn Performance Fund	-2.5	17.5	4.3	-1.4	.....	.....	.....	.....	.....	.....
All-Canadian CapitalFund	7.8	22.2	0.4	3.3	2.8	7.0	-9.3	15.3	16.7	17.6
All-Canadian Compound	8.1	21.6	0.4	3.3	2.7	7.1	-9.3	15.3	16.8	17.6
All-Canadian ConsumerFund	5.7	.....	6.5	9.6	9.1	9.0	6.7	9.0	6.1	20.0
Altafund Investment Corp.	2.3	57.5	15.9	.....	.....					
Altamira Capital Growth Fund	6.6	20.8	19.7	3.0	6.2	12.0	-14.5	19.6	10.0	26.2
Altamira Equity Fund	0.4	52.9	42.4	13.7	17.9	32.7	.....	.....	.....	.....
Altamira North American Recovery	.....	.....								
Altamira Special Growth Fund	-9.8	54.2	34.4	14.3	4.6	8.0	-14.8	12.5	.....	.....
Associate Investors Ltd.	0.2	12.8	4.1	4.7	-4.6	14.6	-1.3	14.9	12.4	33.1
ABC Fundamental Value Fund	38.2	66.5	1.0	27.1	6.2	.....	.....	.....	.....	.....
AGF Canadian Equity Fund	1.2	19.5	0.4	-1.2	-9.1	9.2	-7.0	12.0	27.2	35.5
AGF Growth Equity Fund Ltd.	3.0	59.1	14.1	2.4	-4.1	4.4	-17.0	20.3	33.2	21.5
AIC Advantage Fund	10.1	30.3	17.0	14.5	-8.0	11.8	-9.2	16.6	.....	.....
AMI Private Capital Equity	4.3	17.0	-1.0	-3.4	-3.3	15.2	.....	.....	.....	.....
Batirente - Section Actions	-0.8	10.3	-2.5	-1.4	-4.4	13.4	.....	.....	.....	.....
Beutel Goodman Cdn Equity Fund	8.3	9.6	-3.3	.....						
Bissett Canadian Equity Fund	0.2	32.5	4.4	5.3	1.9	12.2	-6.5	12.9	25.8	26.9
Bissett Small Cap Fund	6.7	101.7	.....	.....	.....	.....	.....	.....	.....	.....
Bullock Growth Fund	2.4	42.3	4.8	5.6	-8.3	7.1	-5.6	4.5	34.0	5.6
BNP (Canada) Equity Fund	-2.8	19.5	.....	.....						
BPI Canadian Equity Fund	-3.5	35.9	-4.1	-4.5	-0.6	4.5	-15.0	6.4	.....	.....
BPI Canadian Equity Value Fund	-3.7	30.6	4.9	7.5	-0.1	.....	.....	.....	.....	.....
BPI Canadian Small Cap Fund	-1.6	52.1	7.4	10.8	-9.8	3.4	.....	.....	.....	.....
C.I. Canadian Growth Fund	7.3	.....	.....	.....	.....	.....	.....	.....	.....	.....
C.I. Sector Canadian Fund	6.4	31.7	-7.1	-6.5	-7.3	7.3	.....	.....	.....	.....
Cambridge Growth Fund	-4.4	42.8	9.2	6.3	4.4	12.4	-0.4	26.8	40.7	31.6
Cambridge Special Equity	-14.8	81.3	-17.4	-19.3	-1.7	17.7	-7.1	.....	.....	.....
Canada Life Canadian Equity S-9	0.9	18.5	4.7	0.7	-5.2	16.9	1.3	14.0	23.0	31.0
Canada Trust Everest Special Eqty	-5.3	45.5	7.2	5.6	-3.0	14.7	-19.0	.....	.....	.....
Canada Trust Everest Stock Fund	0.8	30.1	5.2	2.8	-0.3	.....	.....	.....	.....	.....
Canada Trust Investment-Eqty	-0.1	29.2	-1.2	2.5	-0.5	12.6	-9.3	.....	.....	.....
Canadian Investment Fund	-0.1	10.2	-2.6	-1.5	0.4	15.4	-7.7	11.1	15.2	27.4
Canadian Protected Fund	-5.1	30.7	3.8	7.0	6.4	5.8	8.8	6.4	21.7	.....
Chou RRSP Fund	3.1	9.0	5.4	-0.6	-5.5	15.3	7.1	.....	.....	.....
Clean Environment Equity Fund	5.0	31.2	.....	.....	.....	.....	.....	.....	.....	.....
Colonia Equity Fund	-3.3	14.4	.....	.....	.....	.....	.....	.....	.....	.....
Colonia Special Growth Fund	.....	.....	.....	.....	.....	.....	.....	.....	.....	.....
Concorde Croissance	1.5	14.2	.....	.....	.....	.....	.....	.....	.....	.....

NOTE: An interruption in the historical flow of data indicates that the fund's objectives changed during that twelve month period. If current information is not provided the fund company did not submit the net asset value per share for the fund for June 30, 1994.

Fund	1994	1993	1992	1991	1990	1989	1988	1987	1986	1985
Confed Equity Fund	3.3	12.5	7.8	-1.1	-6.8	15.8	-1.6	16.4	15.7	31.4
Confed Growth Fund	4.8	13.2	6.8	-0.4	-7.0	14.6	-3.4	16.3	24.9	34.0
Confed Life B	4.0	13.6	9.2	0.3	-5.9	17.0	-0.5	17.6	16.9	32.8
Cornerstone Cdn Growth	-3.9	18.6	12.9	3.3	-8.5	13.0	-9.8	.....	.....	.....
Corporate Investors Stock Fund	-1.5	43.6	8.5	5.1	-8.0	-9.8	-31.4	13.9	43.0	26.4
Cundill Security Fund	17.9	25.2	-16.2	-1.8	-4.5	9.7	2.1	22.6	10.3	24.2
CAMAF(Cdn-Anaest)	-1.8	16.3	-3.2	1.7	0.6	11.9	-3.5	20.4	22.0	27.2
CCPE Growth Fund R	4.8	10.5	-1.8	3.5	-2.6	18.9	-4.1	18.1	.....	.....
CDA Aggressive Equity Fund	.....	.....	.....	.....	.....	.....	.....	.....	.....	.....
CDA Common Stock Fund	3.2	23.0	3.8	5.1	-2.2	16.8	-4.8	22.4	25.7	31.4
CIBC Canadian Equity Fund	-4.7	18.5	-6.2	1.4	2.8	.....	.....	.....	.....	.....
CIBC Capital Appreciation Fund	-6.2	44.2	.....	.....	.....	.....	.....	.....	.....	.....
Dynamic Canadian Growth Fund	1.7	106.8	6.4	16.3	-4.6	4.1	-28.6	23.9	.....	.....
Dynamic Fund of Canada	-6.9	51.9	5.9	2.3	1.2	12.5	-1.9	25.3	15.2	23.0
Elliott & Page Equity Fund	-2.0	28.0	13.1	8.6	-6.4	20.7	.....	.....	.....	.....
Empire Elite Equity Fund 5	-1.7	22.0	9.4	1.2	-2.0	10.3	-13.7	17.0	24.2	43.9
Empire Equity Growth Fund 3	3.5	26.8	1.3	6.1	-4.1	18.2	0.9	7.2	44.2	27.3
Empire Premier Equity Fund 1	1.6	21.7	4.4	3.0	-1.8	14.6	3.5	16.9	23.5	31.9
Equitable Life Canadian Stock	4.0	.....	.....	.....	.....	.....	.....	.....	.....	.....
Equitable Life Seg. Common Stock	6.9	14.5	1.8	1.5	-5.6	10.9	-10.1	21.8	21.4	27.0
Ethical Growth Fund	-1.7	19.2	-0.8	7.3	4.0	16.0	10.9	9.5	.....	.....
Fidelity Capital Builder Fund	-2.9	26.5	-2.1	13.9	1.3	14.3	.....	.....	.....	.....
First Canadian Equity Index	2.4	17.2	0.5	-0.5	-3.7	11.0	.....	.....	.....	.....
First Cdn. Growth Fund	.....	.....	.....	.....	.....	.....	.....	.....	.....	.....
First Cdn. Special Growth Fund	.....	.....	.....	.....	.....	.....	.....	.....	.....	.....
Fonds de Prof. Cdn. Equity	-1.7	14.3	-0.3	4.7	-4.0	14.7	.....	.....	.....	.....
Fonds Desjardins Actions	-3.1	20.3	-0.8	3.2	-4.7	15.2	-11.0	.....	.....	.....
Fonds Desjardins Croissance	.....	.....	.....	.....	.....	.....	.....	.....	.....	.....
Fonds Desjardins Environnement	0.2	10.6	1.9	.....	.....	.....	.....	.....	.....	.....
Fonds Ficadre Actions	3.0	12.3	2.3	-2.7	-15.0	2.7	-25.6	.....	.....	.....
General Trust of Canada Cdn Eqty	-1.1	12.8	-2.3	2.3	-5.8	10.9	-8.2	14.8	19.7	26.1
General Trust of Canada Growth	-2.6	45.6	15.9	2.7	-10.5	25.2	.....	.....	.....	.....
Global Strategy Canada Growth	0.7	18.2	.....	.....	.....	.....	.....	.....	.....	.....
Great-West Life Canadian Equity	-3.0	33.0	6.8	3.7	1.8	9.9	-12.5	.....	.....	.....
Great-West Life Eqty Index Invest	1.6	17.9	-0.8	0.0	-3.9	11.2	-6.8	22.5	14.0	24.1
Green Line Blue Chip Equity Fund	0.1	10.9	4.2	1.8	-1.0	15.2	.....	.....	.....	.....
Green Line Canadian Equity Fund	1.7	26.3	-1.7	1.4	-5.6	19.0	.....	.....	.....	.....
Green Line Canadian Index Fund	2.7	19.1	-0.1	0.4	-3.5	11.5	-6.2	23.4	.....	.....
Green Line Canadian Value Fund	.....	.....	.....	.....	.....	.....	.....	.....	.....	.....
Guardian Canadian Equity Fund	-2.4	22.4	-2.6	-2.4	-4.2	7.1	-7.6	14.4	34.8	23.8
Guardian Enterprise Fund	-0.2	26.5	-1.8	1.5	5.7	2.5	-1.9	5.0	29.0	24.8
Guardian Growth Equity Fund	1.2	41.4	7.2	4.2	6.5	.....	.....	.....	.....	.....
Gyro Equity Fund	-2.0	34.2	-1.3	-3.4	-0.7	9.0	-1.0	28.4	.....	.....
GBC Canadian Growth Fund	-4.1	49.0	16.9	15.2	10.4	.....	.....	.....	.....	.....
Hongkong Bank Equity Fund	4.7	43.8	-1.3	2.7	-2.1	.....	.....	.....	.....	.....
Hyperion Aurora Trust	.....	.....	.....	.....	.....	.....	.....	.....	.....	.....
HRL Canadian Fund	1.6	15.7	-4.8	5.4	0.1	12.8	-2.6	.....	.....	.....
Imperial Growth Canadian Equity	1.5	19.3	5.4	3.1	-5.9	27.4	17.3	31.3	23.1	28.9
Industrial Alliance Ecoflex Fund A	6.1	.....	.....	.....	.....	.....	.....	.....	.....	.....
Industrial Equity Fund Ltd.	3.6	91.9	-0.2	-12.6	-13.0	-2.9	-0.5	31.4	18.1	16.8
Industrial Future Fund	5.3	37.5	-5.3	-0.9	-2.6	11.0	.....	.....	.....	.....
Industrial Growth Fund	4.2	32.5	-8.8	-1.5	-2.5	8.4	4.5	27.7	16.4	27.1
Industrial Horizon Fund	6.2	21.5	-2.3	0.4	-1.7	10.1	15.2	.....	.....	.....
Industrial Pension Fund	11.4	26.1	-7.2	-9.8	-7.9	3.5	4.3	23.4	20.8	30.6
Industrial Strategic Cap Protection	3.5	18.9	.....	.....	.....	.....	.....	.....	.....	.....
Investors Canadian Equity Fund	5.3	28.6	4.7	6.6	1.0	8.5	-5.7	10.1	27.8	25.4
Investors Retirement Gth. Portfolio	6.3	17.9	2.4	2.7	1.0	.....	.....	.....	.....	.....
Investors Retirement Mutual Fund	5.3	18.1	-0.8	1.9	-2.7	12.7	4.6	20.4	13.6	26.7
Investors Summa Fund Ltd.	3.2	14.3	5.7	1.8	-3.2	12.5	-3.1	.....	.....	.....
InvesNat Equity Fund	-2.1	20.5	4.9	3.4	1.4	.....	.....	.....	.....	.....
Ivy Canadian Fund	3.8	.....	.....	.....	.....	.....	.....	.....	.....	.....

Fund	1994	1993	1992	1991	1990	1989	1988	1987	1986	1985
Ivy Capital Protection Fund	-0.7	.....	.....	.....	.....	.....	.....	.....	.....	.....
Ivy Capital Protection Fund 1994	.....	.....	.....	.....	.....	.....	.....	.....	.....	.....
Jarislowsky Finsco Canadian Equity	1.9	6.9	-1.5	3.6	-0.8	13.5	-9.2	13.3	.....	.....
Jones Heward Fund Ltd.	-5.1	41.8	8.8	4.5	-9.7	10.7	-3.8	11.8	29.4	31.6
Laurentian Canadian Equity Fund	-0.5	16.8	1.3	1.6	-11.1	16.9	-2.6	11.1	20.6	25.9
Laurentian Special Equity Fund	11.7	24.6	1.8	3.4	.....	.....	.....	.....	.....	.....
Leith Wheeler Canadian Equity	.....	.....	.....	.....	.....	.....	.....	.....	.....	.....
London Life Canadian Equity	-1.5	27.2	5.7	1.1	-8.2	15.0	-0.3	21.0	19.0	28.7
Lotus (MKW) Canadian Equity	.....	.....	.....	.....	.....	.....	.....	.....	.....	.....
Mackenzie Equity Fund	9.9	24.7	-7.5	-8.6	-7.1	6.5	4.8	20.8	23.1	29.6
Mackenzie Sentinel Canada Equity	13.3	46.0	-7.6	-6.2	-4.4	6.1	-15.6	42.1	.....	.....
Manulife Vistafund 1 Cap. Gains Gth	-2.7	35.3	8.3	2.3	0.3	11.8	-8.0	24.3	14.4	28.6
Manulife Vistafund 1 Equity Fund	-0.5	21.5	5.1	3.7	-1.9	10.5	-6.1	20.3	9.8	22.5
Manulife Vistafund 2 Cap. Gains Gth	-3.4	34.2	7.5	1.5	-0.4	11.0	-8.7	23.4	13.6	27.7
Manulife Vistafund 2 Equity Fund	-1.2	20.6	4.3	2.9	-2.7	9.7	-6.8	19.4	9.0	21.6
Marathon Equity Fund	11.3	105.7	26.9	-7.3	-5.9	35.6	-33.0	3.7	.....	.....
Maritime Life Growth Fund	-2.6	25.0	0.1	-1.0	-4.0	13.5	-11.1	15.2	24.7	34.8
Mawer Canadian Equity Fund	-2.7	21.5	.....	.....	.....	.....	.....	.....	.....	.....
Mawer New Canada Fund	16.2	49.1	6.1	7.8	11.3	9.4	.....	.....	.....	.....
McLean Budden Equity Growth	1.0	19.6	6.0	1.3	-3.6	.....	.....	.....	.....	.....
Metlife MVP Equity Fund	1.1	13.4	-3.3	-1.4	-0.5	12.9	-11.8	.....	.....	.....
Metlife MVP Growth Fund	10.6	.....	.....	.....	.....	.....	.....	.....	.....	.....
Middlefield Growth Fund	-10.2	57.2	4.9	.....	.....	.....	.....	.....	.....	.....
Montreal Trust Excelsior Equity	5.9	17.7	-0.2	5.8	-2.0	10.1	-4.0	22.1	14.5	22.3
Multiple Opportunities Fund	47.0	66.5	-2.1	-3.9	27.3	-35.9	-27.2	93.5	.....	.....
Mutual Canadian Indexfund	3.5	9.2	-0.9	1.0	-0.4	10.4	.....	.....	.....	.....
Mutual Equifund	0.8	15.3	-2.0	-1.9	-8.2	20.4	-6.2	8.2	26.7	.....
Mutual Premier Blue Chip Fund	1.0	.....	.....	.....	.....	.....	.....	.....	.....	.....
Mutual Premier Growth Fund	2.6	.....	.....	.....	.....	.....	.....	.....	.....	.....
MD Equity Fund	11.0	29.3	-1.8	0.9	-0.4	11.1	6.1	20.5	20.5	33.9
MD Select Fund	.....	.....	.....	.....	.....	.....	.....	.....	.....	.....
National Life Equities Fund	6.0	23.8	3.1	8.7	-2.6	12.5	-1.3	23.7	17.5	34.3
National Trust Canadian Equity	-4.3	18.5	5.1	6.7	0.8	10.8	-9.7	14.6	24.9	31.0
National Trust Special Equity Fund	-0.9	.....	.....	.....	.....	.....	.....	.....	.....	.....
NatCan Canadian Equity Fund	-1.9	.....	.....	.....	.....	.....	.....	.....	.....	.....
NAL-Investor Equity Fund	-4.5	20.2	-0.7	4.1	-0.8	12.0	-7.6	.....	.....	.....
NN Canadian Growth	0.5	16.8	0.0	4.7	-6.5	9.9	-16.6	20.3	14.6	34.2
NN Canadian 35 Index	3.2	8.4	-1.0	1.2	-1.3	.....	.....	.....	.....	.....
Ontario Teachers Group Div.	1.4	17.3	-3.1	-0.8	-0.8	16.9	-4.7	17.3	21.3	34.8
Ontario Teachers Group Growth	1.7	17.6	-4.2	-0.6	0.9	16.9	-4.6	17.6	24.9	38.4
Optima Strategy Canadian Equity	7.6	7.0	3.6	1.4	-2.9	15.5	-9.4	11.9	19.8	31.0
Optimum Fonds d'Actions	.....	.....	.....	.....	.....	.....	.....	.....	.....	.....
OHA Canadian Equity Fund	-15.1	.....	.....	.....	.....	.....	.....	.....	.....	.....
PH&N RSP/RIF Eqt.	6.4	16.5	0.6	1.1	5.2	17.9	-6.3	16.5	29.0	29.3
PH&N Cdn. Equity	5.7	16.1	-1.2	1.3	4.1	18.2	-2.9	16.1	29.7	28.1
PH&N Vintage	4.9	23.0	8.2	10.5	13.3	17.2	-10.2	25.2	.....	.....
Polymetric Performance Fund	-1.1	9.4	-2.7	.....	.....	.....	.....	.....	.....	.....
Prudential Growth Fund Canada	-7.9	50.5	8.7	-0.9	-4.0	10.8	-14.6	28.0	23.7	27.8
Pursuit Canadian Equity Fund	-3.1	31.1	5.8	10.3	-8.9	0.6	.....	.....	.....	.....
Resolute Growth Fund	.....	.....	.....	.....	.....	.....	.....	.....	.....	.....
Royal Life Equity Fund	5.0	12.8	4.0	11.6	.....	.....	.....	.....	.....	.....
Royal Trust Cdn Special Growth	0.9	.....	.....	.....	.....	.....	.....	.....	.....	.....
Royal Trust Canadian Stock Fund	2.5	16.2	3.2	2.6	-4.3	15.1	-5.7	17.6	11.2	24.6
Royfund Equity Ltd.	5.0	27.5	-1.4	-6.3	0.1	10.2	-8.4	11.8	34.9	35.0
Royfund Growth Fund	0.7	.....	.....	.....	.....	.....	.....	.....	.....	.....
Saxon Small Cap	6.8	38.4	6.0	-1.9	-13.4	9.1	-9.1	11.9	.....	.....
Saxon Stock Fund	-2.0	51.9	0.1	1.6	-5.4	2.0	-12.9	5.5	.....	.....
Sceptre Equity Fund	22.7	15.0	-2.2	3.2	0.1	13.4	4.8	.....	.....	.....
Scotia Canadian Equity Growth	-3.0	16.7	7.9	7.6	-2.4	9.9	-10.9	.....	.....	.....
Spectrum Canadian Equity Fund	3.9	14.5	-1.4	2.6	-4.3	10.1	-3.3	.....	.....	.....
Standard Life Equity Mutual Fund	4.5	.....	.....	.....	.....	.....	.....	.....	.....	.....

Fund	1994	1993	1992	1991	1990	1989	1988	1987	1986	1985
Standard Life Ideal Equity Fund	4.0	14.3	4.2	5.0	0.9	7.7	-8.9	.....	.....	.....
Strata Canadian Fund	.....	.....	.....	.....	.....	.....	.....	.....	.....	.....
Strata Growth Fund	0.7	15.8	6.8	2.8	-5.1	.....	.....	.....	.....	.....
Talvest Growth Fund Inc.	1.3	10.6	2.4	10.6	-1.3	8.8	-0.6	25.7	15.4	27.5
Talvest New Economy	.....	.....	.....	.....	.....	.....	.....	.....	.....	.....
Templeton Heritage Retirement	10.4	10.9	-0.6	-3.4	-1.0	.....	.....	.....	.....	.....
Top Fifty Equity Fund	-2.4	8.3	3.0	2.2	-5.3	.....	.....	.....	.....	.....
Tradex Equity Fund Ltd.	5.8	20.6	-3.3	0.6	1.0	12.1	-3.2	20.4	20.7	26.1
Trans-Canada Equity Fund	-0.4	35.2	-11.8	1.4	-1.0	11.0	-0.9	26.5	47.0	34.3
Trans-Canada Pension Fund	2.6	36.2	-9.5	6.4	1.4	10.2	-6.0	15.4	23.2	25.6
Trimark Canadian Fund	10.7	22.8	8.0	5.1	3.1	16.9	1.6	19.6	18.1	31.5
Trimark RSP Equity Fund	8.8	17.5	6.6	8.0	1.4	.....	.....	.....	.....	.....
Trimark Select Canadian Growth	9.2	.....	.....	.....	.....	.....	.....	.....	.....	.....
Trust Pret & Revenu Canadian	-0.8	21.5	8.9	3.1	-3.2	12.5	-14.8	17.8	11.1	12.2
United Canadian Equity Fund	5.5	29.2	8.5	9.6	-4.2	16.1	-2.2	4.8	22.4	43.1
United Canadian Growth Fund	4.6	43.9	10.7	3.3	-11.8	13.1	-9.7	13.8	28.9	31.9
Universal Canadian Equity Fund	10.5	34.9	-7.2	-6.5	-7.0	7.6	11.0	17.2	24.3	31.1
University Avenue Canadian Fund	-4.1	56.4	26.8	14.6	.....	.....	.....	.....	.....	.....
Working Opportunity Fund	1.6	0.8	.....	.....	.....	.....	.....	.....	.....	.....
Working Ventures Canadian Fund	1.2	2.9	5.0	8.5	.....	.....	.....	.....	.....	.....
20/20 Canadian Growth Fund	7.9	9.7	2.9	7.7	1.9	.....	.....	.....	.....	.....
20/20 RSP Aggressive Equity	.....	.....	.....	.....	.....	.....	.....	.....	.....	.....
HIGHEST IN GROUP	47.0	106.8	42.4	27.1	27.3	35.6	17.3	93.5	47.0	43.9
AVERAGE IN GROUP	2.4	27.7	3.1	2.8	-1.9	11.6	-5.9	18.4	22.0	28.1
LOWEST IN GROUP	-15.1	0.8	-17.4	-19.3	-15.0	-35.9	-33.0	3.7	6.1	5.6

Special Equity Funds

Fund	1994	1993	1992	1991	1990	1989	1988	1987	1986	1985
All-Canadian Resources Corp.	11.3	54.9	-7.4	-8.9	-15.4	-2.7	-12.4	50.3	-8.1	0.1
Altamira Resource Fund	-5.7	108.8	47.0	8.7	.....	.....	.....	.....	.....	.....
AGF Canadian Resources Fund	-9.2	117.2	-2.8	-11.8	15.8	-6.1	-15.5	69.4	-15.4	-3.5
BPI Canadian Resource Fund Inc.	-9.4	102.3	9.8	7.4	0.5	2.7	-14.0	25.0	5.9	4.1
BPI Global Real Estate Securities	.....	.....	.....	.....	.....	.....	.....	.....	.....	.....
Cambridge Resource Fund	-19.9	202.4	-17.3	-8.4	-7.8	-2.2	-7.7	27.7	17.9	10.6
CIS Global Telecommunications	.....	.....	.....	.....	.....	.....	.....	.....	.....	.....
Dominion Equity Resource Fund	-17.6	163.0	2.1	-7.3	3.1	-37.9	-30.7	39.0	.....	.....
Dynamic Precious Metals Fund	23.1	75.0	-1.9	-3.6	3.1	-12.7	-7.2	73.2	.....	.....
First Cdn. Resource Fund	.....	.....	.....	.....	.....	.....	.....	.....	.....	.....
First Heritage Fund	-3.8	57.6	-3.8	-11.2	-5.1	4.0	-14.4	.....	.....	.....
Global Strategy Div. Gold Plus	.....	.....	.....	.....	.....	.....	.....	.....	.....	.....
Goldfund Ltd.	34.6	65.5	-7.8	-1.1	3.4	-20.4	-20.0	63.8	7.8	-10.6
Goldtrust	22.0	67.2	-6.1	-3.2	3.1	-18.2	-21.0	56.8	17.4	-7.1
Green Line Resource Fund	.....	.....	.....	.....	.....	.....	.....	.....	.....	.....
Green Line Science & Tech. Fund	.....	.....	.....	.....	.....	.....	.....	.....	.....	.....
Investors Real Property Fund	-0.3	-2.1	2.1	5.3	7.3	11.6	9.2	10.2	10.0	9.9
MD Realty Fund A Units	-4.6	-25.9	-5.1	-0.1	14.4	14.8	7.7	19.9	5.4	10.1
MD Realty Fund B Units	-1.1	-27.3	-5.4	-0.7	14.4	14.8	7.5	19.1	4.1	8.7
Prudential Nat'l Resource of Can.	-7.8	125.6	14.1	-6.4	14.4	18.7	.....	.....	.....	.....
Prudential Precious Metals of Can.	15.4	62.5	3.0	-15.7	12.2	2.1	.....	.....	.....	.....
Royal Lepage Comm. Real Estate	-0.4	-2.9	-2.1	8.6	7.6	.....	.....	.....	.....	.....
Royal Trust Energy Fund	-7.7	115.6	3.6	-7.4	9.4	5.2	-11.4	66.6	-23.3	0.1
Royal Trust Precious Metals Fund	1.0	40.9	0.6	-3.1	-7.6	.....	.....	.....	.....	.....
Roycom-Summit Realty Fund	10.0	0.6	6.3	7.5	12.1	10.7	11.9	.....	.....	.....
Roycom-Summit TDF Fund	3.9	4.7	6.7	7.0	9.9	12.5	14.5	.....	.....	.....
Scotia CanAm Growth Fund	.....	.....	.....	.....	.....	.....	.....	.....	.....	.....
Scotia Precious Metals Fund	.....	.....	.....	.....	.....	.....	.....	.....	.....	.....
Universal Canadian Resource Fund	-0.1	177.2	-9.5	-14.0	-3.6	-8.8	-4.0	53.9	-13.2	4.2
Universal World Precious Metals	.....	.....	.....	.....	.....	.....	.....	.....	.....	.....
HIGHEST IN GROUP	34.6	202.4	47.0	8.7	15.8	18.7	14.5	73.2	17.9	10.6
AVERAGE IN GROUP	1.6	70.6	1.2	-2.8	4.6	-0.7	-6.7	44.2	0.8	2.4
LOWEST IN GROUP	-19.9	-27.3	-17.3	-15.7	-15.4	-37.9	-30.7	10.2	-23.3	-10.6

Fund	1994	1993	1992	1991	1990	1989	1988	1987	1986	1985
U.S. Equity Funds										
Admax American Performance	2.0	6.1	7.5	-2.5	.....	.....	.....	.....	.....	.....
Altamira Select American Fund	17.2	40.7	24.1	.....	.....	.....	.....	.....	.....	.....
Altamira U.S. Larger Company	.....	.....	.....	.....	.....	.....	.....	.....	.....	.....
AGF American Growth Fund Ltd.	9.7	22.1	9.9	-2.6	5.0	21.2	-15.0	8.4	27.0	33.3
AGF Special Fund Ltd.	7.8	20.8	11.8	4.7	8.2	15.3	-8.2	10.5	31.2	23.4
AIC Value Fund	9.1	27.2	16.6	3.7	.....	.....	.....	.....	.....	.....
Beutel Goodman American Equity	11.3	30.1	7.9	.....	.....	.....	.....	.....	.....	.....
Bissett American Equity Fund	7.6	13.2	12.6	6.8	4.0	8.1	-11.5	13.2	13.9	.....
Bullock American Fund	-1.4	19.8	23.5	22.4	32.1	15.8	-20.7	21.2	56.0	16.8
Bullock Optimax U.S.A. Fund 'A'	.....	.....	.....	.....	.....	.....	.....	.....	.....	.....
Bullock Optimax U.S.A. Fund 'B'	.....	.....	.....	.....	.....	.....	.....	.....	.....	.....
Bullock Optimax U.S.A. Fund 'C'	.....	.....	.....	.....	.....	.....	.....	.....	.....	.....
BPI American Equity Growth Fund	17.2	53.2	4.6	7.0	12.7	-17.9	-18.0	.....	.....	.....
BPI American Equity Value Fund	7.3	17.1	9.8	7.4	7.0	.....	.....	.....	.....	.....
C.I. American Fund	16.5	.....	.....	.....	.....	.....	.....	.....	.....	.....
C.I. Sector North American	16.0	.....	.....	.....	.....	.....	.....	.....	.....	.....
Cambridge American Growth	1.4	4.8	.....	.....	.....	.....	.....	.....	.....	.....
Canada Trust Everest AmeriGrowth	0.4	.....	.....	.....	.....	.....	.....	.....	.....	.....
Canada Trust Everest U.S. Equity	0.6	19.4	6.8	.....	.....	.....	.....	.....	.....	.....
Cassels Blaikie Am. Fund ($US)	-5.9	8.5	5.6	2.5	28.0	24.9	-14.8	11.9	51.2	36.4
Century DJ Fund	2.8	9.5	4.6	3.3	17.7	5.2	-25.1	14.3	.....	.....
Chou Associates Fund	4.8	24.2	16.9	5.1	-4.1	18.6	-5.2	.....	.....	.....
Cornerstone U.S. Fund	7.8	13.7	10.9	0.5	15.1	11.4	-27.7	6.1	27.6	14.9
CIBC U.S. Equity Fund	3.6	16.9	16.6	.....	.....	.....	.....	.....	.....	.....
Dynamic American Fund	4.3	15.7	11.8	-4.0	7.5	16.4	-8.1	22.7	22.3	31.1
Elliott & Page American Growth	8.6	15.7	8.3	-0.9	14.7	8.9	-21.6	17.8	35.1	11.9
Ethical North American Equity	3.6	14.1	6.4	3.2	-3.6	9.3	-10.7	12.9	24.3	28.2
Fidelity Growth America Fund	8.6	28.4	23.2	.....	.....	.....	.....	.....	.....	.....
Fidelity Small Cap America Fund	.....	.....	.....	.....	.....	.....	.....	.....	.....	.....
First American	-7.4	32.9	.....	.....	.....	.....	.....	.....	.....	.....
First Cdn. U.S. Growth Fund	.....	.....	.....	.....	.....	.....	.....	.....	.....	.....
General Trust of Canada U.S. Eqty	2.8	35.2	20.0	-0.3	10.5	19.2	-20.9	18.3	39.9	29.6
Global Strategy Div. Americas	-3.0	12.6	3.4	1.0	6.9	10.0	-18.1	.....	.....	.....
Global Strategy U.S. Growth	-3.2	.....	.....	.....	.....	.....	.....	.....	.....	.....
Green Line US Index Fund ($US)	0.6	11.2	11.7	5.5	13.7	18.2	-8.6	.....	.....	.....
Guardian American Equity Fund	11.8	22.7	16.1	4.2	11.3	12.3	-13.1	12.5	22.3	10.5
Guardian North American Fund	11.9	23.1	16.2	0.3	5.7	14.5	-24.0	3.1	25.2	13.3
Guardian Vantage U.S. Equity	9.4	18.9	14.9	6.7	12.1	.....	.....	.....	.....	.....
GBC North AmFund Inc.	4.6	36.3	25.0	-5.5	-1.8	16.1	-7.2	11.2	29.0	23.7
Hyperion Value Line Equity Trust	-3.3	35.7	16.9	.....	.....	.....	.....	.....	.....	.....
Imperial Growth North Am. Eqt.	11.8	21.1	8.2	-12.1	-5.7	12.1	-6.8	24.2	24.3	28.0
Industrial American Fund	11.0	19.4	10.5	-1.1	7.7	8.3	-6.3	18.4	26.3	29.9
Investors U.S. Growth Fund Ltd.	15.9	18.6	21.7	8.1	7.7	15.8	-14.4	18.5	25.3	27.2
InvesNat Am.Equity Fund (US$)	-4.3	.....	.....	.....	.....	.....	.....	.....	.....	.....
Jarislowsky Finsco American Equity	1.9	10.9	12.2	6.0	9.1	5.6	-14.8	11.9	.....	.....
Jones Heward American Fund	2.6	26.2	9.4	3.6	5.2	20.9	-17.5	14.6	39.0	20.2
Laurentian American Equity Fund	8.5	18.2	8.6	-4.3	1.6	15.6	-8.5	15.2	42.2	27.7
Leith Wheeler U.S. Equity Fund	.....	.....	.....	.....	.....	.....	.....	.....	.....	.....
London Life U.S. Equity	4.9	18.4	14.3	-2.9	-7.5	18.6	.....	.....	.....	.....
Mackenzie Sentinel Am. Equity	9.1	17.8	9.7	-3.8	10.2	19.7	.....	.....	.....	.....
Margin of Safety Fund	7.6	14.1	3.9	16.3	5.2	.....	.....	.....	.....	.....
Mawer U.S. Equity Fund	4.7	.....	.....	.....	.....	.....	.....	.....	.....	.....
McLean Budden Am. Growth Fund	6.2	8.4	15.3	15.1	17.6	.....	.....	.....	.....	.....
Metlife MVP U.S. Equity Fund	7.2	.....	.....	.....	.....	.....	.....	.....	.....	.....
Mutual Amerifund	9.2	17.1	6.4	-2.6	3.4	10.4	-3.6	9.6	.....	.....
Mutual Premier American Fund	9.0	.....	.....	.....	.....	.....	.....	.....	.....	.....
MD U.S. Equity Fund	9.6	.....	.....	.....	.....	.....	.....	.....	.....	.....
National Trust American Equity	4.9	.....	.....	.....	.....	.....	.....	.....	.....	.....

Fund	1994	1993	1992	1991	1990	1989	1988	1987	1986	1985
NatCan American Equity ($US)	0.3	.....	.....	.....	.....	.....	.....	.....	.....	.....
NAL-Investor U.S. Equity Fund	.....	.....	.....	.....	.....	.....	.....	.....	.....	.....
NN Can-Am Fund	-0.5	.....	.....	.....	.....	.....	.....	.....	.....	.....
Optima Strategy U.S. Equity	.....	.....	.....	.....	.....	.....	.....	.....	.....	.....
PH&N U.S. Equity	12.4	23.2	12.8	9.7	17.6	13.1	-10.6	8.1	28.8	32.4
Prosperity American Performance	.....	.....	.....	.....	.....	.....	.....	.....	.....	.....
Pursuit American Fund ($US)	-7.3	-5.8	13.3	24.6	15.1	9.0	.....	.....	.....	.....
Royal Trust American Stock Fund	8.7	19.6	12.9	1.8	18.2	16.1	-15.6	16.8	31.8	21.9
Royal Trust Zweig Strat. Growth	13.1	27.3	.....	.....	.....	.....	.....	.....	.....	.....
Royfund U.S. Equity Fund	11.1	29.3	.....	.....	.....	.....	.....	.....	.....	.....
Scotia American Equity Growth	11.3	16.7	8.3	6.8	11.5	-5.9	-22.9	.....	.....	.....
Talvest U.S. Growth Fund Ltd.	4.8	15.0	16.7	8.7	20.4	14.4	-15.0	6.6	25.8	26.6
Top Fifty U.S. Equity Fund	-3.1	27.0	.....	.....	.....	.....	.....	.....	.....	.....
Trust Pret & Revenu American	4.6	7.6	20.4	3.1	13.6	11.2	-22.3	15.0	35.4	24.2
U.S. Polymetric Performance	3.1	8.8	.....	.....	.....	.....	.....	.....	.....	.....
United American Growth Fund	7.3	22.7	13.1	12.6	2.3	19.8	-17.1	6.4	32.2	29.2
Universal U.S. Emerging Growth	3.6	44.1	.....	.....	.....	.....	.....	.....	.....	.....
University Avenue Growth Fund	-0.5	-6.3	-6.1	2.0	0.6	18.1	-19.7	32.8	.....	.....
20/20 Aggressive Growth Fund	8.7	.....	.....	.....	.....	.....	.....	.....	.....	.....
20/20 U.S. Growth Fund	15.4	21.9	5.5	5.1	10.0	.....	.....	.....	.....	.....
HIGHEST IN GROUP	17.2	53.2	25.0	24.6	32.1	24.9	0.0	32.8	56.0	36.4
AVERAGE IN GROUP	5.9	19.8	12.1	3.9	9.2	12.9	-14.8	14.2	31.1	24.6
LOWEST IN GROUP	-7.4	-6.3	-6.1	-12.1	-7.5	-17.9	-27.7	3.1	13.9	10.5

International Equity Funds

Fund	1994	1993	1992	1991	1990	1989	1988	1987	1986	1985
Admax Global Health Sciences	16.2	.....	.....	.....	.....	.....	.....	.....	.....	.....
Altamira Asia Pacific Fund	31.4	.....	.....	.....	.....	.....	.....	.....	.....	.....
Altamira Diversified Fund	17.9	7.3	12.2	-10.2	-9.3	5.7	-22.4	2.7	42.3	.....
Altamira European Equity Fund	.....	.....	.....	.....	.....	.....	.....	.....	.....	.....
AGF Asian Growth Fund Limited	38.7	21.3	.....	.....	.....	.....	.....	.....	.....	.....
AGF China Focus Fund 'A'	.....	.....	.....	.....	.....	.....	.....	.....	.....	.....
AGF China Focus Fund 'B & C'	.....	.....	.....	.....	.....	.....	.....	.....	.....	.....
AGF European Growth Ltd 'B & C'	.....	.....	.....	.....	.....	.....	.....	.....	.....	.....
AGF European Growth 'A'	.....	.....	.....	.....	.....	.....	.....	.....	.....	.....
AGF Japan Fund Ltd.	21.8	32.9	-13.0	-16.3	16.1	-6.8	4.6	31.8	92.9	15.9
AIC World Fund	.....	.....	.....	.....	.....	.....	.....	.....	.....	.....
Beutel Goodman Int'l Equity	37.5	.....	.....	.....	.....	.....	.....	.....	.....	.....
Bullock Asian Dynasty 'A'	.....	.....	.....	.....	.....	.....	.....	.....	.....	.....
Bullock Asian Dynasty 'B'	.....	.....	.....	.....	.....	.....	.....	.....	.....	.....
Bullock Asian Dynasty 'C'	.....	.....	.....	.....	.....	.....	.....	.....	.....	.....
Bullock Emerging Markets 'A'	.....	.....	.....	.....	.....	.....	.....	.....	.....	.....
Bullock Emerging Markets 'B'	.....	.....	.....	.....	.....	.....	.....	.....	.....	.....
Bullock Emerging Markets 'C'	.....	.....	.....	.....	.....	.....	.....	.....	.....	.....
BPI Global Equity Fund	23.1	5.3	18.4	-2.5	17.8	11.3	-17.8	14.7	.....	.....
BPI Global Small Companies Fund	43.1	.....	.....	.....	.....	.....	.....	.....	.....	.....
BPI International Equity Fund	19.6	12.6	13.3	-0.4	17.3	.....	.....	.....	.....	.....
C.I. Emerging Asian Fund	.....	.....	.....	.....	.....	.....	.....	.....	.....	.....
C.I. Emerging Markets Fund	30.5	13.4	.....	.....	.....	.....	.....	.....	.....	.....
C.I. European Fund	13.7	-4.6	.....	.....	.....	.....	.....	.....	.....	.....
C.I. Global Equity RSP Fund	.....	.....	.....	.....	.....	.....	.....	.....	.....	.....
C.I. Global Fund	19.6	17.3	21.7	2.2	10.8	3.0	-11.4	19.0	.....	.....
C.I. Latin American Fund	.....	.....	.....	.....	.....	.....	.....	.....	.....	.....
C.I. Pacific Fund	36.3	24.6	15.4	-7.0	21.4	2.0	-8.0	34.8	110.1	11.9
C.I. Sector Emerging Markets	29.9	.....	.....	.....	.....	.....	.....	.....	.....	.....
C.I. Sector European Fund	13.3	.....	.....	.....	.....	.....	.....	.....	.....	.....
C.I. Sector Global Fund	19.5	17.3	20.7	2.3	10.4	2.1	.....	.....	.....	.....
C.I. Sector Pacific Fund	35.7	24.2	15.3	-7.0	20.6	1.9	.....	.....	.....	.....
Caldwell Securities International	19.9	1.1	.....	.....	.....	.....	.....	.....	.....	.....
Cambridge Americas Fund	-1.6	21.3	12.6	-0.2	10.0	2.9	-14.7	.....	.....	.....
Cambridge Global Fund	8.5	18.9	8.7	-6.9	-2.7	6.5	9.0	20.0	30.8	28.1

Fund	1994	1993	1992	1991	1990	1989	1988	1987	1986	1985
Cambridge Pacific Fund	14.3	19.5	-0.4	1.4	18.4	.....	.....	.....	.....	.....
Canada Life U.S. & Int. Eqty S-34	18.9	18.7	19.7	3.0	13.3	17.5	-7.7	13.3	31.7	27.8
Canada Trust Everest AsiaGrowth	.....	.....	.....	.....	.....	.....	.....	.....	.....	.....
Canada Trust Everest EuroGrowth	.....	.....	.....	.....	.....	.....	.....	.....	.....	.....
Canada Trust Everest International	25.0	11.6	3.1	-5.2	26.0	30.0	.....	.....	.....	.....
Canada Trust Everest North Am.	-1.0	29.8	5.0	2.9	-2.0	11.9	-9.3	10.8	26.8	25.2
Capstone Int. Investment Trust	13.0	19.1	12.9	4.5	14.5	10.4	-6.2	.....	.....	.....
Cassels Blaikie International Fund	18.2	5.3	5.2	-19.5	16.9	-2.5	-24.5	15.6	.....	.....
Clean Environment Int'l Equity	.....	.....	.....	.....	.....	.....	.....	.....	.....	.....
Cornerstone Global Fund	20.5	13.7	10.5	1.3	16.0	7.9	-20.6	.....	.....	.....
Cundill Value Fund Ltd.	23.4	25.1	9.7	-5.7	1.6	10.4	10.3	16.6	22.6	13.6
CIBC Far East Prosperity Fund	.....	.....	.....	.....	.....	.....	.....	.....	.....	.....
CIBC Global Equity Fund	14.7	9.4	23.4	-10.7	13.4	5.8	.....	.....	.....	.....
Dynamic Europe 1992 Fund	21.2	-1.3	8.1	-17.4	.....	.....	.....	.....	.....	.....
Dynamic Far East Fund	.....	.....	.....	.....	.....	.....	.....	.....	.....	.....
Dynamic Global Green Fund	-8.3	25.1	-0.4	-11.4	16.4	3.7	-13.9	.....	.....	.....
Dynamic Global Partners Fund	.....	.....	.....	.....	.....	.....	.....	.....	.....	.....
Dynamic International Fund	8.5	28.2	9.5	10.9	-9.6	-2.6	-27.7	47.0	.....	.....
Empire International Fund	15.7	16.7	17.3	3.2	13.2	.....	.....	.....	.....	.....
Fidelity European Growth Fund	22.7	6.6	.....	.....	.....	.....	.....	.....	.....	.....
Fidelity Far East Fund	24.7	29.1	.....	.....	.....	.....	.....	.....	.....	.....
Fidelity International Portfolio	19.7	23.2	10.3	-7.4	22.8	11.6	.....	.....	.....	.....
Fidelity Japanese Growth Fund	.....	.....	.....	.....	.....	.....	.....	.....	.....	.....
Fidelity Latin American Growth	.....	.....	.....	.....	.....	.....	.....	.....	.....	.....
Finsco Global Fund	25.9	15.2	15.8	-7.3	.....	.....	.....	.....	.....	.....
First Canadian Int'l Growth	26.2	.....	.....	.....	.....	.....	.....	.....	.....	.....
Fonds de Professionnels Intl Equity	.....	.....	.....	.....	.....	.....	.....	.....	.....	.....
Fonds Desjardins International	24.9	16.3	15.3	-2.1	15.8	17.1	-16.9	.....	.....	.....
General Trust of Canada Intl.	27.4	12.0	13.0	-10.2	21.5	5.3	.....	.....	.....	.....
Global Strategy Asia Fund	.....	.....	.....	.....	.....	.....	.....	.....	.....	.....
Global Strategy Div. Japan Plus	.....	.....	.....	.....	.....	.....	.....	.....	.....	.....
Global Strategy Diversified Asia	.....	.....	.....	.....	.....	.....	.....	.....	.....	.....
Global Strategy Diversified Europe	6.0	.....	.....	.....	.....	.....	.....	.....	.....	.....
Global Strategy Diversified Latin	.....	.....	.....	.....	.....	.....	.....	.....	.....	.....
Global Strategy Europe	4.5	7.8	11.0	-13.1	14.4	11.6	-25.8	.....	.....	.....
Global Strategy Fund	6.7	16.0	3.3	-7.3	12.1	11.3	-17.3	24.7	.....	.....
Global Strategy Japan Plus Fund	20.1	13.6	1.4	-10.0	19.7	12.1	-8.9	.....	.....	.....
Global Strategy Latin Fund	.....	.....	.....	.....	.....	.....	.....	.....	.....	.....
Global Strategy Real Estate Sec.	1.4	12.5	-8.1	-14.3	.....	.....	.....	.....	.....	.....
Green Line Asian Growth Fund	.....	.....	.....	.....	.....	.....	.....	.....	.....	.....
Green Line Emerging Markets	27.8	.....	.....	.....	.....	.....	.....	.....	.....	.....
Green Line Global Select Fund	.....	.....	.....	.....	.....	.....	.....	.....	.....	.....
Green Line International Equity	27.5	.....	.....	.....	.....	.....	.....	.....	.....	.....
Green Line North Amer. Growth	.....	.....	.....	.....	.....	.....	.....	.....	.....	.....
Guardian Global Equity (EAFE)	26.2	6.4	0.7	-12.1	10.0	8.8	-13.9	12.7	52.7	20.6
Guardian Pacific Rim Corporation	24.8	28.6	-2.8	-6.2	2.0	-2.1	.....	.....	.....	.....
GBC International Growth Fund	13.6	11.8	2.0	-12.5	.....	.....	.....	.....	.....	.....
Hercules European Value Fund	.....	.....	.....	.....	.....	.....	.....	.....	.....	.....
Hercules Latin American Value	.....	.....	.....	.....	.....	.....	.....	.....	.....	.....
Hercules N. Am. Growth and Inc.	.....	.....	.....	.....	.....	.....	.....	.....	.....	.....
Hercules Pacific Basin Value Fund	.....	.....	.....	.....	.....	.....	.....	.....	.....	.....
Hongkong Bank Asian Growth	.....	.....	.....	.....	.....	.....	.....	.....	.....	.....
Hyperion Asian Trust	42.0	16.7	23.6	-11.6	.....	.....	.....	.....	.....	.....
Hyperion European Trust	17.5	0.5	29.4	.....	.....	.....	.....	.....	.....	.....
HRL Overseas Growth Fund	24.7	.....	.....	.....	.....	.....	.....	.....	.....	.....
Investors European Growth Fund	18.6	-2.0	24.5	.....	.....	.....	.....	.....	.....	.....
Investors Global Fund Ltd.	23.4	8.4	14.3	-6.4	20.5	3.0	-14.9	.....	.....	.....
Investors Growth Portfolio Fund	17.7	22.8	8.5	-1.1	7.1	.....	.....	.....	.....	.....
Investors Japanese Growth Fund	30.4	37.7	-6.7	-9.4	-1.7	-2.6	4.5	31.8	87.9	7.2
Investors North American Growth	5.7	23.7	13.9	7.1	7.9	21.8	-9.8	18.8	25.5	28.5
Investors Pacific International	43.6	17.0	26.4	.....	.....	.....	.....	.....	.....	.....

Fund	1994	1993	1992	1991	1990	1989	1988	1987	1986	1985
Investors Special Fund Ltd.	-0.6	36.4	11.8	9.5	12.0	18.3	-10.0	16.6	21.3	17.7
Investors World Growth Portfolio	18.5	.....	.....	.....	.....	.....	.....	.....	.....	.....
InvesNat European Equity Fund	27.6	.....	.....	.....	.....	.....	.....	.....	.....	.....
Ivy Foreign Equity Fund	10.2	.....	.....	.....	.....	.....	.....	.....	.....	.....
Laurentian Commonwealth Fund	14.0	15.8	11.2	-1.7	6.6	14.4	-3.7	21.4	30.4	24.2
Laurentian Global Balanced Fund	8.8	15.6	7.2	-2.6	.....	.....	.....	.....	.....	.....
Laurentian International Fund Ltd	18.0	17.7	8.2	-4.8	9.4	9.9	-5.2	10.4	32.3	21.1
Mackenzie Sentinel Global Fund	27.0	17.2	1.3	-15.3	10.0	4.7	-21.3	.....	.....	.....
Mawer World Investment Fund	26.6	5.1	25.0	0.7	10.1	.....	.....	.....	.....	.....
Montreal Trust Excelsior Intl	19.5	19.6	10.1	-1.3	12.6	7.3	-15.7	18.7	37.7	36.0
Mutual Premier International Fund	23.5	.....	.....	.....	.....	.....	.....	.....	.....	.....
MD Growth Investments Ltd.	28.4	14.9	21.3	-9.6	10.1	8.7	-5.2	25.3	37.5	36.8
National Life Global Equities Fund	.....	.....	.....	.....	.....	.....	.....	.....	.....	.....
NAL-Investor Global Equity Fund	29.6	20.7	.....	.....	.....	.....	.....	.....	.....	.....
NN Can-Asian Fund	.....	.....	.....	.....	.....	.....	.....	.....	.....	.....
Ontario Teachers Group Global	7.6	17.1	6.3	.....	.....	.....	.....	.....	.....	.....
Optima Strategy Int'l Equity	.....	.....	.....	.....	.....	.....	.....	.....	.....	.....
Orbit World Fund	18.6	14.2	6.3	1.9	9.2	.....	.....	.....	.....	.....
OHA Foreign Equity Fund	20.9	.....	.....	.....	.....	.....	.....	.....	.....	.....
PH&N North American Equity	7.3	.....	.....	.....	.....	.....	.....	.....	.....	.....
Regent Dragon 888 Fund	.....	.....	.....	.....	.....	.....	.....	.....	.....	.....
Regent Europa Performance Fund	3.0	.....	.....	.....	.....	.....	.....	.....	.....	.....
Regent International Fund	36.1	20.3	10.5	-13.2	17.4	-1.6	.....	.....	.....	.....
Regent Korea Fund	32.7	8.7	.....	.....	.....	.....	.....	.....	.....	.....
Regent Nippon Fund	11.2	.....	.....	.....	.....	.....	.....	.....	.....	.....
Regent Tiger Fund	38.1	16.4	13.3	-8.9	.....	.....	.....	.....	.....	.....
Royal Trust Asian Growth Fund	.....	.....	.....	.....	.....	.....	.....	.....	.....	.....
Royal Trust European Growth	24.5	5.7	18.9	-11.8	0.3	3.4	.....	.....	.....	.....
Royal Trust Japanese Stock Fund	32.4	32.8	-16.9	-8.5	-4.7	-6.9	-4.7	42.4	87.7	.....
Royfund International Equity Fund	24.6	.....	.....	.....	.....	.....	.....	.....	.....	.....
Saxon World Growth	16.0	32.6	9.1	-5.3	-5.1	29.1	-10.8	31.6	.....	.....
Sceptre Asian Growth Fund	50.3	.....	.....	.....	.....	.....	.....	.....	.....	.....
Sceptre International Fund	29.5	27.0	23.9	-4.7	19.1	19.5	-4.4	.....	.....	.....
Scotia Global Growth Fund	.....	.....	.....	.....	.....	.....	.....	.....	.....	.....
Special Opportunities Fund	6.7	26.1	-11.4	5.8	.....	.....	.....	.....	.....	.....
Spectrum International Equity	17.2	9.1	19.7	-5.1	11.2	6.9	-17.7	.....	.....	.....
Talvest Global Diversified Fund	19.7	11.2	17.6	-8.0	14.9	6.1	.....	.....	.....	.....
Talvest Global Growth Fund Inc.	19.1	.....	.....	.....	.....	.....	.....	.....	.....	.....
Templeton Emerging Markets	29.5	19.6	.....	.....	.....	.....	.....	.....	.....	.....
Templeton Global Smaller Companies	18.1	23.9	10.1	-0.9	8.1	.....	.....	.....	.....	.....
Templeton Growth Fund Ltd.	23.9	16.3	28.0	-4.0	11.0	15.4	-10.4	19.3	31.8	28.2
Templeton International Stock	32.8	24.1	20.1	-5.7	7.9	.....	.....	.....	.....	.....
Total Return Fund Inc.	1.5	21.3	13.4	0.7	-1.2	.....	.....	.....	.....	.....
Trimark - The Americas Fund	11.7	.....	.....	.....	.....	.....	.....	.....	.....	.....
Trimark Fund	23.2	28.6	20.0	0.7	8.6	14.9	-0.5	17.5	31.2	26.5
Trimark Select Growth Fund	19.2	25.9	20.3	0.0	11.4	.....	.....	.....	.....	.....
United American Equity Fund	2.0	7.0	13.8	8.4	3.6	25.7	-14.9	11.7	34.2	32.9
United Global Equity Fund	12.5	13.5	13.4	.....	.....	.....	.....	.....	.....	.....
United Global Growth Fund	21.0	20.4	14.5	-2.5	-14.5	11.4	-18.9	4.3	27.4	30.3
United Global Telecommunications	.....	.....	.....	.....	.....	.....	.....	.....	.....	.....
Universal Americas Fund	12.1	22.0	13.6	0.0	9.4	8.8	-5.8	18.9	26.6	27.3
Universal Far East Fund	.....	.....	.....	.....	.....	.....	.....	.....	.....	.....
Universal Japan Fund	.....	.....	.....	.....	.....	.....	.....	.....	.....	.....
Universal World Asset Allocation	.....	.....	.....	.....	.....	.....	.....	.....	.....	.....
Universal World Emerging Growth	.....	.....	.....	.....	.....	.....	.....	.....	.....	.....
Universal World Equity Fund	29.0	18.5	1.9	-14.1	8.6	2.8	-1.4	32.1	.....	.....
Vision Europe Fund	16.4	-2.2	.....	.....	.....	.....	.....	.....	.....	.....
20/20 Asia Pacific Fund	29.5	.....	.....	.....	.....	.....	.....	.....	.....	.....
20/20 Latin America	.....	.....	.....	.....	.....	.....	.....	.....	.....	.....
20/20 Multimanager Emerging Mkts	.....	.....	.....	.....	.....	.....	.....	.....	.....	.....
20/20 RSP Int'l Equity Allocation	.....	.....	.....	.....	.....	.....	.....	.....	.....	.....

Fund	1994	1993	1992	1991	1990	1989	1988	1987	1986	1985
HIGHEST IN GROUP	50.3	37.7	29.4	10.9	26.0	30.0	10.3	47.0	110.1	36.8
AVERAGE IN GROUP	20.4	16.8	11.2	-4.7	10.0	8.5	-10.6	20.9	43.9	24.2
LOWEST IN GROUP	-8.3	-4.6	-16.9	-19.5	-14.5	-6.9	-27.7	2.7	21.3	7.2

Balanced Funds

Fund	1994	1993	1992	1991	1990	1989	1988	1987	1986	1985
Admax Asset Allocation Fund	5.6	.....	.....	.....	.....	.....	.....	.....	.....	.....
Altamira Balanced Fund	-4.4	33.4	9.0	-0.9	-5.0	8.6	-13.6	11.6	21.1	.....
Altamira Growth & Income Fund	8.9	18.5	18.3	10.8	3.5	12.3	12.6	12.3	.....	.....
ABC Fully-Managed Fund	20.2	38.2	-1.1	17.7	5.3	22.5	.....	.....	.....	.....
AMI Private Capital Optimix	2.0	13.8	8.3	5.3	1.3	11.3	.....	.....	.....	.....
Batirente - Section Diversifiee	-1.1	13.5	12.9	8.7	0.2	13.5	.....	.....	.....	.....
Beutel Goodman Balanced Fund	5.2	11.2	8.4	.....	.....	.....	.....	.....	.....	.....
Bissett Retirement Fund	1.9	20.4	.....	.....	.....	.....	.....	.....	.....	.....
Bullock Asset Strategy Fund	1.6	.....	7.7	5.6	0.7	9.3	.....	.....	.....	.....
BPI Balanced Fund	-2.4	21.0	11.6	6.2	-0.2	10.6	.....	.....	.....	.....
BPI Global Balanced Fund	10.2	30.1	10.3	1.0	-0.2	0.7	.....	.....	.....	.....
BPI North American TAA RSP Fund	-2.8	.....	.....	.....	.....	.....	.....	.....	.....	.....
BPI One Decision Balanced Fund	-2.1	20.2	7.1	4.1	1.2	.....	.....	.....	.....	.....
BPI World TAA RSP Fund	5.3	.....	.....	.....	.....	.....	.....	.....	.....	.....
C.I. Canadian Balanced	8.4	.....	.....	.....	.....	.....	.....	.....	.....	.....
Caldwell Securities Associate Fund	16.8	6.1	8.0	.....	.....	.....	.....	.....	.....	.....
Cambridge Balanced Fund	-2.4	37.5	10.8	12.7	2.3	8.5	6.9	10.3	29.4	26.7
Canada Life Managed Fund S-35	1.3	15.4	10.9	6.1	-0.7	13.3	3.2	11.4	20.0	27.4
Canada Trust Everest Balanced	-0.5	18.7	9.4	8.3	2.2	18.5	.....	.....	.....	.....
Capstone Investment Trust	3.6	16.2	2.9	10.3	5.5	9.8	-10.6	10.1	24.7	26.9
Cassels Blaikie Canadian Fund	2.6	10.5	12.6	10.8	2.3	12.4	1.8	11.5	14.1	.....
Clean Environment Balanced Fund	9.1	28.4	.....	.....	.....	.....	.....	.....	.....	.....
Common Sense Asset Builder 1	.....	.....	.....	.....	.....	.....	.....	.....	.....	.....
Cornerstone Balanced Fund	-4.2	14.4	5.9	6.5	0.1	9.2	-17.1	7.0	24.5	21.3
CCPE Diversified Growth Fund R	2.8	11.7	8.6	7.6	2.3	14.5	1.0	11.0	.....	.....
CDA Balanced Fund	0.8	12.4	10.2	8.5	2.5	14.2	0.5	13.0	19.2	24.5
CIBC Balanced Inc. and Growth	-2.8	13.1	6.7	8.7	3.2	11.9	.....	.....	.....	.....
CIS Commax Hedge Fund	.....	.....	.....	.....	.....	.....	.....	.....	.....	.....
Dynamic Managed Portfolio Inc.	1.6	38.9	8.3	1.9	1.3	9.2	-2.3	30.0	.....	.....
Dynamic Partners Fund	6.7	40.5	14.4	5.9	4.1	.....	.....	.....	.....	.....
Elliott & Page Balanced Fund	2.4	26.1	9.1	9.0	-0.9	12.4	.....	.....	.....	.....
Empire Balanced Fund	0.1	15.5	8.7	8.1	3.4	.....	.....	.....	.....	.....
Ethical Balanced Fund	0.7	10.4	5.7	11.5	.....	.....	.....	.....	.....	.....
Fidelity Asset Manager Fund	9.3	.....	.....	.....	.....	.....	.....	.....	.....	.....
Fidelity Growth & Income Fund	4.3	16.9	1.6	6.7	0.4	11.0	.....	.....	.....	.....
First Cdn. Asset Allocation	-5.6	12.2	9.3	8.4	-0.6	10.1	.....	.....	.....	.....
Fonds de Professionnels Balanced	0.3	10.6	13.9	14.0	3.6	10.8	4.2	8.7	15.9	21.5
Fonds Desjardins Equilibre	1.0	14.6	8.6	8.5	0.9	12.2	-0.7	.....	.....	.....
Fonds Ficadre Equilibre	2.4	6.3	11.2	5.4	0.9	9.2	-9.5	14.8	23.6	26.5
General Trust of Canada Balanced	-0.5	13.2	9.5	7.6	-1.3	12.0	-0.2	.....	.....	.....
Global Strategy Diversified Growth	5.1	9.1	-5.4	4.2	-0.1	13.0	.....	.....	.....	.....
Global Strategy Income Plus Fund	5.7	18.0	.....	.....	.....	.....	.....	.....	.....	.....
Great-West Life Diversified RS Inv.	-0.8	15.7	9.1	6.0	2.7	10.6	0.4	12.1	14.6	.....
Great-West Life Equity/Bond	-2.9	21.2	11.5	8.8	1.9	10.8	.....	.....	.....	.....
Green Line Balanced Growth	-4.2	10.6	10.0	5.3	-0.3	12.6	.....	.....	.....	.....
Green Line Balanced Income Fund	-0.7	9.3	8.2	6.6	-1.6	14.1	.....	.....	.....	.....
Guardian Balanced Fund	3.5	13.2	12.3	12.2	5.8	9.7	5.9	14.7	11.5	24.4
Guardian International Balanced	.....	15.4	0.1	6.9	8.9	.....	.....	.....	.....	.....
Hongkong Bank Balanced Fund	2.2	20.6	14.7	6.7	2.1	.....	.....	.....	.....	.....
Hyperion Managed Trust	-2.3	12.5	6.7	8.5	6.9	.....	.....	.....	.....	.....
HRL Balanced Fund	2.9	8.0	3.4	9.8	1.5	12.0	1.0	13.3	16.8	21.1
Imperial Growth Diversified Fund	0.8	11.3	10.1	7.4	2.5	.....	.....	.....	.....	.....
Industrial Alliance Ecoflex Fund D	2.3	.....	.....	.....	.....	.....	.....	.....	.....	.....
Industrial Balanced Fund	-0.5	19.7	6.6	.....	.....	.....	.....	.....	.....	.....
Industrial Income Fund	-4.1	16.5	13.3	8.8	-1.4	12.6	13.2	12.3	18.6	38.0

Fund	1994	1993	1992	1991	1990	1989	1988	1987	1986	1985
Integra Balanced Fund	1.9	16.7	12.6	9.4	-3.1	8.8	.....	.....	.....	.....
Investors Asset Allocation Fund	.....	.....	.....	.....	.....	.....	.....	.....	.....	.....
Investors Growth Plus Portfolio	8.8	17.1	9.5	5.2	4.9	.....	.....	.....	.....	.....
Investors Income Plus Portfolio	-0.8	8.9	11.8	11.7	3.5	.....	.....	.....	.....	.....
Investors Retirement Plus Portfolio	3.8	14.1	7.0	6.7	3.4	.....	.....	.....	.....	.....
InvesNat Retirement Balanced	-3.0	13.5	10.1	10.1	-0.9	.....	.....	.....	.....	.....
Jarislowsky Finsco Balanced Fund	1.0	10.0	7.6	6.5	-0.1	6.0	1.1	6.3	8.6	.....
Jones Heward Canadian Balanced	-2.6	24.0	12.9	7.8	-0.3	8.7	-2.3	6.5	22.0	18.4
Laurentian Canadian Balanced	-0.8	9.7	7.6	7.8	2.9	.....	.....	.....	.....	.....
Leith Wheeler Balanced Fund	4.5	13.6	12.0	11.7	-1.2	8.0	.....	.....	.....	.....
London Life Diversified	-0.5	18.9	11.7	5.7	0.8	12.4	.....	.....	.....	.....
Lotus (MKW) Fund	-0.5	24.4	8.2	7.6	0.4	9.0	-6.1	10.4	19.6	25.7
Manulife Vistafund 1 Diversified	-1.7	17.7	9.5	6.4	0.5	10.7	-1.2	18.3	13.1	21.6
Manulife Vistafund 2 Diversified	-2.5	16.8	8.7	5.6	-0.3	9.9	-2.0	17.5	12.3	20.7
Maritime Life Balanced Fund	0.4	12.8	6.4	8.7	0.7	11.2	1.9	.....	.....	.....
Mawer Cdn. Bal. Rtmt Savings	-0.1	14.9	12.4	9.4	2.8	.....	.....	.....	.....	.....
Mawer Cdn. Div. Investment	-0.7	14.2	11.2	10.0	2.5	.....	.....	.....	.....	.....
McLean Budden Balanced Fund	-0.2	15.1	12.5	9.5	2.1	.....	.....	.....	.....	.....
Metlife MVP Balanced Fund	-0.3	10.8	6.1	5.5	2.2	11.0	-4.1	.....	.....	.....
Montreal Tr. Excelsior Total Return	9.0	20.2	15.3	11.4	1.8	.....	.....	.....	.....	.....
Montreal Trust Excelsior Balanced	4.1	14.1	8.2	9.0	8.4	.....	.....	.....	.....	.....
Mutual Diversifund 25	1.0	9.8	9.1	9.0	1.5	11.1	3.0	6.6	15.9	.....
Mutual Diversifund 40	0.1	13.5	7.3	6.3	-2.9	14.1	0.6	6.9	19.7	.....
Mutual Diversifund 55	0.4	14.4	4.6	3.9	-4.2	16.0	-0.9	7.8	20.9	.....
MD Balanced Fund	4.4	.....	.....	.....	.....	.....	.....	.....	.....	.....
National Life Balanced Fund	2.5	18.4	.....	.....	.....	.....	.....	.....	.....	.....
National Trust Balanced Fund	-1.8	15.0	12.2	.....	.....	.....	.....	.....	.....	.....
NAL-Investor Diversified Fund	-3.8	17.1	7.0	7.7	0.4	11.1	1.3	.....	.....	.....
NN Balanced Fund	0.7	15.0	7.4	5.9	0.3	8.1	0.5	.....	.....	.....
Ontario Teachers Group Balanced	1.8	18.5	4.5	7.5	3.2	14.0	2.0	13.2	.....	.....
Optimum Fonds Equilibre	-0.4	14.3	12.6	8.5	0.0	12.3	5.0	8.1	.....	.....
OHA Balanced Fund	-5.4	.....	.....	.....	.....	.....	.....	.....	.....	.....
PH&N Bal Pens Trust	5.0	14.4	11.7	9.5	5.7	.....	.....	.....	.....	.....
PH&N Balanced	4.4	14.3	.....	.....	.....	.....	.....	.....	.....	.....
Protected American Fund	-3.2	37.3	6.4	9.1	8.3	-2.3	7.2	3.1	.....	.....
Prudential Diversified Invest Fund	-4.7	26.8	14.1	9.6	-2.3	13.7	.....	.....	.....	.....
Royal Life Balanced Fund	0.1	13.3	7.9	11.8	.....	.....	.....	.....	.....	.....
Royal Trust Advantage Balanced	2.3	14.2	10.9	8.4	3.2	12.0	0.2	.....	.....	.....
Royal Trust Advantage Growth	-2.9	16.0	8.5	5.8	2.9	10.7	-4.4	.....	.....	.....
Royal Trust Advantage Income	1.7	12.4	12.6	10.3	4.3	11.4	3.1	.....	.....	.....
Royfund Balanced Fund	3.6	19.5	13.0	4.3	3.8	9.8	.....	.....	.....	.....
Saxon Balanced Fund	-1.0	38.6	6.1	3.9	-8.0	3.8	-13.1	4.5	.....	.....
Sceptre Balanced Fund	6.2	13.2	10.2	8.7	0.9	11.8	3.4	13.3	.....	.....
Scotia Stock & Bond Fund	0.5	12.5	4.6	4.3	0.6	12.6	-0.8	.....	.....	.....
Spectrum Diversified Fund	-2.4	13.6	8.8	7.2	-0.1	10.2	1.6	.....	.....	.....
Standard Life Balanced Mutual	-0.9	.....	.....	.....	.....	.....	.....	.....	.....	.....
Standard Life Ideal Balanced Fund	0.9	12.3	14.2	9.9	1.5	8.4	-0.6	.....	.....	.....
Strata Tactical Fund	.....	.....	.....	.....	.....	.....	.....	.....	.....	.....
Stratafund 40	-1.8	13.6	12.8	10.2	-0.5	.....	.....	.....	.....	.....
Stratafund 60	-0.1	14.6	10.6	7.4	-1.9	.....	.....	.....	.....	.....
Talvest Diversified Fund	3.4	12.4	7.6	8.4	3.2	9.1	6.3	13.9	.....	.....
Talvest U.S. Diversified Fund	3.7	16.8	.....	.....	9.5	7.8	-14.3	15.9	.....	.....
Templeton Balanced Fund	7.6	10.9	7.3	.....	-3.7	8.7	-11.4	19.0	23.0	20.9
Trimark Income Growth Fund	6.0	18.4	12.4	7.2	2.6	13.2	.....	.....	.....	.....
Trimark Select Balanced Fund	5.3	17.9	12.2	10.1	.....	.....	.....	.....	.....	.....
Trust Pret & Revenu Retirement	-0.2	13.3	15.3	8.9	3.7	10.0	-1.4	11.1	16.0	17.2
United Cdn Portfolio of Funds	1.6	20.7	11.3	10.4	0.1	.....	.....	.....	.....	.....
United Global Portfolio of Funds	2.6	16.3	12.4	7.8	2.2	.....	.....	.....	.....	.....
Universal World Balanced RRSP	.....	.....	.....	.....	.....	.....	.....	.....	.....	.....
20/20 Am. Tactical Asset Alloc.	4.6	23.4	17.6	4.7	4.2	.....	.....	.....	.....	.....
20/20 Canadian Asset Allocation	4.6	10.6	9.6	8.9	3.1	.....	.....	.....	.....	.....

Fund	1994	1993	1992	1991	1990	1989	1988	1987	1986	1985
20/20 European Asset Allocation	.....	.....	.....	.....	.....	.....	.....	.....	.....	.....
20/20 World Fund	25.1	14.9	18.7	-11.6	10.5	4.0	.....	.....	.....	.....
HIGHEST IN GROUP	25.1	40.5	18.7	17.7	10.5	22.5	13.2	30.0	29.4	38.0
AVERAGE IN GROUP	1.8	16.8	9.5	7.7	1.7	10.8	-0.6	11.7	18.5	23.9
LOWEST IN GROUP	-5.6	6.1	-5.4	-11.6	-8.0	-2.3	-17.1	3.1	8.6	17.2

Canadian Bond Funds

Fund	1994	1993	1992	1991	1990	1989	1988	1987	1986	1985
Admax Canadian Income Fund	0.1	9.4	10.0	9.9	3.3	.....	.....	.....	.....	.....
Altamira Bond Fund	-5.6	19.2	18.3	11.7	3.6	11.8	.....	.....	.....	.....
Altamira Income Fund	-3.1	16.8	21.4	14.9	5.7	13.6	10.4	7.5	11.8	21.8
AGF Canadian Bond Fund	-3.9	14.6	21.7	10.0	1.4	12.2	7.5	5.8	20.4	31.6
AMI Private Capital Income	-1.7	12.1	17.2	13.6	2.5	10.3	.....	.....	.....	.....
Batirente - Section Obligations	-2.2	15.1	20.3	12.8	0.1	13.7	.....	.....	.....	.....
Beutel Goodman Income Fund	-3.4	11.9	18.5	.....	.....	.....	.....	.....	.....	.....
Bissett Bond Fund	0.3	9.9	17.4	14.4	2.6	11.8	8.5	.....	.....	.....
BNP (Canada) Bond Fund	-1.8	11.2	.....	.....	.....	.....	.....	.....	.....	.....
BPI Bond Fund	-3.9	10.9	17.0	12.9	2.3	.....	.....	.....	.....	.....
BPI Canadian Bond Fund	1.4	6.5	15.1	9.3	4.1	7.9	6.6	1.7	.....	.....
BPI RSP Bond Fund	-3.0	11.6	17.9	14.6	2.5	12.0	.....	.....	.....	.....
C.I. Canadian Bond Fund	-1.3	.....	.....	.....	.....	.....	.....	.....	.....	.....
Canada Life Fixed Income S-19	-2.1	11.4	16.6	12.3	3.4	9.6	6.7	6.4	14.8	24.7
Canada Trust Everest Bond Fund	-2.8	11.4	20.0	13.0	3.0	12.9	11.3	.....	.....	.....
Canada Trust Income Investments	-0.9	12.6	14.0	13.8	3.0	11.0	7.8	.....	.....	.....
Canada Trust Inv. Fund-Income	-5.3	12.7	15.5	11.6	2.3	9.2	6.9	.....	.....	.....
Clean Environment Income Fund	.....	.....	.....	.....	.....	.....	.....	.....	.....	.....
Colonia Bond Fund	-0.2	11.2	.....	.....	.....	.....	.....	.....	.....	.....
Concorde Revenu	-2.5	8.1	.....	.....	.....	.....	.....	.....	.....	.....
Confed Fixed Income	-2.5	10.9	17.3	12.1	2.1	11.9	9.6	10.2	14.0	42.3
Confed Life C	-2.2	11.4	18.0	12.7	2.6	12.6	10.2	10.8	14.7	43.1
Cornerstone Bond Fund	-1.8	11.0	16.1	13.1	7.9	10.4	6.5	.....	.....	.....
CCPE Fixed Income Fund	-0.1	13.7	18.0	12.8	3.9	10.6	4.9	4.8	.....	.....
CDA Bond and Mortgage Fund	-0.4	10.9	16.9	14.1	5.4	11.5	8.2	8.1	14.0	21.3
CIBC Canadian Bond Fund	-7.2	12.9	20.1	12.8	2.6	11.3	.....	.....	.....	.....
CIBC Canadian Income Fund	.....	.....	.....	.....	.....	.....	.....	.....	.....	.....
Dynamic Government Income	.....	14.5	33.8	.....	.....	.....	.....	.....	.....	.....
Dynamic Income Fund	8.5	12.6	16.5	11.6	4.8	13.9	6.6	8.2	14.0	30.3
Elliott & Page Bond Fund	-4.9	10.2	16.2	11.7	6.1	11.8	.....	.....	.....	.....
Empire Bond Fund	-2.0	9.4	17.7	14.0	2.6	11.4	3.0	6.5	.....	.....
Equitable Life Canadian Bond Fund	-1.9	.....	.....	.....	.....	.....	.....	.....	.....	.....
Equitable Life Segregated Accum	-1.7	11.8	19.6	15.9	5.2	10.6	8.7	7.5	15.6	27.4
Ethical Income Fund	-2.0	8.6	8.8	12.8	10.0	7.5	6.8	5.2	10.7	25.5
Fidelity Government Bond Fund	0.3	12.5	13.9	6.5	4.6	7.0	.....	.....	.....	.....
First Canadian Bond Fund	-2.9	11.3	19.2	13.6	0.9	10.2	.....	.....	.....	.....
Fonds de Professionnels Bond	-2.0	10.4	16.7	15.5	3.7	10.3	7.3	8.7	15.1	21.0
Fonds Desjardins Obligations	-2.3	11.6	14.8	13.8	1.1	10.7	7.1	5.4	15.7	29.6
Fonds Ficadre Obligations	-3.3	9.0	16.7	14.0	2.3	10.3	.....	.....	.....	.....
General Trust of Canada Bond	-2.8	12.4	18.1	13.6	0.7	11.6	7.3	5.4	17.8	32.9
Global Strategy Bond Fund	.....	.....	.....	.....	.....	.....	.....	.....	.....	.....
Great-West Life Canadian Bond	-3.6	11.2	17.6	13.3	0.0	10.6	7.4	5.9	14.7	26.0
Green Line Canadian Bond Fund	-3.3	12.3	18.1	12.2	2.5	7.4	.....	.....	.....	.....
Green Line Canadian Govt. Bond	-2.4	11.3	14.4	11.4	-0.8	12.8	.....	.....	.....	.....
Green Line Short Term Income	-0.4	6.3	8.3	11.3	12.2	.....	.....	.....	.....	.....
Guardian Canada Bond Fund	0.8	8.5	6.8	11.4	10.8	10.3	8.4	.....	.....	.....
Gyro Bond Fund	-2.1	11.4	20.8	12.5	.....	.....	.....	.....	.....	.....
GBC Canadian Bond Fund	-1.9	13.0	19.4	14.0	1.4	13.1	8.9	7.0	16.1	.....
Hyperion Fixed Income Trust	-7.4	13.2	19.4	12.3	.....	.....	.....	.....	.....	.....
HRL Bond Fund	-3.2	11.3	14.9	9.7	2.8	11.1	2.9	.....	.....	.....
Industrial Alliance Ecoflex Fund B	-3.5	.....	.....	.....	.....	.....	.....	.....	.....	.....
Industrial Bond Fund	-5.2	12.4	18.3	12.6	1.2	.....	.....	.....	.....	.....
Investors Bond Fund	-2.6	10.9	16.6	13.3	3.3	11.5	7.4	6.4	16.3	28.5

Fund	1994	1993	1992	1991	1990	1989	1988	1987	1986	1985
Investors Corporate Bond Fund	.....	.....	.....	.....	.....	.....	.....	.....	.....	.....
InvesNat Bond Fund	0.0	9.1	17.3	14.2	2.6	.....	.....	.....	.....	.....
Ivy Growth & Income Fund	-1.0	.....	.....	.....	.....	.....	.....	.....	.....	.....
Jarislowsky Finsco Bond Fund	-1.4	11.4	17.5	11.3	1.6	9.5	7.9	5.0	14.9	.....
Jones Heward Bond Fund	-3.8	11.4	15.8	12.5	2.4	11.5	7.7	.....	.....	.....
Laurentian Government Bond	-0.3	8.0	13.5	13.8	4.7	.....	.....	.....	.....	.....
Laurentian Income Fund	-2.3	11.0	15.0	13.0	2.4	10.4	7.7	7.2	16.7	31.0
Leith Wheeler Fixed Income Fund	.....	.....	.....	.....	.....	.....	.....	.....	.....	.....
London Life Bond	-3.1	11.2	17.7	5.2	3.1	13.2	5.3	4.2	21.2	41.3
Lotus (MKW) Bond Fund	.....	.....	.....	.....	.....	.....	.....	.....	.....	.....
Mackenzie Sentinel Canada Bond	-5.8	14.9	18.0	12.3	0.6	10.8	7.4	8.4	.....	.....
Manulife Vistafund 1 Bond Fund	-5.9	14.1	18.1	14.2	2.9	11.8	8.5	7.3	14.8	22.9
Manulife Vistafund 2 Bond Fund	-6.6	13.3	17.2	13.4	2.2	11.0	7.7	6.6	14.0	22.0
Maritime Life Bond Fund	-2.5	11.0	17.0	13.4	.....	.....	.....	.....	.....	.....
Mawer Canadian Bond Fund	-2.5	11.2	.....	.....	.....	.....	.....	.....	.....	.....
McLean Budden Fixed Income	-2.4	12.3	17.6	14.3	5.1	.....	.....	.....	.....	.....
Metlife MVP Bond Fund	-3.3	9.2	14.5	12.3	3.8	11.2	2.1	.....	.....	.....
Montreal Trust Excelsior Income	-1.4	12.0	19.3	13.2	0.9	11.7	6.6	7.6	19.3	24.9
Mutual Bond Fund	-2.0	11.1	16.2	.....	.....	.....	.....	.....	.....	.....
Mutual Premier Bond Fund	-2.0	.....	.....	.....	.....	.....	.....	.....	.....	.....
MD Bond Fund	-1.0	12.2	18.2	13.5	3.8	12.3	.....	.....	.....	.....
National Life Fixed Income Fund	0.4	13.6	19.6	16.0	5.0	12.7	9.0	8.2	17.7	29.8
National Trust Canadian Bond	-3.2	11.7	17.0	13.0	0.7	10.7	7.8	7.3	16.3	30.0
NatCan Canadian Bond Fund	-2.6	.....	.....	.....	.....	.....	.....	.....	.....	.....
NAL-Investor Bond Fund	-1.2	10.9	16.7	12.2	1.8	9.6	9.0	.....	.....	.....
NN Bond Fund	-1.8	11.6	15.2	13.4	3.6	9.6	4.7	.....	.....	.....
Optima Strategy Canadian Income	-2.8	10.3	17.2	12.5	0.1	12.9	1.0	4.9	16.9	22.9
Optima Strategy Sht Term Income	1.4	.....	.....	.....	.....	.....	.....	.....	.....	.....
Optimum Fonds d'Obligations	-2.6	14.2	20.7	12.5	0.4	12.8	7.9	7.4	.....	.....
OHA Bond Fund	-4.4	.....	.....	.....	.....	.....	.....	.....	.....	.....
PH&N Bond Fund	-0.5	12.9	19.8	15.2	3.4	13.2	9.4	9.3	18.6	34.0
Prudential Income Fund of Canada	-3.5	12.2	14.5	12.5	1.7	13.2	9.3	7.3	13.4	22.5
Pursuit Income Fund	4.2	10.8	15.3	8.9	0.6	10.4	.....	.....	.....	.....
PH &N Sht Term Bond & Mort.	.....	.....	.....	.....	.....	.....	.....	.....	.....	.....
Royal Life Income Fund	-4.1	12.0	13.1	10.0	.....	.....	.....	.....	.....	.....
Royal Trust Bond Fund	-1.5	11.9	18.4	13.6	1.9	11.0	7.4	6.2	16.4	29.9
Royfund Bond Fund	-1.1	11.0	19.0	13.4	3.0	9.4	7.8	6.9	15.7	23.9
Sceptre Bond Fund	-5.5	11.4	17.2	16.1	5.8	8.4	8.6	7.1	.....	.....
Scotia Defensive Income Fund	0.9	7.9	12.3	12.3	3.7	8.3	.....	.....	.....	.....
Scotia Income Fund	-0.9	9.7	12.3	11.4	4.5	10.0	7.0	.....	.....	.....
Spectrum Government Bond Fund	-5.7	13.8	19.9	10.7	2.3	.....	.....	.....	.....	.....
Spectrum Interest Fund	-4.6	11.7	17.1	12.1	3.7	9.8	6.0	.....	.....	.....
Standard Life Bond Mutual Fund	-2.6	.....	.....	.....	.....	.....	.....	.....	.....	.....
Standard Life Ideal Bond Fund	-2.6	12.3	18.8	13.3	1.8	8.9	8.6	.....	.....	.....
Strata Government Bond Fund	.....	.....	.....	.....	.....	.....	.....	.....	.....	.....
Strata Income Fund	-3.8	11.3	17.5	14.0	2.5	.....	.....	.....	.....	.....
Talvest Bond Fund	-2.4	11.2	17.7	12.9	2.3	11.6	8.0	9.3	15.9	30.2
Talvest Income Fund	-0.2	10.0	13.7	13.5	5.6	9.1	8.3	8.6	10.3	19.1
Templeton Heritage Bond Fund	1.1	9.2	16.4	7.9	.....	.....	.....	.....	.....	.....
Top Fifty T-Bill/Bond Fund	-8.1	9.5	15.3	11.7	10.4	.....	.....	.....	.....	.....
Tradex Bond Fund	-4.9	10.2	12.7	11.3	.....	.....	.....	.....	.....	.....
Trans-Canada Bond Fund	-1.0	6.1	14.8	11.9	3.9	6.2	9.0	.....	.....	.....
Trimark Government Income Fund	.....	.....	.....	.....	.....	.....	.....	.....	.....	.....
Trust Pret & Revenu Bond Fund	-1.9	9.5	20.0	12.6	4.4	8.6	.....	.....	.....	.....
United Canadian Bond Fund	-4.8	13.4	17.0	14.0	8.4	2.7	5.1	8.0	14.2	29.5
Universal Canadian Bond Fund	-5.6	14.3	17.2	12.0	0.8	13.6	12.1	6.9	15.7	36.4
University Avenue Bond Fund	0.4	.....	.....	.....	.....	.....	.....	.....	.....	.....
20/20 Income Fund	-3.9	11.4	16.6	10.3	1.7	8.5	1.7	12.0	.....	.....
HIGHEST IN GROUP	8.5	19.2	33.8	16.1	12.2	13.9	12.1	12.0	21.2	43.1
AVERAGE IN GROUP	-2.3	11.4	16.9	12.6	3.3	10.7	7.3	7.1	15.6	28.5
LOWEST IN GROUP	-8.1	6.1	6.8	5.2	-0.8	2.7	1.0	1.7	10.3	19.1

Fund	1994	1993	1992	1991	1990	1989	1988	1987	1986	1985
Canadian Mortgage Funds										
Canada Trust Everest Mortgage	3.4	8.6	11.1	15.4	8.4	9.2	9.1	8.4	10.9	17.0
Colonia Mortgage Fund	1.7	6.7	.....	.....	.....	.....	.....	.....	.....	.....
Concorde Hypotheques	1.0	9.0	12.8	.....	.....	.....	.....	.....	.....	.....
Confed Mortgage Fund	1.3	8.2	10.2	14.5	9.5	9.1	8.7	8.6	10.5	16.5
CIBC Mortgage Investment Fund	1.2	9.1	14.5	17.1	7.2	9.4	7.6	8.8	10.3	15.3
First Canadian Mortgage Fund	0.9	8.5	13.9	19.1	7.7	8.9	9.1	9.1	11.4	18.2
Fonds Desjardins Hypotheques	2.2	7.8	10.7	14.7	8.5	9.0	9.4	.....	.....	.....
General Trust of Canada Mortgage	8.1	7.3	13.3	15.3	8.0	8.0	7.9	9.2	12.8	21.7
Great-West Life Mort. Investment	-0.6	9.2	15.7	13.3	3.5	10.8	7.8	6.7	12.5	18.8
Green Line Canadian Mortgage	1.0	9.1	12.5	16.2	9.4	9.8	9.7	8.5	10.5	13.7
Green Line Mortgage-Backed	1.1	6.8	11.6	15.0	11.8	.....	.....	.....	.....	.....
Hongkong Bank Mortgage Fund	7.5	.....	.....	.....	.....	.....	.....	.....	.....	.....
Industrial Alliance Ecoflex Fund H	1.0	.....	.....	.....	.....	.....	.....	.....	.....	.....
Industrial Mortgage Securities	-2.3	17.9	14.0	9.6	-1.0	12.9	13.0	12.5	17.6	30.3
Investors Income Portfolio Fund	-1.8	9.2	13.4	14.2	4.6	.....	.....	.....	.....	.....
Investors Mortgage Fund	-0.7	7.8	10.5	15.7	7.1	9.0	8.8	8.4	11.4	18.5
InvesNat Mortgage Fund	3.3	8.0	.....	.....	.....	.....	.....	.....	.....	.....
Ivy Mortgage Fund	.....	.....	.....	.....	.....	.....	.....	.....	.....	.....
London Life Mortgage	1.0	10.6	12.7	15.7	7.3	8.9	8.7	9.3	13.7	22.9
Mandate National Mortgage Corp.	.....	9.1	9.5	11.2	16.9	16.7	14.6	14.1	15.7	17.3
Montreal Trust Excelsior Mortgage	2.9	8.6	10.1	14.5	8.9	8.8	8.8	8.1	10.6	16.4
Mutual Premier Mortgage Fund	1.6	.....	.....	.....	.....	.....	.....	.....	.....	.....
National Trust Mortgage Fund	-0.2	.....	.....	.....	.....	.....	.....	.....	.....	.....
Ont. Teachers Grp Mortgage Inc	3.8	11.4	9.1	10.5	10.3	9.7	9.2	9.0	10.2	15.5
Royal Trust Mortgage Fund	-0.4	7.7	10.9	15.7	8.6	8.5	9.2	8.7	11.2	16.8
Royfund Mortgage Fund	3.4	9.4	.....	.....	.....	.....	.....	.....	.....	.....
Scotia Mortgage Fund	1.4	.....	.....	.....	.....	.....	.....	.....	.....	.....
Trust Pret & Revenu H Fund	0.1	9.1	12.0	15.7	7.6	9.2	8.5	9.6	10.7	17.5
United Canadian Mortgage Fund	-1.4	6.5	9.4	14.9	7.2	9.0	7.8	7.5	8.7	14.9
HIGHEST IN GROUP	8.1	17.9	15.7	19.1	16.9	16.7	14.6	14.1	17.6	30.3
AVERAGE IN GROUP	1.5	8.9	11.9	14.6	8.0	9.8	9.3	9.2	11.8	18.2
LOWEST IN GROUP	-2.3	6.5	9.1	9.6	-1.0	8.0	7.6	6.7	8.7	13.7
U.S. and International Bond Funds										
Altamira Global Bond Fund	.....	.....	.....	.....	.....	.....	.....	.....	.....	.....
AGF Global Government Bond	7.2	7.4	28.5	4.4	11.2	2.6	1.6	.....	.....	.....
AGF Strategic Income Fund	.....	16.5	14.1	3.5	-6.2	11.1	.....	.....	.....	.....
AGF U.S. Income Fund	1.4	.....	.....	.....	.....	.....	.....	.....	.....	.....
Bullock Global Bond 'A'	.....	.....	.....	.....	.....	.....	.....	.....	.....	.....
Bullock Global Bond 'B'	.....	.....	.....	.....	.....	.....	.....	.....	.....	.....
Bullock Global Bond 'C'	.....	.....	.....	.....	.....	.....	.....	.....	.....	.....
C.I. Global Bond RSP Fund	.....	.....	.....	.....	.....	.....	.....	.....	.....	.....
C.I. World Bond Fund	4.2	.....	.....	.....	.....	.....	.....	.....	.....	.....
Canada Life Int'l Bond S-36	.....	.....	.....	.....	.....	.....	.....	.....	.....	.....
Dynamic Global Bond Fund	11.3	11.4	25.3	-0.7	5.4	2.3	.....	.....	.....	.....
Fidelity Emerging Markets Bond	.....	.....	.....	.....	.....	.....	.....	.....	.....	.....
Fidelity Global Bond Fund	.....	.....	.....	.....	.....	.....	.....	.....	.....	.....
Fidelity North American Income	2.6	.....	.....	.....	.....	.....	.....	.....	.....	.....
First Cdn. International Bond Fund	.....	.....	.....	.....	.....	.....	.....	.....	.....	.....
Global Strategy Diversified Bond	-3.3	14.6	19.9	.....	.....	.....	.....	.....	.....	.....
Global Strategy World Bond Fund	-4.3	19.0	20.4	6.9	1.5	6.3	.....	.....	.....	.....
Green Line Global Gov't Bond	6.6	.....	.....	.....	.....	.....	.....	.....	.....	.....
Green Line Global RSP Bond Fund	.....	.....	.....	.....	.....	.....	.....	.....	.....	.....
Guardian International Income	3.1	16.1	17.2	3.9	3.4	2.1	-1.4	.....	.....	.....
Hercules World Bond Fund	.....	.....	.....	.....	.....	.....	.....	.....	.....	.....
Investors Global Bond Fund	7.1	.....	.....	.....	.....	.....	.....	.....	.....	.....
Lotus (MKW) International Bond	.....	.....	.....	.....	.....	.....	.....	.....	.....	.....
Optima Strat. Global Fixed Income	.....	.....	.....	.....	.....	.....	.....	.....	.....	.....
Regent World Income Fund	3.2	26.1	.....	.....	.....	.....	.....	.....	.....	.....

Fund	1994	1993	1992	1991	1990	1989	1988	1987	1986	1985
Royal Trust International Bond	6.9	20.6	.....	.....	.....	.....	.....	.....	.....	.....
Royfund International Income	10.7	.....	.....	.....	.....	.....	.....	.....	.....	.....
Scotia Canam Income Fund ($US)	-2.0	8.8	.....	.....	.....	.....	.....	.....	.....	.....
Spectrum International Bond Fund	8.9	.....	.....	.....	.....	.....	.....	.....	.....	.....
Talvest Foreign Pay Bond Fund	6.3	.....	.....	.....	.....	.....	.....	.....	.....	.....
Templeton Global Income Fund	3.3	11.5	16.8	10.0	9.7	.....	.....	.....	.....	.....
20/20 Foreign RSP Bond Fund	.....	.....	.....	.....	.....	.....	.....	.....	.....	.....
20/20 World Bond Fund	0.1	.....	.....	.....	.....	.....	.....	.....	.....	.....
HIGHEST IN GROUP	11.3	26.1	28.5	10.0	11.2	11.1	1.6	.....	.....	.....
AVERAGE IN GROUP	4.1	15.2	20.3	4.7	4.2	4.9	0.1	.....	.....	.....
LOWEST IN GROUP	-4.3	7.4	14.1	-0.7	-6.2	2.1	-1.4	.....	.....	.....

Canadian Money Market Funds

Fund	1994	1993	1992	1991	1990	1989	1988	1987	1986	1985
Admax Cash Performance Fund	3.1	.....	.....	.....	.....	.....	.....	.....	.....	.....
AGF Money Market Account	3.6	5.3	7.3	11.3	12.0	10.4	8.4	7.8	9.3	10.8
AMI Private Capital Money Market	4.4	5.9	7.9	11.4	11.4	9.6	.....	.....	.....	.....
Batirente - Sec. Marche Monetaire	3.7	5.5	8.7	12.8	9.7	9.7	.....	.....	.....	.....
Beutel Goodman Money Market	4.6	6.2	9.0	.....	.....	.....	.....	.....	.....	.....
Bissett Money Market Fund	4.5	5.9	.....	.....	.....	.....	.....	.....	.....	.....
BNP (Canada) Cdn Money Market	3.6	4.9	.....	.....	.....	.....	.....	.....	.....	.....
BPI Money Market Fund	3.1	4.4	6.6	10.5	12.1	8.8	7.6	7.0	.....	.....
BPI Short Term Interest Fund	.....	5.0	6.4	9.5	10.4	.....	.....	.....	.....	.....
BPI T-Bill Fund	.....	5.5	7.5	11.4	12.2	10.6	8.6	8.1	9.3	10.9
C.I. Money Market Fund	4.1	5.7	7.8	.....	.....	.....	.....	.....	.....	.....
C.I. Sector Short-Term	2.4	3.3	4.1	6.8	7.1	5.1	.....	.....	.....	.....
Canada Life Money Market S-29	4.0	5.3	7.2	11.7	11.1	9.9	7.1	6.0	7.7	10.0
Canada Trust Everest Money Mkt	3.6	4.6	7.6	11.9	12.6	11.5	8.1	.....	.....	.....
Capstone Cash Management Fund	3.6	6.0	8.2	11.9	12.3	10.0	.....	.....	.....	.....
Colonia Money Market Fund	3.2	5.0	.....	.....	.....	.....	.....	.....	.....	.....
Concorde Monetaire	4.2	4.8	.....	.....	.....	.....	.....	.....	.....	.....
Cornerstone Gov Money	3.7	5.1	7.3	11.5	.....	.....	.....	.....	.....	.....
CDA Money Market Fund	3.9	5.8	8.0	11.8	12.0	10.8	8.2	7.5	9.6	11.0
CIBC Canadian T-Bill Fund	3.1	4.6	6.7	.....	.....	.....	.....	.....	.....	.....
CIBC Money Market Fund	3.3	4.5	7.2	11.2	12.4	.....	.....	.....	.....	.....
CIBC Premium T-Bill Fund	3.8	5.3	7.3	.....	.....	.....	.....	.....	.....	.....
Dynamic Money Market Fund	3.7	5.1	7.5	12.0	11.7	8.9	8.0	7.2	8.9	10.3
Elliott & Page Money Fund	4.3	5.4	8.5	12.4	12.5	10.8	8.8	8.5	10.1	.....
Elliott & Page T-Bill Fund	.....	.....	.....	.....	.....	.....	.....	.....	.....	.....
Empire Money Market Fund	3.2	4.6	7.5	11.6	10.0	.....	.....	.....	.....	.....
Ethical Money Market Fund	3.6	5.3	7.2	11.4	12.7	10.5	8.6	7.7	9.2	10.8
Fidelity Short Term Asset Fund	3.3	4.9	7.4	.....	.....	.....	.....	.....	.....	.....
Finsco Money Market Fund	3.8	5.1	7.3	11.3	12.2	9.9	8.4	7.9	9.5	.....
Finsco T-Bill Fund	3.4	4.8	6.9	10.8	11.9	9.9	.....	.....	.....	.....
First Canadian Money Market	3.6	5.1	7.5	11.1	11.3	9.1	.....	.....	.....	.....
First Cdn. T-Bill Fund	.....	.....	.....	.....	.....	.....	.....	.....	.....	.....
Fonds de Prof. Short Term	3.9	6.0	9.7	12.8	9.6	9.9	.....	.....	.....	.....
Fonds Desjardins Monetaire	3.7	5.3	7.0	10.8	11.5	.....	.....	.....	.....	.....
Fonds Ficadre Money Market	3.7	5.9	7.5	11.1	.....	.....	.....	.....	.....	.....
General Trust of Cda Money Mkt	3.5	5.4	8.3	12.2	10.7	8.2	11.2	.....	.....	.....
Global Strategy T-Bill Savings Fund	4.1	5.7	7.5	10.2	11.5	9.6	.....	.....	.....	.....
Great-West Life Money Mkt Invest	3.1	4.6	6.9	10.9	12.0	9.9	7.8	7.0	8.9	10.7
Green Line Canadian Money Mkt	4.2	5.5	8.1	11.7	12.7	10.4	.....	.....	.....	.....
Green Line Canadian T-Bill Fund	3.8	4.9	.....	.....	.....	.....	.....	.....	.....	.....
Guardian Canadian Money Mkt	3.9	5.4	7.2	11.8	13.0	10.9	8.7	7.7	9.3	10.7
GBC Money Market Fund	4.0	5.6	7.5	11.6	12.4	.....	.....	.....	.....	.....
Hongkong Bank Money Market	3.5	5.0	6.5	10.7	11.4	.....	.....	.....	.....	.....
HRL Instant $$ Fund	4.2	5.3	7.5	11.6	12.1	10.5	.....	.....	.....	.....
Imperial Growth Money Market	3.0	4.9	6.2	10.8	10.1	.....	.....	.....	.....	.....
Industrial Alliance Ecoflex Fund M	12.9	-4.7	.....	.....	.....	.....	.....	.....	.....	.....
Industrial Cash Management	4.0	5.6	7.5	11.6	12.5	10.9	8.1	7.8	9.4	.....

Fund	1994	1993	1992	1991	1990	1989	1988	1987	1986	1985
Industrial Short-Term Fund	3.1	4.3	6.4	.....	.....	.....	.....	.....	.....	.....
Integra Short Term Investment	5.2	.....	.....	.....	.....	.....	.....	.....	.....	.....
Investors Money Market Fund	3.6	5.0	7.0	11.2	11.9	10.1	8.3	7.3	9.0	.....
InvesNat Money Market Fund	3.7	5.3	7.5	.....	.....	.....	.....	.....	.....	.....
Ivy Short-Term Fund	3.1	.....	.....	.....	.....	.....	.....	.....	.....	.....
Laurentian Money Market Fund	3.5	5.0	7.0	11.1	11.9	10.7	8.4	8.0	9.4	.....
Leith Wheeler Money Market	.....	.....	.....	.....	.....	.....	.....	.....	.....	.....
London Life Money Market	3.4	5.2	10.4	11.6	11.5	.....	.....	.....	.....	.....
Lotus (MKW) Income Fund	4.2	5.3	7.9	12.1	13.2	10.9	.....	.....	.....	.....
Mackenzie Sentinel Cda Money Mkt	4.0	5.5	7.6	11.6	11.8	9.2	8.2	.....	.....	.....
Manulife Vistafund 1 Sht Term Sec	3.1	4.9	7.5	11.6	11.9	10.2	8.0	7.6	8.9	10.4
Manulife Vistafund 2 Sht Term Sec	2.3	4.1	6.7	10.7	11.1	9.4	7.2	6.8	8.1	9.6
Maritime Life Money Market Fund	3.0	4.4	7.9	10.6	11.0	9.3	7.4	7.3	9.2	9.7
Mawer Canadian Money Market	3.7	5.3	7.3	11.2	12.1	9.9	.....	.....	.....	.....
McLean Budden Money Market	3.9	4.9	7.3	11.1	11.9	.....	.....	.....	.....	.....
Metlife MVP Money Market Fund	3.1	4.1	.....	.....	.....	.....	.....	.....	.....	.....
Montreal Trust Exc. Money Mkt	3.8	5.1	7.3	11.3	11.9	10.2	.....	.....	.....	.....
Mutual Money Market	3.8	5.2	6.9	10.7	11.5	9.8	7.7	6.8	8.7	.....
MD Money Fund	4.0	5.4	7.6	11.4	11.6	9.3	7.6	7.1	9.0	10.5
Natcan Treasury Bill Fund	3.8	5.4	7.5	.....	.....	.....	.....	.....	.....	.....
National Life Money Market Fund	4.7	6.2	.....	.....	.....	.....	.....	.....	.....	.....
National Trust Money Market	3.5	5.3	7.0	.....	.....	.....	.....	.....	.....	.....
NAL-Investor Money Market Fund	3.2	5.1	7.3	11.2	12.3	.....	.....	.....	.....	.....
NN Money Market Fund	4.0	5.7	7.8	11.6	.....	.....	.....	.....	.....	.....
NN T-Bill Fund	3.1	5.0	7.7	11.0	9.7	8.7	.....	.....	.....	.....
Ont.Teachers Group Fixed Value	4.3	8.6	8.3	11.1	11.1	9.8	8.7	7.6	9.1	10.5
Optimum Fonds d'Epargne	3.9	5.6	9.0	13.2	9.6	10.0	8.3	9.0	.....	.....
OHA Short Term Fund	4.2	.....	.....	.....	.....	.....	.....	.....	.....	.....
Prudential Money Mkt Fd of Can.	4.4	5.7	8.2	11.9	12.2	10.0	8.8	.....	.....	.....
Pursuit Money Market Fund	4.6	6.7	8.0	12.7	11.0	9.5	.....	.....	.....	.....
PH & N Canadian Money Market	4.1	5.8	7.9	11.7	12.7	10.6	8.3	.....	.....	.....
Royal Life Money Market Fund	5.0	.....	.....	.....	.....	.....	.....	.....	.....	.....
Royal Trust Canadian Money Mkt	3.4	4.8	7.4	11.4	11.4	9.7	.....	.....	.....	.....
Royal Trust Cdn T-Bill Money Mkt	2.7	3.9	.....	.....	.....	.....	.....	.....	.....	.....
Royfund Canadian T-Bill Fund	3.7	5.2	7.8	.....	.....	.....	.....	.....	.....	.....
Royfund Money Market Fund	3.4	5.1	7.8	11.4	12.2	10.0	7.8	.....	.....	.....
Sceptre Money Market Fund	3.9	5.7	7.4	11.5	12.1	10.0	.....	.....	.....	.....
Scotia Gov. of Can. Treasury Bill	3.8	4.7	.....	.....	.....	.....	.....	.....	.....	.....
Scotia Money Market Fund	3.7	4.7	7.3	.....	.....	.....	.....	.....	.....	.....
Scotia Premium T-Bill Fund	4.1	.....	.....	.....	.....	.....	.....	.....	.....	.....
Spectrum Cash Reserve Fund	3.7	5.0	7.2	11.2	12.1	10.3	8.0	.....	.....	.....
Spectrum Savings Fund	3.8	4.9	7.4	11.4	12.3	10.6	.....	.....	.....	.....
Standard Life Ideal Money Market	.....	.....	.....	.....	.....	.....	.....	.....	.....	.....
Standard Life Money Market Fund	3.4	.....	.....	.....	.....	.....	.....	.....	.....	.....
Strata Money Market Fund	3.6	5.0	7.0	10.8	11.3	.....	.....	.....	.....	.....
Talvest Money Fund	4.3	5.7	8.1	12.1	12.2	10.8	7.8	2.7	.....	.....
Templeton Treasury Bill Fund	3.9	5.3	7.4	11.4	12.2	10.2	.....	.....	.....	.....
Trans-Canada Money Market	4.5	5.2	7.7	11.2	10.8	.....	.....	.....	.....	.....
Trimark Interest Fund	3.8	5.5	7.3	11.6	12.8	9.6	8.6	.....	.....	.....
Trust Pret & Revenu Money Mkt	4.1	5.3	7.3	11.4	11.1	.....	.....	.....	.....	.....
United Canadian Interest Fund	4.8	6.1	8.5	11.6	12.9	11.6	.....	.....	.....	.....
20/20 Money Market Fund	4.3	5.8	8.0	10.9	.....	.....	.....	.....	.....	.....
HIGHEST IN GROUP	12.9	8.6	10.4	13.2	13.2	11.6	11.2	9.0	10.1	11.0
AVERAGE IN GROUP	3.9	5.1	7.5	11.4	11.6	9.9	8.2	7.3	9.1	10.5
LOWEST IN GROUP	2.3	-4.7	4.1	6.8	7.1	5.1	7.1	2.7	7.7	9.6

U.S. and International Money Market Funds

Fund	1994	1993	1992	1991	1990	1989	1988	1987	1986	1985
Altamira Short Term Global Inc	11.6	8.8	16.2	.....	.....	.....	.....	.....	.....	.....
AGF U.S. Dollar Money Market	2.7	2.8	4.4	6.7	8.7	.....	.....	.....	.....	.....
BNP (Canada) US$ Money Mkt	2.1	1.9	.....	.....	.....	.....	.....	.....	.....	.....

Fund	1994	1993	1992	1991	1990	1989	1988	1987	1986	1985
CIBC U.S. Dollar Money Mkt ($US)	2.3	2.3	4.0	.....	.....	.....	.....	.....	.....	.....
Finsco U.S. Money Mkt Fund ($US)	2.5	2.2	3.9	6.5	7.9	7.2	6.3	.....	.....	.....
Global Strategy Diversified Savings	3.5	6.8	13.6	5.9	9.4	5.9	.....	.....	.....	.....
Global Strategy U.S. Savings ($US)	2.8	2.6	4.1	6.1	7.2	7.3	.....	.....	.....	.....
Green Line U.S. Money Mkt ($US)	2.3	2.4	4.2	6.6	7.8	8.1	.....	.....	.....	.....
Guardian U.S. Money Mkt ($US)	2.7	2.6	4.3	6.7	8.4	8.7	5.9	5.8	.....	.....
Hercules Global Short-Term Fund	.....	.....	.....	.....	.....	.....	.....	.....	.....	.....
InvesNat U.S. Money Mkt $US	2.1	2.1	.....	.....	.....	.....	.....	.....	.....	.....
PH & N $US Money Market	2.9	2.9	4.7	.....	.....	.....	.....	.....	.....	.....
Royal Trust U.S. Money Mkt ($US)	2.2	2.3	4.0	.....	.....	.....	.....	.....	.....	.....
Royfund U.S. Dollar Money ($US)	2.3	2.2	4.0	.....	.....	.....	.....	.....	.....	.....
United U.S. Dollar Money Market	2.9	2.7	2.5	4.7	7.4	9.4	.....	.....	.....	.....
HIGHEST IN GROUP	11.6	8.8	16.2	6.7	9.4	9.4	6.3	5.8	.....	.....
AVERAGE IN GROUP	3.2	3.2	5.8	6.2	8.1	7.8	6.1	5.8	.....	.....
LOWEST IN GROUP	2.1	1.9	2.5	4.7	7.2	5.9	5.9	5.8	.....	.....

Dividend Funds

Fund	1994	1993	1992	1991	1990	1989	1988	1987	1986	1985
AGF High Income Fund	3.6	6.6	14.9	7.9	6.7	7.4	3.6	7.6	10.2	15.1
Bissett Dividend Income Fund	3.5	.....	5.3	2.9	-0.1	7.9	.....	.....	.....	.....
BPI Income Fund	1.6	6.2	3.9	9.8	0.1	9.2	3.1	9.7	7.6	13.4
Corporate Investors Ltd.	6.8	14.5	10.5	1.7	-2.6	10.3	-2.0	22.3	2.4	27.7
CIBC Equity Income Fund	-1.4	18.1	.....	.....	.....	.....	.....	.....	.....	.....
Dynamic Dividend Fund	3.0	14.6	9.6	7.2	2.0	10.1	5.8	11.1	.....	.....
Dynamic Dividend Growth Fund	5.2	13.5	9.7	-2.6	0.8	12.6	0.5	5.5	.....	.....
Fonds Desjardins Dividendes	.....	.....	.....	.....	.....	.....	.....	.....	.....	.....
Green Line Dividend Fund	1.4	13.8	11.7	13.4	0.1	13.3	.....	.....	.....	.....
Guardian Preferred Dividend Fund	1.0	12.5	10.1	5.7	1.6	8.4	4.0	9.1	.....	.....
Industrial Dividend Fund Ltd.	7.1	40.0	-8.3	-8.7	-5.8	2.7	6.1	27.4	16.5	33.2
Investors Dividend Fund	0.6	11.3	12.0	10.6	1.5	12.9	3.6	9.9	9.8	24.2
Investors Mutual of Canada Ltd.	4.3	21.5	6.4	5.8	-0.6	11.6	-1.9	18.4	12.7	21.6
Laurentian Dividend Fund Ltd.	1.0	11.0	8.0	6.2	1.8	14.0	3.6	11.6	15.2	23.5
Mawer Canadian Income Fund	-1.0	.....	.....	.....	.....	.....	.....	.....	.....	.....
Montreal Trust Excelsior Dividend	2.6	13.2	6.0	9.3	1.4	10.0	-0.2	.....	.....	.....
MD Dividend Fund	2.7	.....	.....	.....	.....	.....	.....	.....	.....	.....
National Trust Dividend Fund	4.1	.....	.....	.....	.....	.....	.....	.....	.....	.....
NatCan Dividend Fund	2.4	.....	.....	.....	.....	.....	.....	.....	.....	.....
PH&N Div. Income	5.4	14.7	5.7	5.3	3.5	14.7	2.0	18.8	10.2	20.3
Prudential Dividend Fund of Cda	9.2	34.8	6.1	5.5	-11.8	8.0	6.3	.....	.....	.....
Royal Trust Growth and Income	0.2	10.8	4.7	5.5	-0.6	8.2	0.7	7.2	.....	.....
Royfund Dividend Fund	2.2	.....	.....	.....	.....	.....	.....	.....	.....	.....
Spectrum Dividend Fund	2.5	9.7	4.9	8.9	1.9	12.7	3.4	.....	.....	.....
Trans-Canada Income Fund	6.5	5.0	-7.0	5.0	-2.0	10.9	3.7	17.1	30.3	32.4
20/20 Dividend Fund	3.6	14.5	7.4	6.4	2.9	14.0	1.0	14.3	.....	.....
HIGHEST IN GROUP	9.2	40.0	14.9	13.4	6.7	14.7	6.3	27.4	30.3	33.2
AVERAGE IN GROUP	3.1	15.1	6.4	5.6	0.0	10.5	2.5	13.6	12.8	23.5
LOWEST IN GROUP	-1.4	5.0	-8.3	-8.7	-11.8	2.7	-2.0	5.5	2.4	13.4

Benchmarks

	1994	1993	1992	1991	1990	1989	1988	1987	1986	1985
91-Day Canada T-Bill	4.8	6.5	7.3	10.9	12.8	11.1	8.7	8.0	9.3	10.7
Consumer Price Index	0.0	1.8	1.3	6.1	4.5	4.9	4.1	4.6	4.1	4.0
ScotiaMcLeod Universe Bond Index	-0.8	13.2	20.1	15.3	2.8	12.3	8.7	8.4	18.2	31.9
Standard & Poor's 500 Index(Cdn$)	9.3	21.5	15.2	0.3	11.9	18.9	-5.7	20.6	38.2	34.9
TSE Total Return Index	3.9	20.8	1.1	1.9	-2.4	13.5	-5.2	24.6	17.4	26.7

Survey of Fund Volatility and Compound Performance

(for periods ending June 30, 1994)

This survey provides the total return for the year ended June 30, 1994 and the average annual compound return over three, five and ten years. The star-rating used by the *Financial Times of Canada* ranks funds on their average monthly performance over the past 36 months. The top 10% in a category earn five stars. The bottom 10% earn one star. The variation in a fund's monthly rate of return, the standard deviation, is used to rank the volatility of funds in a category from HIGH to LOW. Under the column labelled RRSP: "R" = 100% eligible for an RRSP or RRIF, "F" = eligible as foreign content, "N" = not eligible at all. Under the column labelled Fees: N = no sales fees, F = front-end load, D = deferred load, O = option, B = both, usually a front-end and back-end fee but can be a redemption fee and a deferred load. MER represents the management expense ratio. An "m" indicates the ratio represents the management fee only. An * indicates additional fees might be charged directly to the investor.

Return	Vol.	Fund	RRSP	Fees	MER	1yr	3yr	5yr	10yr
Canadian Equity Funds									
★★	AV-	20/20 Canadian Growth Fund	R	O	2.50*	7.9	6.8	6.0	NA
NA	NA	20/20 RSP Aggressive Equity	R	O	2.50*	NA	NA	NA	NA
★★★★★	HIGH	ABC Fundamental Value Fund	R	N	2.00	38.2	32.4	25.7	NA
★★	AV-	Admax Cdn Performance Fund	R	O	2.46*	-2.5	6.1	NA	NA
★★	AV-	AGF Canadian Equity Fund	R	O	2.38*	1.2	6.7	1.8	7.9
★★★★	AV+	AGF Growth Equity Fund Ltd.	R	O	2.38*	3.0	23.2	12.9	12.0
★★★★	AV+	AIC Advantage Fund	R	D	2.73*	10.1	18.8	12.1	NA
★★★	AV-	All-Canadian CapitalFund	R	F	2.00*	7.8	9.8	7.0	8.0
★★★	AV-	All-Canadian Compound	R	N	0.00*	8.1	9.7	7.0	8.0
NA	NA	All-Canadian ConsumerFund	R	F	1.97*	5.7	NA	NA	NA
★★★★	AV+	Altafund Investment Corp.	R	N	2.28*	2.3	23.1	NA	NA
★★★★	AV	Altamira Capital Growth Fund	R	N	2.03*	6.6	15.5	11.0	10.4
★★★★★	AV+	Altamira Equity Fund	R	N	2.37*	0.4	29.8	24.0	NA
NA	NA	Altamira N. American Recovery	R	N	2.37*	NA	NA	NA	NA
★★★★	AV+	Altamira Special Growth Fund	R	N	1.81*	-9.8	23.2	17.4	NA
★★	AV-	AMI Private Capital Equity	R	N	1.75*	4.3	6.5	2.4	NA
★	LOW	Associate Investors Ltd.	R	N	2.06	0.2	5.6	3.3	8.6
★	LOW	Batirente - Section Actions	R	N	1.61	-0.8	2.2	0.1	NA
★	AV	Beutel Goodman Cdn Equity	R	N	2.50*	8.3	4.7	NA	NA
★★★	LOW	Bissett Canadian Equity Fund	R	N	1.41	0.2	11.5	8.3	10.9
NA	NA	Bissett Small Cap Fund	R	N	1.5.0	6.7	NA	NA	NA
NA	NA	BNP (Canada) Equity Fund	R	N	2.45	-2.8	NA	NA	NA
★★	AV+	BPI Canadian Equity Fund	R	O	2.81*	-3.5	7.9	3.6	NA
★★★	LOW	BPI Cdn Equity Value Fund	R	O	2.45*	-3.7	9.7	7.2	NA
★★★★	AV	BPI Canadian Small Cap Fund	R	O	2.60*	-1.6	17.1	10.0	NA

Return	Vol.	Fund	RRSP	Fees	MER	1yr	3yr	5yr	10yr
★★★★	AV	Bullock Growth Fund	R	O	2.25	2.4	15.1	8.1	8.2
NA	NA	C.I. Canadian Growth Fund	R	O	2.45	7.3	NA	NA	NA
★★★	AV+	C.I. Sector Canadian Fund	F	O	2.45	6.4	9.2	2.4	NA
★	AV-	CAMAF	R	N	1.31*	-1.8	3.4	2.5	8.6
★★★★	AV+	Cambridge Growth Fund	R	O	2.66*	-4.4	14.2	10.6	15.8
★★★	HIGH	Cambridge Special Equity	R	O	2.66*	-14.8	8.5	0.2	NA
★★	AV-	Canada Life Cdn Equity S-9	R	R	2.00	0.9	7.8	3.6	10.0
★★★★	AV+	Canada Trust Everest Spec. Eqty	R	N	2.09	-5.3	13.9	8.7	NA
★★★	AV-	Canada Trust Everest Stock	R	N	1.94	0.8	11.3	7.2	NA
★★★	AV-	Canada Trust Investment -Eqty	R	N	1.25	-0.1	8.4	5.4	NA
★	LOW	Canadian Investment Fund	R	O	2.25	-0.1	2.3	1.2	6.3
★★★	LOW	Canadian Protected Fund	R	R	2.10	-5.1	8.8	7.9	NA
★	LOW	CCPE Growth Fund R	R	N	1.31	4.8	4.4	2.8	NA
NA	NA	CDA Aggressive Equity Fund	R	N	1.00	NA	NA	NA	NA
★★★	AV-	CDA Common Stock Fund	R	N	0.87	3.2	9.6	6.2	11.8
★	AV-	Chou RRSP Fund	R	F	2.44*	3.1	5.8	2.2	NA
★	AV	CIBC Canadian Equity Fund	R	N	2.25*	-4.7	1.9	2.0	NA
NA	NA	CIBC Capital Appreciation	R	N	2.50*	-6.2	NA	NA	NA
NA	NA	Clean Environment Equity	R	O	2.98*	5.0	NA	NA	NA
NA	NA	Colonia Equity Fund	R	D	2.00	-3.3	NA	NA	NA
NA	NA	Colonia Special Growth Fund	R	D	2.00	NA	NA	NA	NA
NA	NA	Concorde Croissance	R	O	2.10	1.5	NA	NA	NA
★★	AV-	Confed Equity Fund	R	N	2.00	3.3	7.8	2.9	8.8
★★	LOW	Confed Growth Fund	R	F	2.00	4.8	8.2	3.3	9.7
★★★	AV-	Confed Life B	R	F	0.96	4.0	8.8	4.0	10.0
★★★	AV-	Cornerstone Cdn Growth	R	N	2.13*	-3.9	8.8	4.0	NA
★★★★	AV+	Corporate Investors Stock Fund	R	F	2.45*	-1.5	15.3	8.2	6.6
★★	AV	Cundill Security Fund	R	F	2.16*	17.9	7.4	3.0	8.1
★★★★★	HIGH	Dynamic Cdn Growth Fund	R	O	2.75*	1.7	30.8	19.9	NA
★★★★	AV+	Dynamic Fund of Canada	R	O	2.56*	-6.9	14.4	9.2	11.8
★★★★	AV+	Elliott & Page Equity Fund	R	O	1.75*	-2.0	12.3	7.6	NA
★★★	LOW	Empire Elite Equity Fund 5	R	D	2.59	-1.7	9.5	5.4	10.0
★★★	AV	Empire Equity Growth Fund 3	R	F	1.30	3.5	9.9	6.2	12.2
★★★	LOW	Empire Premier Equity Fund 1	R	F	1.56	1.6	8.9	5.5	11.4
NA	NA	Equitable Life Cdn Stock Fund	R	D	2.25	4.0	NA	NA	NA
★★	LOW	Equitable Life Seg. Common Stk	R	F	1.04m*	6.9	7.6	3.6	8.4
★	LOW	Ethical Growth Fund	R	O	2.39*	-1.7	5.1	5.3	NA
★★	AV	Fidelity Capital Builder Fund	R	O	2.21*	-2.9	6.3	6.8	NA
★★	AV	First Canadian Equity Index	R	N	1.44*	2.4	6.4	2.9	NA
NA	NA	First Cdn. Growth Fund	R	N	2.20*	NA	NA	NA	NA
NA	NA	First Cdn. Special Growth Fund	R	N	2.24*	NA	NA	NA	NA
★	LOW	Fonds de Prof. Cdn. Equity	R	N	0.75	-1.7	3.9	2.4	NA
★	AV	Fonds Desjardins Actions	R	N	1.98	-3.1	5.0	2.6	NA
NA	NA	Fonds Desjardins Croissance	R	N	1.80m	NA	NA	NA	NA
★	AV+	Fonds Desjardins Environnement	R	N	1.98	0.2	4.1	NA	NA
★	AV	Fonds Ficadre Actions	R	R	2.75	3.0	5.8	-0.4	NA
★★★★	AV+	GBC Canadian Growth Fund	R	N	1.96	-4.1	18.7	16.3	NA
★	AV-	General Trust of Canada Cdn Equity	R	N	1.50	-1.1	2.9	1.0	6.4
★★★★	AV	General Trust of Canada Growth	R	N	1.83	-2.6	18.0	8.6	NA
NA	NA	Global Strategy Cda Growth	R	O	2.89	0.7	NA	NA	NA
★★★	AV-	Great-West Life Cdn Equity	R	N	2.64	-3.0	11.3	7.8	NA
★	AV	Great-West Life Equity Index	R	N	2.64	1.6	5.9	2.7	7.5
★	LOW	Green Line Blue Chip Equity	R	N	2.27	0.1	4.9	3.1	NA
★★	AV	Green Line Cdn Equity Fund	R	N	2.15	1.7	8.0	3.8	NA

Return	Vol.	Fund	RRSP	Fees	MER	1yr	3yr	5yr	10yr
★★	AV	Green Line Canadian Index	R	N	1.06	2.7	6.9	3.4	NA
NA	NA	Green Line Value Fund	R	N	2.14	NA	NA	NA	NA
★	LOW	Guardian Canadian Equity	R	O	2.64*	-2.4	5.1	1.7	7.4
★★	LOW	Guardian Enterprise Fund	R	O	2.60*	-0.2	7.4	5.9	8.5
★★★★	LOW	Guardian Growth Equity Fund	R	O	2.54*	1.2	15.3	11.2	NA
★★★	AV	Gyro Equity Fund	R	N	0.90*	-2.0	9.1	4.5	NA
★★★★	AV+	Hongkong Bank Equity Fund	R	N	1.53*	4.7	14.1	8.4	NA
★	AV	HRL Canadian Fund	R	N	1.75	1.6	3.8	3.4	NA
NA	NA	Hyperion Aurora Trust	R	F	2.50	NA	NA	NA	NA
★★★	LOW	Imperial Growth Cdn Equity	R	F	2.10	1.5	8.5	4.4	14.4
NA	NA	Industrial Alliance Ecoflex A	R	R	2.00*	6.1	NA	NA	NA
★★★★★	AV+	Industrial Equity Fund Ltd.	R	O	2.63*	3.6	25.7	8.6	10.2
★★★	AV+	Industrial Future Fund	R	O	2.55*	5.3	11.1	5.8	NA
★★	AV+	Industrial Growth Fund	R	O	2.48*	4.2	8.0	3.9	10.0
★★	AV	Industrial Horizon Fund	R	O	2.48*	6.2	8.0	4.5	NA
★★★	AV+	Industrial Pension Fund	R	O	2.59*	11.4	9.2	1.6	8.6
NA	NA	Industrial Strat. Cap Protection	R	O	2.00m*	3.5	NA	NA	NA
★★	AV-	InvesNat Equity Fund	R	N	2.18*	-2.1	7.4	5.3	NA
★★★★	LOW	Investors Canadian Equity	R	B	2.08	5.3	12.3	8.8	10.7
★★★	LOW	Investors Rtmt Gth. Portfolio	R	B	0.18	6.3	8.7	5.9	NA
★★	LOW	Investors Rtmt Mutual Fund	R	B	2.08	5.3	7.2	4.1	9.6
★★	LOW	Investors Summa Fund Ltd.	R	B	2.09	3.2	7.6	4.2	NA
NA	NA	Ivy Canadian Fund	R	O	2.00m*	3.8	NA	NA	NA
NA	NA	Ivy Capital Protection 1994	R	O	2.00m*	NA	NA	NA	NA
NA	NA	Ivy Capital Protection Fund	R	O	2.00m*	-0.7	NA	NA	NA
★	LOW	Jarislowsky Finsco Cdn Equity	R	F	2.41*	1.9	2.4	2.0	NA
★★★★	AV+	Jones Heward Fund Ltd.	R	O	2.50	-5.1	13.5	6.7	10.8
★	AV-	Laurentian Cdn Equity Fund	R	O	2.70*	-0.5	5.6	1.2	7.4
★★★	AV-	Laurentian Special Equity Fund	R	O	2.70*	11.7	12.3	NA	NA
NA	NA	Leith Wheeler Cdn Equity Fund	R	N	1.40m*	NA	NA	NA	NA
★★★	AV	London Life Canadian Equity	R	R	1.50*	-1.5	9.8	4.2	10.1
NA	NA	Lotus Canadian Equity Fund	R	N	2.00*	NA	NA	NA	NA
★★	AV+	Mackenzie Equity Fund	R	O	2.00*	9.9	8.2	1.5	8.7
★★★★	AV+	Mackenzie Sentinel Cda Equity	R	O	2.36*	13.3	15.2	6.5	NA
★★★★	AV	Manulife Vista 1 Cap. Gains Gth	R	F	1.63*	-2.7	12.6	7.9	10.7
★★★	AV	Manulife Vista 1 Equity Fund	R	F	1.63*	-0.5	8.3	5.3	8.0
★★★	AV	Manulife Vista 2 Cap. Gains Gth	R	R	2.38*	-3.4	11.7	7.1	9.8
★★	AV	Manulife Vista 2 Equity Fund	R	R	2.38*	-1.2	7.5	4.5	7.2
★★★★★	HIGH	Marathon Equity Fund	R	N	2.50	11.3	42.7	20.4	NA
★★	AV	Maritime Life Growth Fund	R	N	2.01*	-2.6	6.8	3.0	8.5
NA	NA	Mawer Canadian Equity Fund	R	N	1.64	-2.7	NA	NA	NA
★★★★	AV-	Mawer New Canada Fund	R	N	1.59	16.2	22.5	17.1	NA
★★★	AV-	McLean Budden Eqty Growth	R	N	1.75	1.0	8.6	4.6	NA
★★★	AV-	MD Equity Fund	R	N	1.00	11.0	12.2	7.2	12.5
NA	NA	MD Select Fund	R	N	1.00	NA	NA	NA	NA
★	AV-	Metlife MVP Equity Fund	R	R	2.00m	1.1	3.5	1.7	NA
NA	NA	Metlife MVP Growth Fund	R	R	2.00m	10.6	NA	NA	NA
★★★★	HIGH	Middlefield Growth Fund	R	O	3.14	-10.2	14.0	NA	NA
★★	AV	Montreal Trust Excelsior Equity	R	N	2.08	5.9	7.5	5.2	8.8
★★★★★	HIGH	Multiple Opportunities Fund	R	F	2.73*	47.0	33.8	24.0	NA
★	AV	Mutual Canadian Indexfund	R	F	1.95	3.5	3.9	2.4	NA
★	AV-	Mutual Equifund	R	F	1.80	0.8	4.4	0.5	NA
NA	NA	Mutual Premier Blue Chip	R	N	2.31	1.0	NA	NA	NA
NA	NA	Mutual Premier Growth Fund	R	N	2.29	2.6	NA	NA	NA

Return	Vol.	Fund	RRSP	Fees	MER	1yr	3yr	5yr	10yr
★	AV	NAL-Investor Equity Fund	R	B	1.75	-4.5	4.5	3.3	NA
NA	NA	NatCan Canadian Equity Fund	R	N	1.53*	-1.9	NA	NA	NA
★★★	AV	National Life Equities Fund	R	D	2.00m	6.0	10.6	7.4	12.0
★	AV	National Trust Cdn Eqty Fund	R	N	1.70	-4.3	6.0	5.1	9.2
NA	NA	National Trust Special Eqty	R	N	2.70	-0.9	NA	NA	NA
★	AV	NN Canadian 35 Index	R	R	2.00*	3.2	3.5	2.1	NA
★	AV-	NN Canadian Growth	R	R	2.25*	0.5	5.5	2.8	6.9
NA	NA	OHA Canadian Equity Fund	R	N	0.50*	-15.1	NA	NA	NA
★	AV-	Ont. Teachers Grp Diversified	R	N	0.90	1.4	4.8	2.5	9.3
★	LOW	Ont. Teachers Group Growth	R	N	0.90	1.7	4.6	2.8	10.0
★★	LOW	Optima Strategy Cdn Equity	R	O	0.39*	7.6	6.1	3.3	8.0
NA	NA	Optimum Fonds d'Actions	R	N	1.50m*	NA	NA	NA	NA
★★	LOW	PH&N RSP/RIF Eqt.	R	N	1.24	6.4	7.7	5.8	11.0
★★	AV-	PH&N Cdn. Equity	R	N	1.16	5.7	6.6	5.0	11.0
★★★	LOW	PH&N Vintage	R	F	1.79	4.9	11.8	11.8	NA
★	LOW	Polymetric Performance Fund	R	O	2.45*	-1.1	1.7	NA	NA
★★★★	AV+	Prudential Growth Canada Ltd.	R	F	1.75*	-7.9	14.6	7.5	10.6
★★★	AV-	Pursuit Canadian Equity Fund	R	F	2.00*	-3.1	10.4	6.2	NA
NA	NA	Resolute Growth Fund	R	F	1.00	NA	NA	NA	NA
★★	LOW	Royal Life Equity Fund	R	D	2.37	5.0	7.2	NA	NA
NA	NA	Royal Trust Cdn Special Grth	R	N	2.05*	0.9	NA	NA	NA
★★	LOW	Royal Trust Canadian Stock	R	N	1.93*	2.5	7.1	3.8	7.9
★★★	AV-	Royfund Equity Ltd.	R	N	2.03	5.0	9.7	4.4	9.8
NA	NA	Royfund Growth Fund	R	N	2.19	0.7	NA	NA	NA
★★★★	AV	Saxon Small Cap	R	N	1.75	6.8	16.1	5.9	NA
★★★★	AV+	Saxon Stock Fund	R	N	1.75	-2.0	14.1	7.4	NA
★★★	AV	Sceptre Equity Fund	R	N	2.00*	22.7	11.3	7.3	NA
★★	AV-	Scotia Canadian Equity Growth	R	N	2.15	-3.0	6.9	5.1	NA
★	LOW	Spectrum Canadian Equity	R	O	1.99	3.9	5.5	2.9	NA
NA	NA	Standard Life Equity Mutual	R	N	2.00	4.5	NA	NA	NA
★★	LOW	Standard Life Ideal Equity Fund	R	D	2.00	4.0	7.4	5.6	NA
NA	NA	Strata Canadian Fund	R	N	2.48*	NA	NA	NA	NA
★★	AV	Strata Growth Fund	R	F	1.53	0.7	7.6	4.0	NA
★	AV-	Talvest Growth Fund Inc.	R	O	2.40*	1.3	4.7	4.6	9.6
NA	NA	Talvest New Economy	R	O	2.50*	NA	NA	NA	NA
★★	AV	Templeton Heritage Rtmt Fund	R	O	2.98	10.4	6.7	3.1	NA
★	AV-	Top Fifty Equity Fund	R	F	2.35*	-2.4	2.9	1.0	NA
★★	LOW	Tradex Equity Fund Ltd.	R	N	1.35*	5.8	7.3	4.6	9.6
★	AV+	Trans-Canada Equity Fund	R	O	2.66*	-0.4	5.9	3.6	12.6
★★	HIGH	Trans-Canada Pension Fund	R	O	2.66*	2.6	8.1	6.4	9.7
★★★★	AV-	Trimark Canadian Fund	R	F	1.56*	10.7	13.7	9.7	13.4
★★★	LOW	Trimark RSP Equity Fund	R	D	2.00*	8.8	10.9	8.3	NA
NA	NA	Trimark Select Cdn Growth	R	O	2.60*	9.2	NA	NA	NA
★★★	AV	Trust Pret & Revenu Cdn Fund	R	N	1.80*	-0.8	9.5	5.5	6.3
★★★★	AV-	United Canadian Equity Fund	R	O	2.21*	5.5	14.0	9.2	12.5
★★★★	AV+	United Canadian Growth Fund	R	O	2.29*	4.6	18.5	8.7	11.6
★★★	AV+	Universal Cdn Equity Fund Ltd.	R	O	2.70*	10.5	11.4	3.7	10.6
★★★★★	AV+	University Avenue Cdn Fund	R	N	2.72	-4.1	23.9	NA	NA
NA	NA	Working Opportunity Fund	R	N		1.6	NA	NA	NA
★	LOW	Working Ventures Cdn Fund	R	R	2.23*	1.2	3.0	NA	NA
		HIGHEST IN GROUP				47.0	42.7	25.7	15.8
		AVERAGE IN GROUP				2.4	10.2	6.0	9.7
		LOWEST IN GROUP				-15.1	1.7	-0.4	6.3

Return	Vol.	Fund	RRSP	Fees	MER	1yr	3yr	5yr	10yr
Special Equity Funds									
★★★	AV	AGF Canadian Resources Fund	R	O	2.52*	-9.2	24.2	14.4	8.0
★★	AV+	All-Canadian Resources Corp	R	F	1.94*	11.3	16.9	4.2	3.8
★★★★★	AV-	Altamira Resource Fund	R	N	2.36*	-5.7	42.5	NA	NA
★★★	AV-	BPI Canadian Resource Fund	R	O	2.50*	-9.4	26.3	16.8	10.2
NA	NA	BPI Global Real Estate Sec	F	O	2.00m	NA	NA	NA	NA
★★★	HIGH	Cambridge Resource Fund	R	O	2.66*	-19.9	26.1	11.1	9.8
NA	NA	CIS Global Telecommunications	R	F	2.40*	NA	NA	NA	NA
★★★★	AV+	Dominion Equity Resource	R	R	1.80	-17.6	30.3	16.2	NA
★★★★	AV+	Dynamic Precious Metals Fund	R	O	2.86*	23.1	28.3	16.0	NA
NA	NA	First Cdn. Resource Fund	R	N	2.26*	NA	NA	NA	NA
★★	AV-	First Heritage Fund	R	F	6.25*	-3.8	13.4	4.2	NA
NA	NA	Global Strategy Div. Gold Plus	R	O	2.59	NA	NA	NA	NA
★★★	AV+	Goldfund Ltd.	F	F	3.38	34.6	27.1	16.0	7.8
★★	AV	Goldtrust	R	F	2.48	22.0	24.2	13.8	7.8
NA	NA	Green Line Resource Fund	R	N	2.20	NA	NA	NA	NA
NA	NA	Green Line Science & Tech.	F	N	2.56	NA	NA	NA	NA
★	LOW	Investors Real Property Fund	R	B	2.13	-0.3	-0.1	2.4	6.2
★★	AV-	MD Realty Fund A Units	R	N	1.50m	-4.6	-12.4	-5.2	2.8
★	AV-	MD Realty Fund B Units	F	N	1.50m	-1.1	-12.0	-5.0	2.5
★★★★	AV	Prudential Natural Resource	R	F	1.77*	-7.8	33.4	20.5	NA
★★★	AV	Prudential Precious Metals	R	F	1.83*	15.4	24.5	12.8	NA
★	LOW	Royal Lepage Comm. Real Estate	R	N	3.24	-0.4	-1.8	2.0	NA
★★★	AV	Royal Trust Energy Fund	R	N	2.17*	-7.7	27.3	15.9	9.6
★★	LOW	Royal Trust Precious Metals	R	N	2.70*	1.0	12.7	5.1	NA
★	LOW	Roycom-Summit Realty Fund	F	D	3.70	10.0	5.5	7.2	NA
★	LOW	Roycom-Summit TDF Fund	R	D	3.29*	3.9	5.1	6.4	NA
NA	NA	Scotia CanAm Growth Fund	R	N	1.25m	NA	NA	NA	NA
NA	NA	Scotia Precious Metals Fund	R	N	1.99	NA	NA	NA	NA
★★★★	AV	Universal Canadian Resource	R	O	2.77*	-0.1	35.8	15.7	9.7
NA	NA	Universal Wld Precious Metals	F	O	2.00m*	NA	NA	NA	NA
		HIGHEST IN GROUP				34.6	42.5	20.5	10.2
		AVERAGE IN GROUP				1.6	18.0	9.5	7.1
		LOWEST IN GROUP				-19.9	-12.4	-5.2	2.5
U.S. Equity Funds									
NA	NA	20/20 Aggressive Growth	F	O	2.50*	8.7	NA	NA	NA
★★★	LOW	20/20 U.S. Growth Fund	F	O	2.48*	15.4	14.1	11.4	NA
★	AV+	Admax American Performance	F	O	2.49	2.0	5.2	NA	NA
★★★	AV	AGF American Growth Fund	F	O	2.29*	9.7	13.8	8.5	11.0
★★★	AV+	AGF Special Fund Ltd.	F	O	2.32*	7.8	13.3	10.5	12.1
★★★★	AV+	AIC Value Fund	F	D	2.81*	9.1	17.4	NA	NA
★★★★★	AV+	Altamira Select American Fund	F	N	2.35*	17.2	26.9	NA	NA
NA	NA	Altamira U.S. Larger Company	F	N	2.40*	NA	NA	NA	NA
★★★★	LOW	Beutel Goodman Am. Equity	F	N	4.50	11.3	16.0	NA	NA
★★	AV-	Bissett American Equity Fund	F	N	1.50	7.6	11.1	8.8	NA
★★★★★	AV	BPI American Equity Growth	F	O	3.10*	17.2	23.4	17.8	NA
★★	LOW	BPI American Equity Value	F	O	2.48*	7.3	11.3	9.6	NA
★★★	HIGH	Bullock American Fund	F	O	2.25	-1.4	13.4	18.7	16.9
NA	NA	Bullock Optimax U.S.A.'A'	F	F	2.21	NA	NA	NA	NA
NA	NA	Bullock Optimax U.S.A. 'B'	F	R	2.53	NA	NA	NA	NA
NA	NA	Bullock Optimax U.S.A. 'C'	F	N	2.77	NA	NA	NA	NA
NA	NA	C.I. American Fund	F	O	2.55	16.5	NA	NA	NA

Return	Vol.	Fund	RRSP	Fees	MER	1yr	3yr	5yr	10yr
NA	NA	C.I. Sector North American	F	O	2.55	16.0	NA	NA	NA
NA	NA	Cambridge American Growth	N	O	2.66*	1.4	NA	NA	NA
NA	NA	Cda Trust Everest AmeriGrowth	R	N	1.38	0.4	NA	NA	NA
★★	AV	Canada Trust Everest U.S. Eqty	F	N	2.11	0.6	8.6	NA	NA
★	AV	Cassels Blaikie American Fund	F	F	1.16	-5.9	2.5	7.2	13.3
★	LOW	Century DJ Fund	F	F	1.80	2.8	5.6	7.5	NA
★★★	AV-	Chou Associates Fund	F	F	2.06*	4.8	15.0	8.9	NA
★★★	AV-	CIBC U.S. Equity Fund	F	N	2.50*	3.6	12.2	NA	NA
★★	AV	Cornerstone U.S. Fund	F	N	2.20*	7.8	10.8	9.5	7.0
★★	AV	Dynamic American Fund	F	O	2.56*	4.3	10.5	6.8	11.3
★★	AV	Elliott & Page Am. Growth	F	O	1.73*	8.6	10.8	9.1	8.9
★	LOW	Ethical North American Equity	F	O	2.55*	3.6	7.9	4.6	8.2
★★★★	AV	Fidelity Growth America Fund	F	O	2.18*	8.6	19.8	NA	NA
NA	NA	Fidelity Small Cap America	F	O	2.33*	NA	NA	NA	NA
NA	NA	First American	R	R	2.30	-7.4	NA	NA	NA
NA	NA	First Cdn. U.S. Growth Fund	F	N	2.20*	NA	NA	NA	NA
★★★★	AV+	GBC North American Growth	F	N	1.84	4.6	21.3	10.6	12.2
★★★★	HIGH	General Trust of Canada U.S. Eqty	F	N	1.62	2.8	18.6	13.0	14.0
★	LOW	Global Strategy Div. Americas	R	O	2.91	-3.0	4.1	4.1	NA
NA	NA	Global Strategy U.S. Growth	F	O	2.84	-3.2	NA	NA	NA
★	LOW	Green Line US Index ($US)	N	N	0.55	0.6	7.7	8.4	NA
★★★★	AV+	Guardian American Equity	F	O	2.99*	11.8	16.8	13.1	10.6
★★★★	AV+	Guardian North American	F		2.61*	11.9	17.0	11.2	8.0
★★★	AV	Guardian Vantage U.S. Equity	F		2.79*	9.4	14.3	12.3	NA
★★★	AV+	Hyperion Value Line Eqty Trust	F	O	3.00	-3.3	15.3	NA	NA
★★★	AV-	Imperial Growth Nth Am. Eqt.	F	F	1.62	11.8	13.6	4.0	9.6
★★★	AV	Industrial American Fund	F	O	2.48*	11.0	13.5	9.3	11.9
NA	NA	InvesNat American Eqty (US$)	F	N	2.66*	-4.3	NA	NA	NA
★★★★	LOW	Investors U.S. Growth Fund	F	B	2.03	15.9	18.7	14.3	13.8
★	AV-	Jarislowsky Finsco American	F	F	2.41	1.9	8.2	8.0	NA
★★★	AV	Jones Heward American Fund	F	O	2.50	2.6	12.3	9.1	11.4
★★	AV	Laurentian American Equity	F	O	2.70	8.5	11.7	6.3	11.6
NA	NA	Leith Wheeler U.S. Equity Fund	F	N	1.25m*	NA	NA	NA	NA
★★★	AV-	London Life U.S. Equity	F	R	1.50*	4.9	12.4	5.0	NA
★★★	AV-	Mackenzie Sentinel Am. Eqty	F		2.48*	9.1	12.2	8.4	NA
★	LOW	Margin of Safety Fund	N	N	1.91	7.6	8.5	9.3	NA
NA	NA	Mawer U.S. Equity Fund	F	N	2.07	4.7	NA	NA	NA
★★	AV	McLean Budden Am. Growth	F	N	1.75	6.2	9.9	12.4	NA
NA	NA	MD U.S. Equity Fund	F	N	1.00	9.6	NA	NA	NA
NA	NA	Metlife MVP U.S. Equity Fund	N	R	2.00m	7.2	NA	NA	NA
★★	AV	Mutual Amerifund	F	F	2.06	9.2	10.8	6.5	NA
NA	NA	Mutual Premier American Fund	N	N	2.35	9.0	NA	NA	NA
NA	NA	NAL-Investor U.S. Equity Fund	F	B	2.25	NA	NA	NA	NA
NA	NA	NatCan American Eqty ($US)	F	N	1.82*	0.3	NA	NA	NA
NA	NA	National Trust Am. Eqty Fund	F	N	2.48	4.9	NA	NA	NA
NA	NA	NN Can-Am Fund	R	R	2.25*	-0.5	NA	NA	NA
NA	NA	Optima Strategy U.S. Equity	F	O	0.18*	NA	NA	NA	NA
★★★	AV	PH&N U.S. Equity	F	N	1.13	12.4	16.0	15.1	14.2
NA	NA	Prosperity Am. Performance	F	O	2.50	NA	NA	NA	NA
★	AV	Pursuit American Fund ($US)	F	F	2.00*	-7.3	-0.3	7.3	NA
★★★	AV	Royal Trust American Stock	F	N	1.87*	8.7	13.7	12.1	12.5
NA	NA	Royal Trust Zweig Strat. Grth	F	N	2.50*	13.1	NA	NA	NA
NA	NA	Royfund U.S. Equity Fund	F	N	2.29	11.1	NA	NA	NA
★★★	LOW	Scotia American Equity Grth	F	N	2.30	11.3	12.0	10.8	NA
★★★	AV	Talvest U.S. Growth Fund Ltd.	F	O	2.25*	4.8	12.0	13.0	11.8

Return	Vol.	Fund	RRSP	Fees	MER	1yr	3yr	5yr	10yr
NA	NA	Top Fifty U.S. Equity Fund	F	F	2.54	-3.1	NA	NA	NA
★★	AV-	Trust Pret & Revenu American	F	N	2.40*	4.6	10.7	9.7	10.3
NA	NA	U.S. Polymetric Performance	F	O	2.40	3.1	NA	NA	NA
★★★	AV-	United American Growth	F	O	2.18*	7.3	14.2	11.4	12.0
NA	NA	Universal U.S. Emerging Grth	F	O	3.03*	3.6	NA	NA	NA
★	AV-	University Avenue Growth	F	N	2.83	-0.5	-4.3	-2.1	NA
		HIGHEST IN GROUP				17.2	26.9	18.7	16.9
		AVERAGE IN GROUP				5.9	12.3	9.5	11.5
		LOWEST IN GROUP				-7.4	-4.3	-2.1	7.0

International Equity Funds

Return	Vol.	Fund	RRSP	Fees	MER	1yr	3yr	5yr	10yr
NA	NA	20/20 Asia Pacific Fund	F	O	2.50*	29.5	NA	NA	NA
NA	NA	20/20 Latin America	F	O	3.50	NA	NA	NA	NA
NA	NA	20/20 Multimanager Em. Mkts	F	O	2.50m*	NA	NA	NA	NA
NA	NA	20/20 RSP Int'l Equity Alloc.	R	O	2.50*	NA	NA	NA	NA
NA	NA	Admax Global Health Sciences	F	O	2.49	16.2	NA	NA	NA
NA	NA	AGF Asian Growth Fund	F	O	2.65*	38.7	NA	NA	NA
NA	NA	AGF China Focus Fund Ltd. 'A'	F	F	2.00m*	NA	NA	NA	NA
NA	NA	AGF China Focus 'B & C'	F	D	2.50m*	NA	NA	NA	NA
NA	NA	AGF European Growth 'B & C'	F	D	2.50m*	NA	NA	NA	NA
NA	NA	AGF European Growth 'A'	F	F	2.00m*	NA	NA	NA	NA
★★	AV+	AGF Japan Fund Ltd.	F	O	2.53*	21.8	12.1	6.5	14.7
NA	NA	AIC World Fund	F	D	2.75m	NA	NA	NA	NA
NA	NA	Altamira Asia Pacific Fund	F	N	2.38*	31.4	NA	NA	NA
★★	AV-	Altamira Diversified Fund	F	N	2.00*	17.9	12.4	3.0	NA
NA	NA	Altamira European Equity Fund	F	N	2.35*	NA	NA	NA	NA
NA	NA	Beutel Goodman Intrn'l Equity	F	N	3.30	37.5	NA	NA	NA
★★★	LOW	BPI Global Equity Fund	F	O	3.40*	23.1	15.4	12.0	NA
NA	NA	BPI Global Small Companies	F	O	2.17*	43.1	NA	NA	NA
★★★	LOW	BPI International Equity Fund	F	O	2.46*	19.6	15.1	12.2	NA
NA	NA	Bullock Asian Dynasty 'A'	F	F	2.12	NA	NA	NA	NA
NA	NA	Bullock Asian Dynasty 'B'	F	R	2.42	NA	NA	NA	NA
NA	NA	Bullock Asian Dynasty 'C'	F	N	2.72	NA	NA	NA	NA
NA	NA	Bullock Emerging Markets 'A'	F	F	2.10	NA	NA	NA	NA
NA	NA	Bullock Emerging Markets 'B'	F	R	2.42	NA	NA	NA	NA
NA	NA	Bullock Emerging Markets 'C'	F	N	2.68	NA	NA	NA	NA
NA	NA	C.I. Emerging Asian Fund	F	O	2.85	NA	NA	NA	NA
NA	NA	C.I. Emerging Markets Fund	F	O	2.85	30.5	NA	NA	NA
NA	NA	C.I. European Fund	F	O	2.55	13.7	NA	NA	NA
NA	NA	C.I. Global Equity RSP Fund	R	O	2.60	NA	NA	NA	NA
★★★★	AV	C.I. Global Fund	F	O	2.60	19.6	19.5	14.1	NA
NA	NA	C.I. Latin American Fund	F	O	2.85	NA	NA	NA	NA
★★★★	AV+	C.I. Pacific Fund	F	O	2.60	36.3	25.1	17.2	20.7
NA	NA	C.I. Sector Emerging Markets	F	O	2.85	29.9	NA	NA	NA
NA	NA	C.I. Sector European Fund	F	O	2.55	13.3	NA	NA	NA
★★★★	AV-	C.I. Sector Global Fund	F	O	2.60	19.5	19.2	13.8	NA
★★★★	AV+	C.I. Sector Pacific Fund	F	O	2.60	35.7	24.8	16.9	NA
NA	NA	Caldwell Securities Intern'l	F	D	3.20	19.9	NA	NA	NA
★	AV+	Cambridge Americas Fund	N	O	2.66*	-1.6	10.3	8.1	NA
★★	AV+	Cambridge Global Fund	N	O	2.66*	8.5	11.9	4.9	11.5
★	AV+	Cambridge Pacific Fund	N	O	2.66*	14.3	10.8	10.3	NA
★★★	LOW	Canada Life U.S.&Int. Eqty S-34	F	R	2.00	18.9	19.1	14.6	15.1
NA	NA	Cda Trust Everest AsiaGrowth	R	N	1.30	NA	NA	NA	NA
NA	NA	Cda Trust Everest EuroGrowth	R	N	1.30	NA	NA	NA	NA
★★	LOW	Cda Trust Everest International	F	N	2.67	25.0	12.9	11.4	NA
★	LOW	Cda Trust Everest N. American	F	N	2.14	-1.0	10.5	6.3	9.3

Return	Vol.	Fund	RRSP	Fees	MER	1yr	3yr	5yr	10yr
★★★	AV-	Capstone Int. Investment Trust	F	N	2.00*	13.0	15.0	12.7	NA
★	AV	Cassels Blaikie International	N	F	1.88	18.2	9.4	4.3	NA
NA	NA	CIBC Far East Prosperity Fund	F	N	2.75	NA	NA	NA	NA
★★★	LOW	CIBC Global Equity Fund	F	N	2.50*	14.7	15.7	9.4	NA
NA	NA	Clean Environment Int'l Equity	F	O	2.00m*	NA	NA	NA	NA
★★	AV	Cornerstone Global Fund	F	N	2.54*	20.5	14.8	12.2	NA
★★★★	LOW	Cundill Value Fund Ltd.	F	F	2.04	23.4	19.2	10.2	12.4
★	AV	Dynamic Europe 1992 Fund	F	O	3.10*	21.2	9.0	NA	NA
NA	NA	Dynamic Far East Fund	N	O	2.60*	NA	NA	NA	NA
★	AV	Dynamic Global Green Fund	F	O	3.41*	-8.3	4.5	3.3	NA
NA	NA	Dynamic Global Partners Fund	F	O	2.60*	NA	NA	NA	NA
★★★	AV	Dynamic International Fund	F	O	2.75*	8.5	15.1	8.8	NA
★★★	LOW	Empire International Fund	F	O	2.59	15.7	16.6	13.1	NA
NA	NA	Fidelity European Growth Fund	F	O	2.63*	22.7	NA	NA	NA
NA	NA	Fidelity Far East Fund	F	O	2.54*	24.7	NA	NA	NA
★★★	AV-	Fidelity International Portfolio	F	O	2.57*	19.7	17.6	13.1	NA
NA	NA	Fidelity Japanese Growth Fund	F	O	2.69*	NA	NA	NA	NA
NA	NA	Fidelity Latin Am. Growth	F	O	3.13*	NA	NA	NA	NA
★★★	AV	Finsco Global Fund	F	F	1.66	25.9	18.9	NA	NA
NA	NA	First Canadian Int'l Growth	F	N	1.88*	26.2	NA	NA	NA
NA	NA	Fonds de Prof. Int'l Equity	N	N	0.75	NA	NA	NA	NA
★★★	AV	Fonds Desjardins International	F	N	2.22	24.9	18.8	13.7	NA
★	AV+	GBC International Growth	F	N	1.31	13.6	9.0	NA	NA
★★★	AV-	General Trust of Canada Intl.	F	N	1.80	27.4	17.3	12.0	NA
NA	NA	Global Strategy Asia Fund	F	O	2.15	NA	NA	NA	NA
NA	NA	Global Strategy Div. Japan Plus	R	O	2.00m	NA	NA	NA	NA
NA	NA	Global Strategy Diversified Asia	R	O	1.25m	NA	NA	NA	NA
NA	NA	Global Strategy Div. Europe	R	O	2.84	6.0	NA	NA	NA
NA	NA	Global Strategy Div. Latin	R	O	2.25m	NA	NA	NA	NA
★	AV-	Global Strategy Europe	F	O	2.72	4.5	7.7	4.5	NA
★	AV	Global Strategy Fund	F	O	2.50	6.7	8.5	5.8	NA
★★	AV+	Global Strategy Japan Plus	F	O	2.90	20.1	11.4	8.3	NA
NA	NA	Global Strategy Latin Fund	F	O	2.25m	NA	NA	NA	NA
★	AV	Global Strategy Real Estate	F	D	2.91	1.4	1.6	NA	NA
NA	NA	Green Line Asian Growth Fund	F	N	2.46	NA	NA	NA	NA
NA	NA	Green Line Emerging Markets	F	N	2.97	27.8	NA	NA	NA
NA	NA	Green Line Global Select Fund	F	N	2.37	NA	NA	NA	NA
NA	NA	Green Line International Equity	F	N	2.37	27.5	NA	NA	NA
NA	NA	Green Line North Am. Growth	F	N	2.32	NA	NA	NA	NA
★	AV	Guardian Global Equity (EAFE)	F	O	2.52*	26.2	10.6	5.5	9.8
★★★	AV	Guardian Pacific Rim Corp.	F		2.80*	24.8	16.0	8.4	NA
NA	NA	Hercules European Value Fund	F	N	2.00m	NA	NA	NA	NA
NA	NA	Hercules Latin American Value	F	N	2.00m	NA	NA	NA	NA
NA	NA	Hercules N. Amer. Grth & Inc.	F	N	2.00m	NA	NA	NA	NA
NA	NA	Hercules Pacific Basin Value	F	N	2.00m	NA	NA	NA	NA
NA	NA	Hongkong Bank Asian Growth	F	N	2.32*	NA	NA	NA	NA
NA	NA	HRL Overseas Growth Fund	N	N	1.75m	24.7	NA	NA	NA
★★★★★	HIGH	Hyperion Asian Trust	F	O	3.25	42.0	27.0	NA	NA
★★★	AV	Hyperion European Trust	F	O	3.00	17.5	15.2	NA	NA
NA	NA	InvesNat Eur. Equity Fund	F	N	2.88*	27.6	NA	NA	NA
★★	AV	Investors Eur. Growth Fund	F	B	2.16	18.6	13.1	NA	NA
★★★	AV-	Investors Global Fund Ltd.	F	B	2.07	23.4	15.2	11.5	NA
★★★	AV-	Investors Growth Portfolio	F	B	0.18	17.7	16.2	10.7	NA
★★★	HIGH	Investors Japanese Growth	F	B	2.08	30.4	18.8	8.3	14.9
★★	LOW	Investors North Am. Growth	F	B	2.05	5.7	14.2	11.5	13.7

Return	Vol.	Fund	RRSP	Fees	MER	1yr	3yr	5yr	10yr
★★★★★	AV+	Investors Pacific International	F	B	2.24	43.6	28.6	NA	NA
★★★	AV	Investors Special Fund Ltd.	F	B	2.07	-0.6	14.9	13.2	12.7
NA	NA	Investors World Grth Portfolio	F	B	0.40	18.5	NA	NA	NA
NA	NA	Ivy Foreign Equity Fund	F	O	2.00m*	10.2	NA	NA	NA
★★	LOW	Laurentian Commonwealth	F	O	2.70	14.0	13.6	9.0	12.8
★	LOW	Laurentian Global Balanced	F	O	2.70	8.8	10.5	NA	NA
★★	AV-	Laurentian International Fund	F	O	2.70	18.0	14.5	9.4	11.2
★★	AV	Mackenzie Sentinel Global	F		2.55*	27.0	14.7	7.0	NA
★★★	AV-	Mawer World Investment	F	N	1.44	26.6	18.5	13.0	NA
★★★★	AV	MD Growth Investments Ltd.	F	N	1.00	28.4	21.5	12.3	15.8
★★★	AV	Montreal Trust Excelsior Intl	F	N	2.11	19.5	16.3	11.8	13.4
NA	NA	Mutual Premier International	N	N	2.33	23.5	NA	NA	NA
NA	NA	NAL-Investor Global Equity	F	B	2.50	29.6	NA	NA	NA
NA	NA	National Life Global Equities	F	D	2.40m	NA	NA	NA	NA
NA	NA	NN Can-Asian Fund	R	R	2.25*	NA	NA	NA	NA
NA	NA	OHA Foreign Equity Fund	F	N	0.50*	20.9	NA	NA	NA
★	LOW	Ontario Teachers Group Global	F	N	1.00	7.6	10.2	NA	NA
NA	NA	Optima Strategy Int'l Equity	F	O	0.18*	NA	NA	NA	NA
★★	LOW	Orbit World Fund	F	F	2.98	18.6	12.9	9.9	NA
NA	NA	PH&N North American Equity	F	N	1.27	7.3	NA	NA	NA
NA	NA	Regent Dragon 888 Fund	F	O	2.75	NA	NA	NA	NA
NA	NA	Regent Europa Performance	F	O	2.90	3.0	NA	NA	NA
★★★★	AV+	Regent International Fund	F	O	2.25	36.1	21.9	13.0	NA
NA	NA	Regent Korea Fund	F	O	3.75	32.7	NA	NA	NA
NA	NA	Regent Nippon Fund	F	O	3.50	11.2	NA	NA	NA
★★★★	AV	Regent Tiger Fund	F	O	3.39	38.1	22.1	NA	NA
NA	NA	Royal Trust Asian Growth Fund	F	N	2.29	NA	NA	NA	NA
★★★	AV+	Royal Trust European Growth	F	N	2.98	24.5	16.1	6.7	NA
★★	HIGH	Royal Trust Japanese Stock	F	N	3.10	32.4	13.5	5.0	NA
NA	NA	Royfund International Equity	F	N	2.47	24.6	NA	NA	NA
★★★	AV	Saxon World Growth	F	N	1.75	16.0	18.8	8.6	NA
NA	NA	Sceptre Asian Growth Fund	F	N	2.42*	50.3	NA	NA	NA
★★★★★	AV	Sceptre International Fund	F	N	2.00*	29.5	26.8	18.3	NA
NA	NA	Scotia Global Growth Fund	F	N	2.48	NA	NA	NA	NA
★	AV-	Special Opportunities Fund	F	F	2.13	6.7	6.0	NA	NA
★★★	AV	Spectrum International Equity	F	O	2.25	17.2	15.2	10.1	NA
★★★	AV-	Talvest Global Diversified Fund	F	O	2.75*	19.7	16.1	10.6	NA
NA	NA	Talvest Global Growth Fund	F	O	2.50*	19.1	NA	NA	NA
NA	NA	Templeton Emerging Markets	F	O	3.14	29.5	NA	NA	NA
★★★	AV-	Templeton Global Smaller Comp.	F	O	2.59	18.1	17.2	11.5	NA
★★★★	LOW	Templeton Growth Fund Ltd.	F	O	1.89*	23.9	22.6	14.5	15.1
★★★★	AV+	Templeton International Stock	F	O	2.54	32.8	25.6	15.0	NA
★★	AV	Total Return Fund Inc.	F	N	2.88	1.5	11.8	6.8	NA
NA	NA	Trimark - The Americas Fund	F	O	2.85*	11.7	NA	NA	NA
★★★★	AV	Trimark Fund	F	F	1.54*	23.2	23.9	15.8	16.6
★★★★	AV	Trimark Select Growth Fund	F	O	2.41*	19.2	21.7	15.0	NA
★	LOW	United American Equity Fund	F	O	2.50*	2.0	7.5	6.9	11.5
★★	AV-	United Global Equity Fund	F	O	2.60*	12.5	13.2	NA	NA
★★★	AV-	United Global Growth Fund	F	O	2.30*	21.0	18.6	6.8	8.1
NA	NA	United Global Telecomm.	F	O	0.03	NA	NA	NA	NA
★★★	AV	Universal Americas Fund	F	O	2.72*	12.1	15.8	11.2	12.8
NA	NA	Universal Far East Fund	F	O	2.00m*	NA	NA	NA	NA
NA	NA	Universal Japan Fund	F	O	2.00m*	NA	NA	NA	NA
NA	NA	Universal World Asset Alloc.	F	O	2.00m*	NA	NA	NA	NA
NA	NA	Universal World Emerging Grth	F	O	2.00m*	NA	NA	NA	NA

Return	Vol.	Fund	RRSP	Fees	MER	1yr	3yr	5yr	10yr
★★★	AV	Universal World Equity Fund	F	O	2.55*	29.0	15.9	7.8	NA
NA	NA	Vision Europe Fund	F	R	3.82	16.4	NA	NA	NA
		HIGHEST IN GROUP				50.3	28.6	18.3	20.7
		AVERAGE IN GROUP				20.4	15.6	10.3	13.3
		LOWEST IN GROUP				-8.3	1.6	3.0	8.1

Balanced Funds

Return	Vol.	Fund	RRSP	Fees	MER	1yr	3yr	5yr	10yr
★★★★	AV+	20/20 Am. Tactical Asset Alloc.	F	O	2.61*	4.6	14.9	10.6	NA
★★★	AV	20/20 Canadian Asset Alloc.	R	O	2.42*	4.6	8.2	7.3	NA
NA	NA	20/20 European Asset Alloc.	F	O	2.50*	NA	NA	NA	NA
★★★★★	HIGH	20/20 World Fund	F	O	2.57*	25.1	19.5	10.8	NA
★★★★★	HIGH	ABC Fully-Managed Fund	R	N	2.00	20.2	18.0	15.3	NA
NA	NA	Admax Asset Allocation Fund	R	O	2.45*	5.6	NA	NA	NA
★★★★	AV+	Altamira Balanced Fund	R	N	2.00*	-4.4	11.6	5.5	NA
★★★★	AV+	Altamira Growth & Income	R	N	1.41*	8.9	15.1	11.8	NA
★★	AV	AMI Private Capital Optimix	R	N	1.75*	2.0	7.9	6.0	NA
★★★	AV	Batirente - Section Diversifiee	R	N	1.61	-1.1	8.2	6.7	NA
★★★	AV	Beutel Goodman Balanced	R	N	2.20*	5.2	8.3	NA	NA
NA	NA	Bissett Retirement Fund	R	N	0.50	1.9	NA	NA	NA
★★★	AV-	BPI Balanced Fund	R	O	2.39*	-2.4	9.7	6.9	NA
★★★★★	AV	BPI Global Balanced Fund	R	O	3.28*	10.2	16.5	9.8	NA
NA	NA	BPI North American TAA RSP	R	O	2.57*	-2.8	NA	NA	NA
★★	AV+	BPI One Decision Balanced	R	O	3.29*	-2.1	8.0	5.8	NA
NA	NA	BPI World TAA RSP Fund	R	O	2.49*	5.3	NA	NA	NA
NA	NA	Bullock Asset Strategy Fund	R	O	2.25	1.6	NA	NA	NA
NA	NA	C.I. Canadian Balanced	R	O	2.30	8.4	NA	NA	NA
★★★	HIGH	Caldwell Securities Associate	R	D	2.34	16.8	10.2	NA	NA
★★★★	HIGH	Cambridge Balanced Fund	R	O	2.66*	-2.4	14.1	11.4	13.7
★★★	AV	Canada Life Mgd Fund S-35	R	R	2.00	1.3	9.0	6.4	10.5
★★★	AV	Canada Trust Everest Balanced	R	N	2.10	-0.5	8.9	7.4	NA
★★	AV-	Capstone Investment Trust	R	N	2.00*	3.6	7.4	7.6	9.4
★★★	LOW	Cassels Blaikie Canadian Fund	R	F	1.21	2.6	8.4	7.7	NA
★★	LOW	CCPE Div. Growth Fund R	R	N	1.31	2.8	7.6	6.5	NA
★★	AV-	CDA Balanced Fund	R	N	0.92	0.8	7.7	6.8	10.3
★	AV	CIBC Balanced Inc. & Growth	R	N	2.25*	-2.8	5.5	5.6	NA
NA	NA	CIS Commax Hedge Fund	R	F	2.40*	NA	NA	NA	NA
NA	NA	Clean Environment Balanced	R	O	2.97*	9.1	NA	NA	NA
NA	NA	Common Sense Asset Builder 1	R	D	2.10m*	NA	NA	NA	NA
★	AV	Cornerstone Balanced Fund	R	N	2.07*	-4.2	5.1	4.4	6.1
★★★★	AV+	Dynamic Managed Portfolio	R	O	1.04*	1.6	15.2	9.5	NA
★★★★★	AV	Dynamic Partners Fund	R	R	2.67*	6.7	19.7	13.6	NA
★★★★	AV+	Elliott & Page Balanced Fund	R	O	1.78*	2.4	12.1	8.8	NA
★★	LOW	Empire Balanced Fund	R	O	2.20	0.1	7.9	7.0	NA
★	LOW	Ethical Balanced Fund	R	O	2.30*	0.7	5.5	NA	NA
NA	NA	Fidelity Asset Manager Fund	F	O	2.76*	9.3	NA	NA	NA
★★	AV+	Fidelity Growth & Income	R	O	2.41*	4.3	7.4	5.8	NA
★	AV+	First Cdn. Asset Allocation	R	N	1.86*	-5.6	5.0	4.5	NA
★★★	LOW	Fonds de Prof. Balanced	R	N	0.75	0.3	8.1	8.3	10.2
★★	AV-	Fonds Desjardins Equilibre	R	N	1.98	1.0	7.9	6.6	NA
★	AV-	Fonds Ficadre Equilibre	R	R	2.37	2.4	6.6	5.2	8.6
★★	LOW	General Trust of Canada Bal.	R	N	1.66	-0.5	7.3	5.5	NA
★	AV+	Global Strategy Div. Grth	R	O	2.91	5.1	2.7	2.5	NA
NA	NA	Global Strategy Income Plus	R	O	1.99	5.7	NA	NA	NA
★★	AV-	Great-West Life Diversified RS	R	N	2.64	-0.8	7.8	6.4	NA

Return	Vol.	Fund	RRSP	Fees	MER	1yr	3yr	5yr	10yr
★★★	AV	Great-West Life Equity/Bond	R	N	2.64	-2.9	9.5	7.8	NA
★	AV	Green Line Balanced Growth	R	N	2.39	-4.2	5.2	4.1	NA
★	AV-	Green Line Balanced Income	R	N	2.39	-0.7	5.5	4.3	NA
★★★	LOW	Guardian Balanced Fund	R	O	1.88*	3.5	9.5	9.3	11.2
NA	NA	Guardian International Bal.	R	O	2.58*	NA	NA	NA	NA
★★★★	AV	Hongkong Bank Balanced	R	N	2.04*	2.2	12.2	9.0	NA
★	AV	HRL Balanced Fund	R	N	1.75	2.9	4.8	5.1	8.8
★	AV+	Hyperion Managed Trust	R	O	2.20	-2.3	5.5	6.4	NA
★★	LOW	Imperial Growth Diversified	R	F	2.00	0.8	7.3	6.3	NA
NA	NA	Industrial Alliance Ecoflex D	R	R	2.00*	2.3	NA	NA	NA
★★★	AV	Industrial Balanced Fund	R	O	2.55*	-0.5	8.2	NA	NA
★★★	AV	Industrial Income Fund	R	O	2.01*	-4.1	8.2	6.3	12.3
★★★	AV-	Integra Balanced Fund	R	N	2.15	1.9	10.2	7.3	NA
★★	LOW	InvesNat Retirement Balanced	R	N	2.97*	-3.0	6.6	5.7	NA
NA	NA	Investors Asset Allocation Fund	R	B	2.30	NA	NA	NA	NA
★★★★	LOW	Investors Growth Plus Portfolio	F	B	0.17	8.8	11.7	9.0	NA
★	LOW	Investors Income Plus Portfolio	R	B	0.17	-0.8	6.5	6.9	NA
★★★	LOW	Investors Rtmt Plus Portfolio	R	B	0.17	3.8	8.2	6.9	NA
★	LOW	Jarislowsky Finsco Balanced	R	F	1.82*	1.0	6.1	4.9	NA
★★★	AV	Jones Heward Canadian Bal'd	R	O	2.40	-2.6	10.9	8.0	9.1
★	LOW	Laurentian Canadian Balanced	R	O	2.70*	-0.8	5.4	5.3	NA
★★★	AV	Leith Wheeler Balanced Fund	R	N	1.10	4.5	10.0	8.0	NA
★★★	AV-	London Life Diversified	R	R	1.50*	-0.5	9.7	7.1	NA
★★★	AV	Lotus Fund	R	N	2.10*	-0.5	10.3	7.7	9.4
★★★	AV	Manulife Vista 1 Diversified	R	F	1.63*	-1.7	8.2	6.2	9.2
★★	AV	Manulife Vista 2 Diversified	R	R	2.38*	-2.5	7.4	5.4	8.4
★	AV-	Maritime Life Balanced Fund	R	N	2.03*	0.4	6.4	5.7	NA
★★★	AV-	Mawer Cdn. Bal. Rtmt Savings	R	N	0.94	-0.1	8.9	7.7	NA
★★	LOW	Mawer Cdn. Div'd Investment	F	N	1.02	-0.7	8.0	7.3	NA
★★★	AV	McLean Budden Balanced	R	N	1.75	-0.2	8.9	7.6	NA
NA	NA	MD Balanced Fund	R	N	1.00	4.4	NA	NA	NA
★	AV-	Metlife MVP Balanced Fund	R	R	2.00m	-0.3	5.4	4.8	NA
★★★★	AV+	Montreal Tr. Exc. Ttl Return	R	N	2.32	9.0	14.8	11.4	NA
★★★	AV-	Montreal Trust Exc. Balanced	R	N	2.33	4.1	8.7	8.7	NA
★	LOW	Mutual Diversifund 25	R	F	1.93	1.0	6.6	6.0	NA
★★	AV-	Mutual Diversifund 40	R	F	1.78	0.1	6.8	4.7	NA
★	AV	Mutual Diversifund 55	R	F	1.80	0.4	6.3	3.6	NA
★	AV	NAL-Investor Diversified Fund	R	B	1.75	-3.8	6.4	5.4	NA
NA	NA	National Life Balanced Fund	R	D	2.00m	2.5	NA	NA	NA
★★★	AV	National Trust Balanced Fund	R	N	2.09	-1.8	8.2	NA	NA
★★	AV-	NN Balanced Fund	R	R	2.25*	0.7	7.6	5.7	NA
NA	NA	OHA Balanced Fund	R	N	0.50*	-5.4	NA	NA	NA
★★★	AV-	Ontario Teachers Grp Balanced	R	N	0.90	1.8	8.0	6.9	NA
★★★	AV	Optimum Fonds Equilibre	R	N	1.50m*	-0.4	8.6	6.8	NA
★★★	LOW	PH&N Bal Pens Trust	R	N		5.0	10.3	9.2	NA
NA	NA	PH&N Balanced	R	N		4.4	NA	NA	NA
★★★★	AV	Protected American Fund	R	R	2.10	-3.2	12.2	10.8	NA
★★★★	AV+	Prudential Diversified Invest	R	F	1.51*	-4.7	11.3	8.1	NA
★★	AV	Royal Life Balanced Fund	R	D	2.34	0.1	6.9	NA	NA
★★★	LOW	Royal Trust Adv. Balanced	R	N	1.68*	2.3	9.0	7.7	NA
★★	AV	Royal Trust Adv. Growth	R	N	1.97*	-2.9	6.9	5.9	NA
★★★	LOW	Royal Trust Adv. Income Fund	R	N	1.69*	1.7	8.8	8.1	NA
★★★★	AV-	Royfund Balanced Fund	R	N	2.25	3.6	11.9	8.7	NA

Return	Vol.	Fund	RRSP	Fees	MER	1yr	3yr	5yr	10yr
★★★★	AV+	Saxon Balanced Fund	R	N	1.75	-1.0	13.4	6.8	NA
★★★	AV-	Sceptre Balanced Fund	R	N	1.62*	6.2	9.8	7.8	NA
★	LOW	Scotia Stock & Bond Fund	R	N	2.09	0.5	5.8	4.4	NA
★	AV	Spectrum Diversified Fund	R	O	2.25	-2.4	6.4	5.3	NA
NA	NA	Standard Life Balanced Mutual	R	N	2.00	-0.9	NA	NA	NA
★★★	AV-	Standard Life Ideal Balanced	R	D	2.00	0.9	9.0	7.6	NA
NA	NA	Strata Tactical Fund	R	N	2.45*	NA	NA	NA	NA
★★	AV+	Stratafund 40	R	F	1.54	-1.8	8.0	6.6	NA
★★★	AV+	Stratafund 60	R	F	1.54	-0.1	8.2	5.9	NA
★★	AV	Talvest Diversified Fund	R	O	2.42*	3.4	7.7	6.9	NA
NA	NA	Talvest U.S. Diversified Fund	F	O	2.25*	3.7	NA	NA	NA
★★★	AV+	Templeton Balanced Fund	R	F	2.57	7.6	8.6	NA	NA
★★★★	AV	Trimark Income Growth Fund	R	F	1.75*	6.0	12.1	9.2	NA
★★★★	AV	Trimark Select Balanced Fund	R	O	2.39*	5.3	11.7	NA	NA
★★★	AV	Trust Pret & Revenu Rtmt	R	N	1.70*	-0.2	9.3	8.1	9.2
★★★★	AV	United Cdn Portfolio of Funds	R	O	0.94*	1.6	10.9	8.5	NA
★★★	AV-	United Global Portf. of Funds	F	O	0.70*	2.6	10.3	8.1	NA
NA	NA	Universal World Bal'd RRSP	R	O	2.00m*	NA	NA	NA	NA
		HIGHEST IN GROUP				25.1	19.7	15.3	13.7
		AVERAGE IN GROUP				1.8	9.0	7.2	9.8
		LOWEST IN GROUP				-5.6	2.7	2.5	6.1

Canadian Bond Funds

Return	Vol.	Fund	RRSP	Fees	MER	1yr	3yr	5yr	10yr
★	LOW	Admax Canadian Income Fund	R	O	2.05*	0.1	6.4	6.5	NA
★★★★	AV+	AGF Canadian Bond Fund	R	O	1.37*	-3.9	10.3	8.4	11.7
★★★★	HIGH	Altamira Bond Fund	R	N	1.33*	-5.6	10.0	9.0	NA
★★★★★	AV+	Altamira Income Fund	R	N	1.00*	-3.1	11.2	10.8	11.9
★★★	AV	AMI Private Capital Income	R	N	1.25*	-1.7	8.9	8.5	NA
★★★★★	AV+	Batirente - Section Obligations	R	N	1.61	-2.2	10.6	8.8	NA
★★★	AV	Beutel Goodman Income Fund	R	N	1.40*	-3.4	8.6	NA	NA
★★★★	AV-	Bissett Bond Fund	R	N	0.75	0.3	8.9	8.7	NA
NA	NA	BNP (Canada) Bond Fund	R	N	1.68	-1.8	NA	NA	NA
★★	AV	BPI Bond Fund	R	O	2.25*	-3.9	7.6	7.6	NA
★★	LOW	BPI Canadian Bond Fund	R	O	3.00*	1.4	7.5	7.2	NA
★★★	AV	BPI RSP Bond Fund	R	F	1.50*	-3.0	8.5	8.4	NA
NA	NA	C.I. Canadian Bond Fund	R	O	1.70	-1.3	NA	NA	NA
★★★	AV	Canada Life Fixed Income S-19	R	R	2.00	-2.1	8.3	8.1	10.2
★★★★	AV	Canada Trust Everest Bond	R	N	1.32	-2.8	9.1	8.6	NA
★★★	AV-	Canada Trust Inc. Investments	R		1.08	-0.9	8.4	8.3	NA
★	HIGH	Canada Trust Inv. Fund-Inc.	R	N	1.25	-5.3	7.2	7.1	NA
★★★★	LOW	CCPE Fixed Income Fund	R	N	1.31	-0.1	10.3	9.5	NA
★★★	LOW	CDA Bond and Mortgage Fund	R	N	0.86	-0.4	8.9	9.2	10.8
★★	AV+	CIBC Canadian Bond Fund	R	N	1.50*	-7.2	8.0	7.8	NA
NA	NA	CIBC Canadian Income Fund	R	N	0.85*	NA	NA	NA	NA
NA	NA	Clean Environment Income	R	O	2.39*	NA	NA	NA	NA
NA	NA	Colonia Bond Fund	R	D	1.50	-0.2	NA	NA	NA
NA	NA	Concorde Revenu	R	O	2.35	-2.5	NA	NA	NA
★★★	AV-	Confed Fixed Income	R	N	2.00	-2.5	8.2	7.7	12.3
★★★	AV-	Confed Life C	R	F	1.44	-2.2	8.7	8.2	12.8
★★★	AV	Cornerstone Bond Fund	R	N	1.36*	-1.8	8.2	9.1	NA
NA	NA	Dynamic Government Income	R	F	0.85*	NA	NA	NA	NA
★★★★★	LOW	Dynamic Income Fund	R	O	1.68*	8.5	12.5	10.7	12.5
★	AV-	Elliott & Page Bond Fund	R	O	1.53*	-4.9	6.8	7.6	NA

Return	Vol.	Fund	RRSP	Fees	MER	1yr	3yr	5yr	10yr
★★	AV-	Empire Bond Fund	R	O	2.20	-2.0	8.1	8.1	NA
NA	NA	Equitable Life Canadian Bond	R	D	2.00	-1.9	NA	NA	NA
★★★★	AV-	Equitable Life Seg. Accum Inc	R	F		-1.7	9.5	9.9	11.8
★	LOW	Ethical Income Fund	R	O	1.70*	-2.0	5.0	7.5	9.2
★★★	AV-	Fidelity Government Bond	R	O	2.06*	0.3	8.7	7.4	NA
★★★	AV+	First Canadian Bond Fund	R	N	1.41*	-2.9	8.8	8.1	NA
★★	LOW	Fonds de Professionnels Bond	R	N	0.75	-2.0	8.1	8.6	10.5
★★	AV-	Fonds Desjardins Obligations	R	N	1.66	-2.3	7.8	7.6	10.5
★	AV-	Fonds Ficadre Obligations	R	R	1.82	-3.3	7.2	7.5	NA
★★★★	AV	GBC Canadian Bond Fund	R	N	1.14	-1.9	9.8	8.9	NA
★★★	AV-	General Trust of Canada Bond	R	N	1.30	-2.8	8.9	8.1	11.3
NA	NA	Global Strategy Bond Fund	R	O	0.63m	NA	NA	NA	NA
★★	AV	Great-West Life Cdn Bond	R	N	2.40	-3.6	8.0	7.4	10.0
★★★	AV	Green Line Canadian Bond	R	N	0.91	-3.3	8.6	8.1	NA
★★	AV	Green Line Cdn Govt. Bond	R	N	2.07	-2.4	7.5	6.5	NA
★	LOW	Green Line Short Term Income	R	N	1.18	-0.4	4.7	7.4	NA
★	LOW	Guardian Canada Bond Fund	R	O	0.01	0.8	5.3	7.6	NA
★★★★	AV	Gyro Bond Fund	R	N	1.30*	-2.1	9.6	NA	NA
★	AV-	HRL Bond Fund	R	N	1.50	-3.2	7.4	6.9	NA
★★	AV+	Hyperion Fixed Income Trust	R	O	2.10	-7.4	7.8	NA	NA
NA	NA	Industrial Alliance Ecoflex B	R	R	2.00*	-3.5	NA	NA	NA
★★	AV+	Industrial Bond Fund	R	O	2.22*	-5.2	8.0	7.5	NA
★★★	LOW	InvesNat Bond Fund	R	N	1.40*	0.0	8.6	8.5	NA
★★	AV-	Investors Bond Fund	R	R	1.82	-2.6	8.0	8.1	10.9
NA	NA	Investors Corporate Bond Fund	R	R	1.80	NA	NA	NA	NA
NA	NA	Ivy Growth & Income Fund	R	O	1.75m*	-1.0	NA	NA	NA
★★★	LOW	Jarislowsky Finsco Bond Fund	R	F	1.92*	-1.4	8.9	7.9	NA
★	AV	Jones Heward Bond Fund	R	O	1.75	-3.8	7.5	7.4	NA
★	LOW	Laurentian Government Bond	R	O	2.20*	-0.3	7.0	7.8	NA
★★	LOW	Laurentian Income Fund	R	O	2.20*	-2.3	7.7	7.6	10.9
NA	NA	Leith Wheeler Fixed Income	R	N	0.75m*	NA	NA	NA	NA
★★★	AV	London Life Bond	R	R	1.50*	-3.1	8.3	6.6	11.3
NA	NA	Lotus Bond Fund	R	N	1.25m*	NA	NA	NA	NA
★★★	AV+	Mackenzie Sentinel Cda Bond	R	O	1.78*	-5.8	8.5	7.6	NA
★★★	AV+	Manulife Vistafund 1 Bond	R	F	1.63*	-5.9	8.2	8.3	10.6
★	AV+	Manulife Vistafund 2 Bond	R	R	2.38*	-6.6	7.4	7.5	9.8
★★★	AV	Maritime Life Bond Fund	R	N	1.98*	-2.5	8.2	NA	NA
NA	NA	Mawer Canadian Bond Fund	R	N	0.96	-2.5	NA	NA	NA
★★★	AV	McLean Budden Fixed Income	R	N	1.30	-2.4	8.8	9.1	NA
★★★★	AV-	MD Bond Fund	R	N	1.00	-1.0	9.5	9.1	NA
★	AV-	Metlife MVP Bond Fund	R	R	2.00m	-3.3	6.6	7.1	NA
★★★★	AV-	Montreal Trust Exc. Income	R	N	1.57	-1.4	9.6	8.5	11.1
★★★	AV	Mutual Bond Fund	R	F	1.87	-2.0	8.2	NA	NA
NA	NA	Mutual Premier Bond Fund	R	N	1.90	-2.0	NA	NA	NA
★★★	AV-	NAL-Investor Bond Fund	R	B	1.75	-1.2	8.5	7.9	NA
NA	NA	NatCan Canadian Bond Fund	R	N	1.24*	-2.6	NA	NA	NA
★★★★★	AV+	National Life Fixed Income	R	D	2.00m	0.4	10.9	10.7	12.9
★★★	AV	National Trust Canadian Bond	R	N	1.41	-3.2	8.2	7.6	10.8
★★	AV-	NN Bond Fund	R	R	2.00*	-1.8	8.1	8.2	NA
NA	NA	OHA Bond Fund	R	N	0.50*	-4.4	NA	NA	NA
★★	AV+	Optima Strategy Cdn Income	R	O	0.43*	-2.8	7.9	7.2	9.3
NA	NA	Optima Strategy Sht Term Inc.	R	O	0.29*	1.4	NA	NA	NA
★★★★	AV	Optimum Fonds d'Obligations	R	N	1.25m*	-2.6	10.3	8.7	NA
NA	NA	PH&N Sht Term Bond & Mortg	R	N	0.50m	NA	NA	NA	NA

Return	Vol.	Fund	RRSP	Fees	MER	1yr	3yr	5yr	10yr
★★★★	AV	PH&N Bond Fund	R	N	0.60	-0.5	10.4	9.9	13.2
★	AV+	Prudential Income Fund of Cda	R	F	1.51*	-3.5	7.5	7.3	10.1
★★★★	AV-	Pursuit Income Fund	R	F	1.00*	4.2	10.0	7.8	NA
★	LOW	Royal Life Income Fund	R	D	1.88	-4.1	6.7	NA	NA
★★★★	AV	Royal Trust Bond Fund	R	N	1.38*	-1.5	9.3	8.6	11.2
★★★★	AV	Royfund Bond Fund	R	N	1.50	-1.1	9.3	8.8	10.7
★	AV	Sceptre Bond Fund	R	N	1.22*	-5.5	7.2	8.7	NA
★	LOW	Scotia Defensive Income Fund	R	N	1.41	0.9	6.9	7.3	NA
★	LOW	Scotia Income Fund	R	N	1.41	-0.9	6.9	7.3	NA
★★★	HIGH	Spectrum Government Bond	R	O	1.70	-5.7	8.8	7.8	NA
★★	AV+	Spectrum Interest Fund	R	O	1.60	-4.6	7.7	7.7	NA
NA	NA	Standard Life Bond Mutual	R	N	1.50	-2.6	NA	NA	NA
★★★★	AV	Standard Life Ideal Bond Fund	R	D	2.00	-2.6	9.1	8.4	NA
NA	NA	Strata Government Bond Fund	R	N	2.15*	NA	NA	NA	NA
★★	AV	Strata Income Fund	R	F	1.53	-3.8	8.0	8.0	NA
★★★	AV	Talvest Bond Fund	R	O	1.99*	-2.4	8.5	8.1	11.4
★★	LOW	Talvest Income Fund	R	O	1.50*	-0.2	7.7	8.4	9.7
★★★	LOW	Templeton Heritage Bond	R	O	2.99	1.1	8.7	NA	NA
★	AV-	Top Fifty T-Bill/Bond Fund	R	F	2.08*	-8.1	5.1	7.4	NA
★	LOW	Tradex Bond Fund	R	N	1.36*	-4.9	5.7	NA	NA
★	LOW	Trans-Canada Bond Fund	R	O	2.66*	-1.0	6.4	7.0	NA
NA	NA	Trimark Government Income	R	O	0.00*	NA	NA	NA	NA
★★★	AV	Trust Pret & Revenu Bond	R	N	1.50*	-1.9	8.8	8.7	NA
★★	HIGH	United Canadian Bond Fund	R	O	1.80*	-4.8	8.1	9.3	10.4
★★	AV+	Universal Canadian Bond Fund	R	O	1.81*	-5.6	8.1	7.4	11.9
NA	NA	University Avenue Bond Fund	R	N	2.19	0.4	NA	NA	NA
★★	AV+	20/20 Income Fund	R	O	1.93*	-3.9	7.7	7.0	NA
		HIGHEST IN GROUP				8.5	12.5	10.8	13.2
		AVERAGE IN GROUP				-2.3	8.3	8.1	11.1
		LOWEST IN GROUP				-8.1	4.7	6.5	9.2

Canadian Mortgage Funds

Return	Vol.	Fund	RRSP	Fees	MER	1yr	3yr	5yr	10yr
★★★	AV-	Canada Trust Everest Mortg	R	N	1.57	3.4	7.7	9.3	10.1
★★★★	AV+	CIBC Mortgage Investment	R	N	1.50*	1.2	8.1	9.7	10.0
NA	NA	Colonia Mortgage Fund	R	D	1.75	1.7	NA	NA	NA
★★★	AV	Concorde Hypotheques	R	O	1.90*	1.0	7.5	NA	NA
★★	LOW	Confed Mortgage Fund	R	F	1.75	1.3	6.5	8.7	9.7
★★★	AV+	First Canadian Mortgage Fund	R	N	1.02*	0.9	7.6	9.9	10.6
★★	AV-	Fonds Desjardins Hypotheques	R	N	1.66	2.2	6.8	8.7	NA
★★★★★	AV-	General Trust of Canada Mort	R	N	1.48	8.1	9.5	10.3	11.1
★★★	AV+	Great-West Life Mortgage Inv.	R	N	2.40	-0.6	7.9	8.1	9.6
★★★	AV	Green Line Cdn Mortgage	R	N	1.50	1.0	7.4	9.5	10.0
★	AV-	Green Line Mortgage-Backed	R	N	1.65	1.1	6.4	9.1	NA
NA	NA	Hongkong Bank Mortgage	R	N	1.65*	7.5	NA	NA	NA
NA	NA	Industrial Alliance Ecoflex H	R	R	2.00*	1.0	NA	NA	NA
★★★★	HIGH	Industrial Mortgage Securities	R	O	1.98*	-2.3	9.5	7.4	12.1
NA	NA	InvesNat Mortgage Fund	R	N	1.33*	3.3	NA	NA	NA
★★	AV+	Investors Income Portfolio	R	R	0.17	-1.8	6.7	7.7	NA
★	AV-	Investors Mortgage Fund	R	R	1.82	-0.7	5.8	7.9	9.5
NA	NA	Ivy Mortgage Fund	R	O	1.50m*	NA	NA	NA	NA
★★★★	LOW	London Life Mortgage	R	R	1.50*	1.0	8.0	9.4	11.0
NA	NA	Mandate National Mortgage	R	N		NA	NA	NA	NA
★★	AV	Montreal Trust Exc. Mortgage	R	N	1.56	2.9	7.2	8.9	9.7

Return	Vol.	Fund	RRSP	Fees	MER	1yr	3yr	5yr	10yr
NA	NA	Mutual Premier Mortgage	R	N	1.63	1.6	NA	NA	NA
NA	NA	National Trust Mortgage Fund	R	N	1.63	-0.2	NA	NA	NA
★★★★	LOW	Ontario Teachers Grp Mortg	R	N	0.65	3.8	8.1	9.0	9.8
★	LOW	Royal Trust Mortgage Fund	R	N	1.94*	-0.4	5.9	8.4	9.6
NA	NA	Royfund Mortgage Fund	R	N	1.73	3.4	NA	NA	NA
NA	NA	Scotia Mortgage Fund	R	N	1.46	1.4	NA	NA	NA
★★	AV	Trust Pret & Revenu H Fund	R	N	1.60*	0.1	7.0	8.8	9.9
★	AV	United Canadian Mortgage	R	O	1.95*	-1.4	4.7	7.2	8.4
		HIGHEST IN GROUP				8.1	9.5	10.3	12.1
		AVERAGE IN GROUP				1.5	7.3	8.8	10.1
		LOWEST IN GROUP				-2.3	4.7	7.2	8.4

U.S. and International Bond Funds

Return	Vol.	Fund	RRSP	Fees	MER	1yr	3yr	5yr	10yr
NA	NA	20/20 Foreign RSP Bond Fund	R	O	2.00*	NA	NA	NA	NA
NA	NA	20/20 World Bond Fund	F	O	2.00*	0.1	NA	NA	NA
★★★★	AV+	AGF Global Government Bond	F	O	1.26*	7.2	13.9	11.4	NA
NA	NA	AGF Strategic Income Fund	R	O	2.10*	NA	NA	NA	NA
NA	NA	AGF U.S. Income Fund	F	O	1.54*	1.4	NA	NA	NA
NA	NA	Altamira Global Bond Fund	R	N	1.84*	NA	NA	NA	NA
NA	NA	Bullock Global Bond 'A'	F	F	1.79	NA	NA	NA	NA
NA	NA	Bullock Global Bond 'B'	F	R	2.15	NA	NA	NA	NA
NA	NA	Bullock Global Bond 'C'	F	N	2.27	NA	NA	NA	NA
NA	NA	C.I. Global Bond RSP Fund	R	O	2.00	NA	NA	NA	NA
NA	NA	C.I. World Bond Fund	F	O	2.00	4.2	NA	NA	NA
NA	NA	Canada Life Int'l Bond S-36	R	R	2.00	NA	NA	NA	NA
★★★★★	HIGH	Dynamic Global Bond Fund	R	O	2.18*	11.3	15.8	10.2	NA
NA	NA	Fidelity Emerging Mkts Bond	F	O	2.44*	NA	NA	NA	NA
NA	NA	Fidelity Global Bond Fund	R	O	2.22*	NA	NA	NA	NA
NA	NA	Fidelity Nth Am. Income Fund	F	O	1.75*	2.6	NA	NA	NA
NA	NA	First Cdn. International Bond	F	N	1.81*	NA	NA	NA	NA
★★★	AV+	Global Strategy Div. Bond	R	O	2.10	-3.3	9.9	NA	NA
★★★★	AV+	Global Strategy World Bond	F	O	2.09	-4.3	11.1	8.2	NA
NA	NA	Green Line Global Gov't Bond	F	N	2.15	6.6	NA	NA	NA
NA	NA	Green Line Global RSP Bond	R	N	1.95	NA	NA	NA	NA
★★★★	AV+	Guardian International Income	R	O	1.68*	3.1	12.0	8.5	NA
NA	NA	Hercules World Bond Fund	R	N	1.50m*	NA	NA	NA	NA
NA	NA	Investors Global Bond Fund	F	R	2.15	7.1	NA	NA	NA
NA	NA	Lotus International Bond Fund	R	N	1.50m*	NA	NA	NA	NA
NA	NA	Optima Strategy Glbl Fixd Inc.	F	O	0.13*	NA	NA	NA	NA
NA	NA	Regent World Income Fund	R	O	2.00*	3.2	NA	NA	NA
NA	NA	Royal Trust International Bond	R	N	1.79*	6.9	NA	NA	NA
NA	NA	Royfund International Income	R	N	1.92	10.7	NA	NA	NA
NA	NA	Scotia Canam Income ($US)	R	N	1.60	-2.0	NA	NA	NA
NA	NA	Spectrum International Bond	R	O	1.90	8.9	NA	NA	NA
NA	NA	Talvest Foreign Pay Bond Fund	R	O	2.15*	6.3	NA	NA	NA
★★★★	AV	Templeton Global Income	F	O	2.25	3.3	10.4	10.2	NA
		HIGHEST IN GROUP				11.3	15.8	11.4	NA
		AVERAGE IN GROUP				4.1	12.2	9.7	NA
		LOWEST IN GROUP				-4.3	9.9	8.2	NA

Canadian Money Market Funds

Return	Vol.	Fund	RRSP	Fees	MER	1yr	3yr	5yr	10yr
★★★★	AV-	20/20 Money Market Fund	R	O	1.04*	4.3	6.0	NA	NA
NA	NA	Admax Cash Performance	R	O	1.20*	3.1	NA	NA	NA
★★★	AV	AGF Money Market Account	R	O	0.83*	3.6	5.4	7.9	8.6
★★★★	AV-	AMI Private Capital Money Mkt	R	N	0.75*	4.4	6.1	8.1	NA

Return	Vol.	Fund	RRSP	Fees	MER	1yr	3yr	5yr	10yr
★★★★	AV+	Batirente - Sec. Marche Mntr.	R	N	1.61	3.7	6.0	8.0	NA
★★★★★	AV	Beutel Goodman Money Mkt	R	N	0.60*	4.6	6.6	NA	NA
NA	NA	Bissett Money Market Fund	R	N	0.50	4.5	NA	NA	NA
NA	NA	BNP (Cda) Cdn Money Mkt	R	N	1.43	3.6	NA	NA	NA
★	AV	BPI Money Market Fund	R	D	1.48*	3.1	4.7	7.3	NA
NA	NA	BPI Short Term Interest Fund	R	D	1.00*	NA	NA	NA	NA
NA	NA	BPI T-Bill Fund	R	F	0.65*	NA	NA	NA	NA
★★★	LOW	C.I. Money Market Fund	R	O	0.59	4.1	5.8	NA	NA
★	AV	C.I. Sector Short-Term	F	O	0.59	2.4	3.3	4.7	NA
★★★	AV+	Canada Life Money Mkt S-29	R	R	1.25	4.0	5.5	7.8	8.0
★★	AV	Cda Trust Everest Money Mkt	R	N	0.75	3.6	5.2	8.0	NA
★★★★	AV+	Capstone Cash Management	R	N	0.60*	3.6	5.9	8.4	NA
★★★	AV+	CDA Money Market Fund	R	N	0.55	3.9	5.9	8.2	8.8
★	AV-	CIBC Canadian T-Bill Fund	R	N	1.20*	3.1	4.8	NA	NA
★	AV	CIBC Money Market Fund	R	N	1.20*	3.3	5.0	7.7	NA
★★★	AV-	CIBC Premium T-Bill Fund	R	N	0.55*	3.8	5.4	NA	NA
NA	NA	Colonia Money Market Fund	R	N	1.00	3.2	NA	NA	NA
NA	NA	Concorde Monetaire	R	O	1.50	4.2	NA	NA	NA
★★	AV	Cornerstone Gov Money	R	N	1.14*	3.7	5.4	NA	NA
★★★	AV	Dynamic Money Market Fund	R	O	0.80*	3.7	5.4	7.9	8.3
★★★★	AV+	Elliott & Page Money Fund	R	F	0.56*	4.3	6.1	8.6	NA
NA	NA	Elliott & Page T-Bill Fund	R	D	1.77*	NA	NA	NA	NA
★	AV+	Empire Money Market Fund	R	N	1.56	3.2	5.1	7.4	NA
★★	AV-	Ethical Money Market Fund	R	O	1.26*	3.6	5.4	8.0	8.7
★	AV	Fidelity Short Term Asset Fund	R	O	1.00*	3.3	5.2	NA	NA
★★	AV-	Finsco Money Market Fund	R	F	1.07*	3.8	5.4	7.9	NA
★	LOW	Finsco T-Bill Fund	R	F	1.29*	3.4	5.0	7.5	NA
★★★	AV	First Canadian Money Market	R	N	0.95*	3.6	5.4	7.7	NA
NA	NA	First Cdn. T-Bill Fund	R	N	1.02*	NA	NA	NA	NA
★★★★★	AV+	Fonds de Prof. Short Term	R	N	0.40	3.9	6.5	8.4	NA
★★	HIGH	Fonds Desjardins Monetaire	R	N	1.10	3.7	5.3	7.6	NA
★★★	AV+	Fonds Ficadre Money Market	R	R	1.21	3.7	5.7	NA	NA
★★★	AV-	GBC Money Market Fund	R	N	0.50	4.0	5.7	8.2	NA
★★★	AV+	Gen'l Trust of Cda Money Mkt	R	N	0.83	3.5	5.7	8.0	NA
★★★	AV-	Global Strategy T-Bill Savings	R	D	0.45	4.1	5.8	7.8	NA
★	AV	Great-West Life Money Mkt	R	N	1.74	3.1	4.9	7.4	8.1
★★★★	AV	Green Line Cdn Money Mkt	R	N	0.66	4.2	5.9	8.4	NA
NA	NA	Green Line Cdn T-Bill Fund	R	N	0.68	3.8	NA	NA	NA
★★★	AV	Guardian Cdn Money Market	R	O	0.72*	3.9	5.5	8.2	8.8
★	LOW	Hongkong Bank Money Mkt	R	N	1.08*	3.5	5.0	7.4	NA
★★★	LOW	HRL Instant $$ Fund	R	N	0.50	4.2	5.7	8.1	NA
★	AV	Imperial Growth Money Mkt	R	F	1.50	3.0	4.7	7.0	NA
NA	NA	Industrial Alliance Ecoflex M	R	R	1.50*	12.9	NA	NA	NA
★★★	LOW	Industrial Cash Management	R	F	0.50*	4.0	5.7	8.2	NA
★	LOW	Industrial Short-Term Fund	R	R	1.54*	3.1	4.6	NA	NA
NA	NA	Integra Short Term Investment	R	N	1.00*	5.2	NA	NA	NA
★★★	AV-	InvesNat Money Market Fund	R	N	1.09*	3.7	5.5	NA	NA
★★	LOW	Investors Money Market Fund	R	R	1.08*	3.6	5.2	7.7	NA
NA	NA	Ivy Short-Term Fund	R	O	1.00*	3.1	NA	NA	NA
★	LOW	Laurentian Money Market	R	N	1.20*	3.5	5.1	7.6	NA
NA	NA	Leith Wheeler Money Market	R	N	0.60m*	NA	NA	NA	NA
★★★★	AV+	London Life Money Market	R	R	1.30*	3.4	6.3	8.4	NA
★★★	AV	Lotus Income Fund	R	N	0.75*	4.2	5.8	8.4	NA
★★★	AV-	Mackenzie Sentinel Cda M. Mkt	R	N	0.96*	4.0	5.7	8.1	NA

Return	Vol.	Fund	RRSP	Fees	MER	1yr	3yr	5yr	10yr
★	HIGH	Manulife Vista 1 Sht Term Sec	R	F	1.63*	3.1	5.2	7.7	8.4
★	AV+	Manulife Vista2 Sht Term Sec	R	R	2.38*	2.3	4.4	6.9	7.6
★	AV	Maritime Life Money Market	R	N	1.75*	3.0	5.1	7.4	8.0
★★★	AV	Mawer Canadian Money Mkt	R	N	0.69	3.7	5.4	7.9	NA
★★★	AV-	McLean Budden Money Mkt	R	N	0.75	3.9	5.4	7.8	NA
★★★	AV	MD Money Fund	R	N	0.50	4.0	5.6	7.9	8.3
NA	NA	Metlife MVP Money Market	R	R	1.50m	3.1	NA	NA	NA
★★★	HIGH	Mont'l Trust Exc. Money Mkt	R	N	1.07	3.8	5.4	7.8	NA
★★	LOW	Mutual Money Market	R	N	1.03	3.8	5.3	7.6	NA
★★	AV	NAL-Investor Money Market	R	B	1.25	3.2	5.2	7.8	NA
★★★	AV-	Natcan Treasury Bill Fund	R	N	0.87*	3.8	5.6	NA	NA
NA	NA	National Life Money Market	R	D	1.60m	4.7	NA	NA	NA
★★	LOW	National Trust Money Market	R	N	1.16	3.5	5.3	NA	NA
★★★	AV-	NN Money Market Fund	R	N	0.75*	4.0	5.8	NA	NA
★★	AV	NN T-Bill Fund	R	R	1.75*	3.1	5.2	7.3	NA
NA	NA	OHA Short Term Fund	R	N	0.50*	4.2	NA	NA	NA
★★★★★	AV	Ont. Teachers Grp Fixed Value	R	N	0.50	4.3	7.0	8.7	8.9
★★★★	AV+	Optimum Fonds d'Epargne	R	N	0.60m*	3.9	6.2	8.2	NA
★★★	AV	PH&N Canadian Money Mkt	R	N	0.52	4.1	5.9	8.4	NA
★★★★	AV	Prudential Money Mkt Fd of Cda	R	N	0.66*	4.4	6.1	8.4	NA
★★★★	AV	Pursuit Money Market Fund	R	N	0.50*	4.6	6.4	8.6	NA
NA	NA	Royal Life Money Market Fund	R	D	1.00	5.0	NA	NA	NA
★★	AV	Royal Trust Cdn Money Mkt	R	N	1.16*	3.4	5.2	7.6	NA
NA	NA	Royal Trust Cdn T-Bill Mon. Mkt	R	N	1.71*	2.7	NA	NA	NA
★★★	AV	Royfund Canadian T-Bill Fund	R	N	0.84	3.7	5.5	NA	NA
★★★	AV	Royfund Money Market Fund	R	N	1.18	3.4	5.4	7.9	NA
★★★	AV	Sceptre Money Market Fund	R	N	0.83*	3.9	5.7	8.1	NA
NA	NA	Scotia Gov. of Can. T-Bill	R	N	0.80	3.8	NA	NA	NA
★★	LOW	Scotia Money Market Fund	R	N	1.00	3.7	5.2	NA	NA
NA	NA	Scotia Premium T-Bill Fund	R	N	0.55	4.1	NA	NA	NA
★★	LOW	Spectrum Cash Reserve Fund	R	O	1.10	3.7	5.3	7.8	NA
★★	AV-	Spectrum Savings Fund	R	N	1.00	3.8	5.4	7.9	NA
NA	NA	Standard Life Ideal Money Mkt	R	D	1.40	NA	NA	NA	NA
NA	NA	Standard Life Money Market	R	N	0.90	3.4	NA	NA	NA
★★	LOW	Strata Money Market Fund	R	N	1.27	3.6	5.2	7.5	NA
★★★★	AV	Talvest Money Fund	R	F	0.75*	4.3	6.0	8.4	NA
★★★	LOW	Templeton Treasury Bill Fund	R	N	0.75	3.9	5.5	8.0	NA
★★★	AV	Trans-Canada Money Market	R	O	0.66*	4.5	5.8	7.8	NA
★★★	AV-	Trimark Interest Fund	R	F	0.75*	3.8	5.5	8.1	NA
★★★	LOW	Trust Pret & Revenu Mny Mkt	R	N	1.20*	4.1	5.5	7.8	NA
★★★★	AV	United Canadian Interest Fund	R	O	1.31*	4.8	6.4	8.7	NA
		HIGHEST IN GROUP				12.9	7.0	8.7	8.9
		AVERAGE IN GROUP				3.9	5.5	7.9	8.4
		LOWEST IN GROUP				2.3	3.3	4.7	7.6

U.S. and International Money Market Funds

Return	Vol.	Fund	RRSP	Fees	MER	1yr	3yr	5yr	10yr
★★★★	AV	AGF U.S. Dollar Money Mkt	F	F	0.36*	2.7	3.3	5.0	NA
★★★★★	HIGH	Altamira Short Term Global Inc	R	N	1.28*	11.6	12.2	NA	NA
NA	NA	BNP (Canada)US$ Money Mkt	R	N	1.46	2.1	NA	NA	NA
★★★	AV	CIBC U.S. Dollar Money Mkt	F	N	0.95*	2.3	2.9	NA	NA
★★★	AV	Finsco U.S. Money Mkt ($US)	F	F	1.05	2.5	2.9	4.6	NA
★★★★	AV+	Global Strategy Div. Savings	R	O	1.50	3.5	7.9	7.8	NA
★★★	AV-	Global Strat. U.S. Savings ($US)	R	D	0.45	2.8	3.2	4.6	NA

Return	Vol.	Fund	RRSP	Fees	MER	1yr	3yr	5yr	10yr
★★★	AV+	Green Line U.S. M. Mkt ($US)	R	N	0.96	2.3	2.9	4.6	NA
★★★★	AV	Guardian U.S. M. Mkt ($US)	R	O	0.54*	2.7	3.2	4.9	NA
NA	NA	Hercules Global Short-Term	F	N	0.75m	NA	NA	NA	NA
NA	NA	InvesNat U.S. Money Mkt $US	F	N	1.19*	2.1	NA	NA	NA
★★★★	AV+	PH&N $US Money Market	R	N	0.53	2.9	3.5	NA	NA
★★★	AV-	Royal Trust U.S. M. Mkt ($US)	F	N	1.20	2.2	2.8	NA	NA
★★	AV	Royfund U.S. Dollar Money	R	N	1.09	2.3	2.8	NA	NA
★★	AV+	United U.S. Dollar Money Mkt	F	O	0.60*	2.9	2.7	4.0	NA
		HIGHEST IN GROUP				11.6	12.2	7.8	NA
		AVERAGE IN GROUP				3.2	4.2	5.1	NA
		LOWEST IN GROUP				2.1	2.7	4.0	NA

Dividend Funds

Return	Vol.	Fund	RRSP	Fees	MER	1yr	3yr	5yr	10yr
★★★	AV+	20/20 Dividend Fund	R	O	2.08*	3.6	8.4	6.9	NA
★★★	LOW	AGF High Income Fund	R	O	1.42*	3.6	8.3	7.9	8.3
NA	NA	Bissett Dividend Income Fund	F	N	1.50	3.5	NA	NA	NA
★	AV-	BPI Income Fund	R	F	1.15*	1.6	3.9	4.3	6.4
NA	NA	CIBC Equity Income Fund	R	N	2.00*	-1.4	NA	NA	NA
★★★★	AV	Corporate Investors Ltd.	R	F	1.35*	6.8	10.6	6.0	8.8
★★★	LOW	Dynamic Dividend Fund	R	O	1.80*	3.0	9.0	7.2	NA
★★★★	AV-	Dynamic Dividend Growth	R	O	1.80*	5.2	9.5	5.2	NA
NA	NA	Fonds Desjardins Dividendes	R	N	1.80m	NA	NA	NA	NA
★★★	AV	Green Line Dividend Fund	R	N	2.20	1.4	8.8	7.9	NA
★★	LOW	Guardian Preferred Dividend	R	O	1.24*	1.0	7.8	6.1	NA
★★★★	HIGH	Industrial Dividend Fund Ltd.	R	O	2.52*	7.1	11.2	3.4	9.8
★★	AV	Investors Dividend Fund	F	B	2.01	0.6	7.8	7.1	9.5
★★★★	AV	Investors Mutual of Canada	F	B	2.03	4.3	10.5	7.2	9.7
★★	AV-	Laurentian Dividend Fund Ltd.	R	O	2.70*	1.0	6.6	5.5	9.4
NA	NA	Mawer Canadian Income Fund	F	N	1.08	-1.0	NA	NA	NA
NA	NA	MD Dividend Fund	R	N	1.00	2.7	NA	NA	NA
★★	AV-	Montreal Trust Exc. Dividend	R	N	1.08	2.6	7.2	6.4	NA
NA	NA	NatCan Dividend Fund	R	N	1.63*	2.4	NA	NA	NA
NA	NA	National Trust Dividend Fund	R	N	2.20	4.1	NA	NA	NA
★★★	AV+	PH&N Div. Income	N	N	1.23	5.4	8.5	6.9	9.9
★★★★★	AV+	Prudential Div. Fund of Cda	R	F	1.53*	9.2	16.0	7.8	NA
★	AV-	Royal Trust Growth & Income	R	N	2.80*	0.2	5.1	4.0	NA
NA	NA	Royfund Dividend Fund	R	N	1.78	2.2	NA	NA	NA
★★	AV	Spectrum Dividend Fund	R	O	1.55	2.5	5.7	5.5	NA
★	AV+	Trans-Canada Income Fund	R	O	2.66*	6.5	1.3	1.4	9.5
		HIGHEST IN GROUP				9.2	16.0	7.9	9.9
		AVERAGE IN GROUP				3.1	8.1	5.9	9.0
		LOWEST IN GROUP				-1.4	1.3	1.4	6.4

Benchmarks

			1yr	3yr	5yr	10yr
91-Day Canada T-Bills			4.8	6.5	8.9	9.4
Consumer Price Index			0.0	0.9	2.6	3.5
ScotiaMcLeod Universe Bond Index			-0.8	10.5	9.8	12.7
Standard & Poor's 500 Index (U.S.$)			1.4	9.3	10.4	15.2
TSE Total Return Index			3.9	8.3	4.8	9.7
Morgan Stanley The World Index			19.5	18.2	10.1	16.9
Morgan Stanley Europe (14)			25.4	19.3	13.5	19.0
Morgan Stanley Japan			24.5	18.2	3.5	19.4
Morgan Stanley EAFE			26.5	19.5	8.4	19.2

Index